MW01537413

# Indigenous Peoples, Environment and Development

## Proceedings of the conference
## Zurich, May 15-18, 1995

edited by
**Silvia Büchi**
**Christian Erni**
**Luzia Jurt**
**Christoph Rüegg**

**International Work Group for Indigenous Affairs and Department of Social Anthropology, University of Zurich**
**IWGIA Document No. 85**
**Copenhagen 1997**

ISSN 0105-4503 ISBN 87-984110-2-0

Published by the International Work Group for Indigenous Affairs, Fiolstræde 10, DK-1171 Copenhagen K, Denmark, in collaboration with the Department of Social Anthropology, University of Zurich, Freiensteinstrasse 5, CH-8032 Zurich, Switzerland.

Translation and proofreading: Jeffrey V. Lazarus

Cover: Jørgen Abelsen

Prepress: Tulugaq and Christensen Fotosats & Repro

Print: Eks-Skolens Trykkeri, Copenhagen, Denmark

# CONTENTS

4

In the beginning, the primary aim of the conference on "Indigenous Peoples, Environment and Development" (IPED) was just to reflect on the indigenous peoples' assessments of developments during the three years since the United Nations Earth Summit on Environment and Development (UNCED) in Rio de Janeiro in 1992. It was thought that these reflections would launch a broader discussion on environmental and development issues in the context of indigenous peoples' rights and demands, addressing the various topics from the angle of the participants' specific experiences, knowledge and theoretical views.

Not yet satisfied, however, with the rather limited impact to be expected from these objectives, the organising committee decided to pursue a more concrete goal. It decided to link up IPED directly with lobbying for indigenous peoples in Switzerland and to identify concrete criteria and principles for co-operation with indigenous peoples in development and environmental protection projects, to be submitted to both the government and Swiss-based NGOs working on environmental and development issues.

Not only did IPED therefore lead to closer co-operation between the various support groups for indigenous peoples in Switzerland, but it is hoped that it initiated the first step in the process towards the drawing up of a Swiss policy on indigenous peoples' rights.

### The Conference Proceedings

The present publication contains a collection of articles written by the participants and presented during the IPED conference in Zurich either in the plenary sessions or workshops. These contributions provide an overview of the conference's main themes and the workshop topics. Indigenous and non-indigenous experts enter into in-depth discussions, reflecting on approaches to development and conservation, on alternative models and implementing strategies for environmental protection and sustainable development on indigenous territories.

The publication is divided into six parts and structured according to the conference's four workshop themes. The first part contains a general introduction on indigenous peoples, the environment and development, as well as an indigenous assessment of developments on indigenous territories three years after the United Nations Earth Summit.

The second part provides some more detailed observations on the concrete situations of and threats to indigenous peoples in different parts of the world, centred around the issues of land rights, self-determination and resource use.

Part three, titled 'Biodiversity Conservation and Indigenous Peoples: Competing Approaches', presents views of indigenous peoples and concerned environmentalists and anthropologists, encompassing both case studies on indigenous resource management or the impact of governmental conservation programmes on indigenous communities, and the discussion of more general issues related to conservation and indigenous peoples.

The articles in the fourth part of the publication, titled "Indigenous Culture and Development: The Question of Identity, Equity, and Cooperation", reflect aspects of indigenous peoples' self-development: the impact of development approaches on the co-operation between indigenous organisations and aid agencies, the role of indigenous women in development processes as well as the importance of intercultural, bilingual education for indigenous peoples in the context of development and conservation.

Based on the preceding parts, part five reflects on non-governmental organisations (NGOs), the state and the "New Partnership" with indigenous peoples, which has been proclaimed by the United Nations for the "International Year of the World's Indigenous Peoples" in 1993 and the following decade. Experiences from the Netherlands during the years of incessant lobbying for indigenous peoples' rights, which led to a policy-paper by the Dutch Parliament in 1994, may constitute a concrete asset for lobbying in Switzerland.

Moreover, in part five, the workshop results are summarised and discussed briefly. These results address fundamental issues that have to be considered when drawing up concrete criteria and suggestions for co-operation between government agencies, NGOs and indigenous peoples.

Part six presents the concluding remarks made by an indigenous representative, reflecting on the IPED conference's procedure and the work achieved during the four days. Ultimately, it contemplates the aims of the conference and its importance.

**Initiating a Process Towards a Swiss Policy-Paper**
It might not come as a surprise that no government policy on indigenous peoples and their role in development co-operation exists in Switzerland. Switzerland has no colonial past and therefore no direct responsibility towards indigenous peoples. Moreover, Switzerland has no indigenous peoples living within its own borders, according to definitions commonly used within the UN system. Nevertheless, through its foreign policy Switzerland is closely linked with indigenous peoples' rights when it comes to development co-operation and activities in international fora such as the UNCED.

The conference organisers are convinced that Switzerland should develop a comprehensive policy on indigenous peoples similar to many other European countries, in order to pursue just and appropriate development co-operation. Such a policy should recognise indigenous peoples as a special partner in development co-operation, based on respecting indigenous peoples' rights.

This publication documents the initial steps in the attempt to establish a Swiss government policy on indigenous peoples and their rights, steps undertaken during the IPED conference. Furthermore, it contributes to the co-operation between the different support groups for indigenous peoples and other NGOs in Switzerland in order to pursue an efficient and systematic lobbying for indigenous peoples. On a more general level, this compilation serves as a means to raise the awareness of a broad spectrum of interested people with respect to indigenous peoples' issues.

This publication is a contribution to the "UN International Decade of the World's Indigenous Peoples". It was born in the warm atmosphere of mutual respect and friendship which was maintained throughout the four days in the Conference Centre Boldern, near Zurich.

**Thanks**
We would like to express our grateful thanks first and foremost to the indigenous participants and speakers who contributed with their presentations and discussions to the success of the

conference. Our thanks go furthermore to all other participants, speakers, chairpersons and workshop facilitators for all their valuable contributions to the conference.

We received technical help from the Department of Social Anthropology of the University in Zurich, which offered its infrastructure for the organisational work and the editing of this publication.

We would like to express our gratitude to the World Wide Fund for Nature WWF (Switzerland), to the Swiss Agency for Development and Co-operation SDC, and to the Royal Ministry of Foreign Affairs (Norway) for their generous funding of the conference and the publication of the proceedings.

Lastly, we would like to thank all the volunteer workers, among them especially the members of IWGIA Basel, who helped in the organisation and carrying-out of the conference. Without their attentive work backstage we would not have been able to build such an atmosphere of friendship during the IPED conference. Furthermore, all the others members of the organising committee, the Society for Threatened Peoples (Switzerland), Bruno Manser Fonds and Incomindios (Switzerland) deserve special thanks.

## Acknowledgements
Finally, we would like to acknowledge the generous financial support of the following institutions, organisations and private persons:

WWF Switzerland; Swiss Agency for Development and Co-operation SDC; Royal Ministry of Foreign Affairs (Norway); Präsidialabteilung der Stadt Zürich; Erziehungsdirektion des Kantons Zürich; Migros-Genossenschaftsbund; The Body Shop; Departement Sicherheit und Umwelt der Stadt Winterthur; Ökofond der Zentralstelle der Studentenschaft der Universität Zürich; Fondation Duchemin; Evangelisch-reformierte Kantonalkirche St. Gallen; Daniel Brunner; World Council of Churches; Swiss Interchurch Aid (HEKS); Bread for the World; Schweizerisches ArbeiterInnenhilfswerk; Seraphisches Liebeswerk Solothurn; Rosenkranzmission Ilanz.

International Work Group for Indigenous Affairs
Zurich, Switzerland

# I
# Introduction

ANDREW GRAY

# WHO ARE INDIGENOUS PEOPLES?

**Identifying Indigenous Peoples**

Defining indigenous characteristics is difficult because the notion of indigenous is polythetic, consisting of a variety of attributes not all of which need be present at any one time (Burger 1987:9). In general terms, indigenous peoples are the disadvantaged inhabitants of a present day country who have lived in the area since before it became a nation-state. Their problems occur from the processes of colonisation or from state formation arising from decolonisation.

Indigenous peoples have prior rights to their territories, lands and resources, but often these have been taken or are threatened by colonisation from the state. They have distinct cultures and economic production methods to those of the dominant society. Although they have their social and political organisations, indigenous peoples' own institutions are often not recognised and they have no means of expressing their desires and aspirations.

Apart from these external characteristics, it is crucial to understand the importance of self-identification for indigenous peoples. This internal aspect of the definition of indigenous is recognised in the ILO Convention 169 on indigenous and tribal peoples, Article 2.2. 'Indigenousness' is, therefore, not just a term which is used to define particular types of people, but also a concept which the peoples themselves recognise and use as a part of their identity.

Indigenous persons number over 300 million and live throughout the world, ranging from the forest peoples of the Amazon to the tribal peoples of India and from the Inuit of the Arctic to the Aboriginal peoples of Australia. They include peoples who are uncontacted, living in remote places, and also a large proportion of migrants to urban areas who have been forced from their territories and find themselves on the margins of national society. Indigenous peoples live in countries of the North and the South and, in spite of the variety of political and economic conditions in the states where they live, they have formed an influential international movement.

15

## Indigenous Peoples, Peasants and the Proletariat

'Indigenous' is not a static concept but a growing phenomenon which is increasingly being adopted throughout the world by vulnerable peoples who claim rights on the basis of occupation prior to the existence of the state. The changing face and definition of indigenous peoples raises the question of what attributes distinguish indigenous from non-indigenous peoples. For example, many of the characteristics of rural indigenous peoples are co-terminous with those of peasant farmers – indeed in certain parts of the world, such as the Andean highlands, local communities can be both.

Whereas lands, resources, culture and political organisation are important for peasant farmers, they take on a different hue from an indigenous perspective which becomes significant in the context of rural development. For example, whereas peasant farmers talk of self-management of their lands and resources, indigenous peoples talk of their rights to self-determination and to control their territories and resources. This is not only a verbal difference, but reflects a distinct perspective on their relationship to resources which includes not only rights to economic access, but also political control.

Another important attribute which can distinguish indigenous peoples from peasant farmers concerns their relationship to the state. Peasant farmers have their own cultures and relate to the state as members of ethnic groups and communities. Indigenous identity, however, includes a political dimension where each person relates to a collectivity as a member of a people, tribe or nation. The effect is that indigenous peoples have a more autonomous notion of their identity and are consequently less integrated into the political and economic system of the national society.

Connected with this distinction is political mobilisation and organisation. Peasant farmers frequently organise themselves within a framework of class consciousness and unionisation. For indigenous peoples, organisation takes the form of different types of self-governing institutions which may or may not be juxtaposed with other unionised or federated models of organisation.

Unlike peasant farmers, indigenous peoples can also live in urban areas where they often appear indistinguishable from other sectors of the urban proletariat. However, even in towns, the concept of the right to self-determination, relationship to their lands and territories and their own forms of government make them less integrated into the urban sectors of the state than those whose recruitment ties them predominantly to class identity.

In rural and urban areas where indigenous peoples have been thrown off their lands and can no longer subsist, they share the characteristics of the poor and oppressed. Indigenous mortality rates are high, indigenous peoples have higher levels of imprisonment than other sectors of society, they lack self-reliance and rapidly become dependent. This does not just occur in countries of the South. Statistics from Canada, New Zealand and Australia demonstrate that these problems are disproportionately high for indigenous peoples living in wealthy countries, and the effects lead to social and personal breakdown. A particularly distressing consequence of encroaching alienation and anomie is the high instances of alcoholism, drug-taking and suicide. This socio-cultural breakdown is a consequence of colonisation which destroys the fabric of indigenous social and personal identity.

The distinction between peasant farmers, members of the urban proletariat and indigenous peoples is a matter of degree and self-awareness. It is possible to be indigenous in one context and a peasant farmer or member of the working class in another. At the same time, what might appear as a difference in degree between indigenous peoples and others becomes a difference in kind the more they assert their identity as distinct from the state. An accumulation of external and internal defining attributes can therefore transform a difference in degree to a difference in kind.

Throughout the world, rural and urban poor are increasingly identifying themselves as indigenous, and peoples are gradually becoming associated into an international movement. For example, in the 1960s the indigenous movement was focused on North America, Australia and Scandinavia; during the 1970s it took root in Latin America; during the 1980s it spread all over Asia and parts of the Pacific; and in the 1990s the emphasis on indigenous mobilisation has been in Africa and Russia.

The indigenous movement is consequently an historical phenomenon which continually broadens in scope as more peoples become associated with its assertion of rights. Since 1977, when the indigenous peoples of the world first crossed the threshold of the United Nations in Geneva, there has been a long process of establishing indigenous rights in international law. The draft Declaration on the Rights of Indigenous Peoples which has recently been completed by the expert UN Working Group on Indigenous Populations is a version of what these rights could be; however, it remains to be seen whether states demonstrate their integrity and recognise them at the higher echelons of the United Nations.

Indigenous peoples are aware that any recognition of their rights by states will be a long and hard struggle. However, they see the possibility of indigenous development as a means of implementing their rights in practice. Some features of development, such as the alleviation of poverty, hunger and oppression, connect indigenous peoples to rural peasants and the urban proletariat. However, at the same time, indigenous development is distinctive because the participants utilise programmes and projects as the means of implementing specific indigenous rights which are designed to respond to their particular needs.[1] Human rights and development can, in this manner, work hand in hand.

### References
Burger, J. 1986. Report from the Frontier: The State of the World's Indigenous Peoples. Zed Books.

### Notes
1. For a more indepth discussion of this issue refer to the author's other article in this volume.

# INDIGENOUS PEOPLES, ENVIRONMENT AND DEVELOPMENT: APPROACHING THE ISSUE

There is a myth told among the Buhid of Mindoro island in the Philippines, which in some respect reminds us of the Judaeo-Christian myth of the fall of man. But whereas in the latter the present day misery of human existence is attributed to the mythical ancestor's disrespect of God's law, the trespass committed in the Buhid myth is the disrespect of the integrity of other creatures, the wild species on which their ancestor's affluence and well-being rested.

> In the old days, people say, there lived two people: Málway and Dáli-Dáli. Those days it was not difficult for the Buhid, the people, to find ufi [1]. Those days the wild chicken were very kind, they gave as many eggs as one wished. Only the chicken used to say: 'Leave me alone while I lay my eggs. Don't watch me!'

While Málway respected the wild chicken's wish, Dáli-Dáli did not. He couldn't hold back his curiosity, peeped through the bushes and was discovered by the chicken.

> 'You are really watching me! From now on you and your descendants will not be able to catch us anymore unless you kill us! We will not help you anymore.' That's why from that time on, wild chicken have been hard to catch.

And the same happened with the wild pig:

> When Málway ran out of dfi, she just went to the forest to ask the wild pig for it. Málway used to say to it: 'My friend, please give me some dfi.' 'Go on! Just cut off a piece of my skin. I'll give it to you,' answered the pig.
>
> When Málway returned home, she carried a lot of meat with her. Dáli-Dáli again wondered: 'How come you have so much meat?' 'Just ask for it,' Málway replied, 'the wild pig will surely give you some, too, if it's just for a dfi. But don't take any from inside, just cut off some from the ouside.'

But Dáli-Dáli could not hold back his greed and cut too deep, hurting the pig and breaking the agreement, after which the pig announced:

> From now on you will not be able to catch us anymore, except with the help of dogs and traps.

Dáli-Dáli also messed it up with the wild *daráyaw*-Palm, whose pith is a favourite side dish among the Buhid. And the story concludes:

> They are still there: the wild pig, the wild chicken and the daráyaw-palm. They haven't disappeared. But they don't help the people anymore.

Of course, the myth could merely be interpreted as a tale about the golden age, the lost paradise, a projection of the human longing for a life without toil. But it is obvious that the myth also contains an educational message.

As in many other human societies, Buhid values contrast uncontrolled tempers, aggression, treachery, egoism and greed with reason, gentleness, honesty, altruism and generosity. So the myth simply teaches us about proper human behaviour. But what is remarkable is that it does not refer to proper behaviour among humans but to the relationship with non-human beings, the animals and plants of the forest. And the message it conveys addresses a problem humans have been confronted with ever since, but which has become critical in the modern world today. It deals with the dilemma between the short-term and the long-term, with forsaking the future for present gains, the problem of sustainability.

The Buhid have had many experiences with unsustainable resource use practices. The most recent one is the combined result of increasing resource scarcity due to logging, the establishment of cattle ranches and landgrabbing by Christian settlers, as well as new economic opportunities that became available in the 1970s. Communities living closer to the lowland Christain settlers and, therefore, with ready market access were lured by attractive prices to adopt intensive commercial corn production. Plough and ox, which allowed a more intensive use of the now also much larger upland fields, were introduced. However, the Buhid had had no previous experience with this new technology. After almost two decades, the impact on the environment was painfully felt. Agricultural expansion into watershed forests, left untouched by logging companies, aggravated annual flash-floods during the rainy season; sheet erosion and overuse led to rapid loss of soil fertility and declining yields. In response, some communities have now reverted to their traditional subsistence agriculture, imposed a ban on swiddening in the remaining forests, begun to reforest marginal land and intensified their already well-developed agroforestry practices in order to meet cash needs. However, these conservation measures were introduced not just out of concern for their immediate economic survival, but explicitly out of concern for their childrens' future. Reforestation and the planting of fruit trees is, for many, an investment whose benefits only the next generation will be able to reap. So, if sustainable development is understood as 'development that meets the needs of the present without compromising the ability of future generations to meet their own needs' (WCED 1987: 8), then it is 'sustainable development' which is now of major concern to these Buhid communities.

The Buhid are just one of six indigenous peoples living on Mindoro island, just one out of more than fifty in the Philippines and one out of more than four thousand worldwide. Each of these peoples has its own distinct culture, social structure and particular way to adapt to their natural and social environment. Nevertheless, many of the features characterising the Buhid's relationship to the natural environment, their experiences with new technologies and the market economy, and, above all, the particular problems and challenges they face due to outsiders' encroachment on their territories are common to most of the world's indigenous peoples today.

### The Politics of Stereotypes: Between 'Primitive Polluters'[2] and the 'Ecologically Noble Savages'

What the recent experiences of the Buhid illustrate – and what is also reflected in their myth – is that they are not and have never been the 'ecologically noble savages' as indigenous peoples are often pictured in the western media today. Nor are they 'primitive polluters' and 'destroyers of the forest', as many governments, especially in Asia, tend to label indigenous swidden farmers (see for example Prasert Trakansuphakon's contribution in this volume). Stereotypes attached to indigenous peoples – whether contemptuous or idealising – have always had a political bearing.

*Old growth forests have become rare on Mindoro island. Aware of their vital role in their domestic economy and in maintaining a healthy environment, Buhid communities have now taken initiatives for their conservation. Photo: Christian Erni*

Scapegoating the indigenous peoples as forest destroyers has led to harsh measures such as relocation of communities or banning of swidden agriculture (as, for example, in Thailand and Vietnam; see IWGIA 1995: 135-139; 1996: 148-158).

On the other hand, idealising them as 'environmental saints' has raised false expectations, and consequently leads to severe criticism if indigenous communities start to commercially exploit some of their resources such as, for example, taking up small-scale logging in their forests. Western industrial civilisation obviously wants to portray indigenous peoples as unchanging 'primitives', living in a pristine state of human existence and 'in harmony with nature'. There is apparently a need for knowing that 'out there somewhere' there are unspoilt human societies, 'peoples close to nature', rejecting the corruptive impact of modern civilisation. Just like 'untouched wildernesses', 'the last paradises' brought to cozy middle class homes by easy consumable 45 minute TV documentaries and glossy coffee-table books, indigenous peoples seem to serve the psychological hygiene of people deeply unsatisfied with the state of their own society.

The peculiarities of indigenous peoples' culture and social and political system are all too often only recognised if they conform to such prevailing prejudices – or to the extent they serve particular interests like those of conservation agencies and develoment NGOs, for example, which may more easily raise funds these days if their programmes are brushed up with an 'indigenous peoples component'.

Far more important, the widespread, highly romanticising preconception of indigenous peoples as pristine 'ecologically noble savages' implies the denial of the right to change, to experiment with new adaptive strategies, to make mistakes and learn in order to be able to cope with the challenges faced by a rapidly changing natural and social environment, in short: to self-development.

There is ample evidence that indigenous peoples' relationships to the environment are different, that their resource use systems are much more sustainable than those dominating the world today. But this is not a given, it is not 'in the genes' nor does it, once attained in the process of a particular indigenous peoples' cultural evolution, remain static. Like in all human societies,

23

indigenous peoples' environmental adaptations are constantly changing, are shifting course in the process of self-development and in response to changing external and internal conditions.

The rich variety of specific forms of cultural adaptations developed by the world's indigenous peoples in this process renders it difficult to make generalisations about indigenous peoples' relationships to the environment. Nevertheless, and even at the risk of having to face the blame for imposing just another outsider's view on indigenous peoples, I would like to draw attention to a few crucial aspects of indigenous peoples' environmental relationship and self-development, features which make them qualitatively different from the dominant models today.

Some of the characteristics outlined in the following may not fully apply any more to indigenous communities who became – by choice or force – more closely integrated into the ever expanding market economy. Furthermore, indigenous peoples' relationships to the natural environment are holistic. They are as much emotional and spiritual as political and economic. Any outsider's attempt to understand and describe the nature of environmental relationships of a particular indigenous people will unavoidably be confined – and distorted – by his or her own culture: specific perceptions and conceptualisations. And because making generalisations means even further abstraction, such an endeavour must leave many – and above all indigenous people – unsatisfied. Nevertheless, as one of the aims of this publication is to further the western development aid and conservation community's understanding of indigenous peoples' relationships with the environment, doing this within western culture's conceptual framework may be a legitimate, and probably the only feasible, way. Even from this perspective, the brief outline given below is far from being exhaustive. It is mainly confined to a few formal and structural aspects of indigenous peoples' traditional resource use systems, aspects which I consider crucial in defining their relationship to the natural environment and the logic of indigenous self-development.

Some basic features of indigenous resource use systems:

1. Indigenous resource use systems are highly decentralised and based on the utilisation of renewable resources, i.e. they rest on tapping biological processes (like forest succession for restoring

soil fertility or population dynamics of game and fish species) rather than on the exploitation of organic and inorganic capital (oil, coal, mineral resources) accumulated in geological time spans.

2. This means that traditional indigenous resource use is not – and even more modern forms only to a very limited extent – dependent on external energy and nutrient subsidy in the form of fuel and agrochemicals.

3. Consequently, traditional indigenous resource use systems are not 'self-poisoning' (Clarke 1977: 389).

4. This means that in indigenous resource use systems, the present generation is bearing the cost of production rather than passing them on to future generations (ibid.: 376). In this way, indigenous resource use systems fulfill the main criteria of the World Commission on Environment and Development's definition of sustainable development.

5. Traditional indigenous economies are usually based on the utilisation of a broad range of domesticated and/or wild animal and plant species. Indigenous peoples manipulate their natural environment accordingly, which increases the complexity of an ecosystem's microhabitat pattern and thereby often enhances, rather than reduces, biodiversity. Many of the so-called 'wildernesses' – like the savannas of East Africa, the woodlands of Northern Australia, the dry forests of mainland South-East Asia or even the Amazon rainforests – should rather be called 'cultural landscapes', as they have been created or at least shaped, and in any case maintained, for centuries through indigenous peoples' constant interaction with their natural environments (see also the contributions of Kamomon and McNeely in this volume; Collins et.al. 1991; Lewis 1989; Posey/BalJe 1989).

6. Closely related to, and in some cases the result of, the use of a broad variety of species and microhabitats is the high degree of decentralisation of indigenous peoples' resource use systems mentioned above. Indigenous communities are, generally, to a large extent economically self-sufficient. They are able to satisfy most household needs locally; both production and consumption occur locally. Little energy and matter leave the local system.

In general, most traditional indigenous resource use systems show properties which largely correspond to those identified as the fundamental principles found in highly sustainable self-regulated systems, like the utilisation of existing natural processes, recycling, symbiosis and small-scale spatial diversity; a high structural and functional compatability with the organisational principles found in nature, etc. (see Vester 1984: 81ff).

7. What is crucial about such small autonomous systems is that they have shown to be more sensitive to ecological problems than larger, more complex ones (Clarke 1977: 382).

For indigenous peoples, to be sensitive to ecological problems is a question of survival. What this of course requires is an intimate knowledge of the natural environments and processes.

> In indigenous cultures, experts exist who are peculiarly aware of Nature's organising principles, sometimes described as entities, spirits, or natural law (Posey 1996: 31).
>
> Although Indigenous Knowledge is highly pragmatic and practical, Indigenous Peoples generally view this knowledge as emanating from a spiritual base: all Creation is sacred, the sacred and the secular are inseperable, spirituality is the highest form of consciousness, and spiritual consciousness is the highest form of awarness. In this sense, a dimension of Indigenous Knowledge is not local knowledge, but knowledge of the universal as expressed in the local (ibid.).

8. Indigenous peoples' traditional economies are so-called subsistence economies, whose functional logic differs fundamentally from the now globalised model of capitalist market economy. Indigenous subsistence economies are *need oriented,* which means that production aims – and therefore the overall level of production – are geared to fulfilling the totality of individual and communal needs, as defined by the prevalent values of the society. The crucial implication is that in contrast to the logic of capitalist commodity production, which is based on the primacy of profit maximisation, production stops when needs are met. Especially in non-monetarised indigenous economies, driving production beyond this level just does not make sense, as there is simply no use for accumulated surplus. The self-amplifying mechanism of profit maximisation, capital accumulation and reinvestment in production, leading to exponantial growth, is

absent. Therefore, subsistence economies have an inherent tendency to rather 'underuse' than fully exploit (or over-exploit) natural resources (Sahlins 1974). This is provided, of course, that the resource base is still sufficient, which again in most cases depends on whether the respective indigenous community retains uncontested control over its territory.

9. But even then, over-exploitation of certain resources is possible – and at times has occured among many indigenous communities. But due to their intimacy with their natural environment and their direct and vital dependence on it, self-regulation processes are more likely to occur in time. Explicit and implicit conservation rules, both age-old and recent, can be found among indigenous peoples all over the world. Often, they are embedded in ritual practices and regulations (see, for example, BalJe 1985; Eder 1995; Sankhala 1985; Reichel-Dolmatoff 1976; Trakansuphakon in this volume).

Nevertheless, just as often, neither explicit nor implicit conservation rules may be found, or, even where prevalent, there may be 'little correlation between beliefs prescribing certain practices and actual behavior' (Colchester 1994: 27). And yet, as among Amazonian Indians, balance is achieved.

Many Amazonian Indians, it has been found, have an opportunistic rather than conservation attitude to the environment and achieve ecological balance because their traditional political systems and settlement patterns encourage mobility. Indians thus move their villages, fields and hunting expeditions to fresh areas once localities are exhausted because it requires less effort than does obtaining diminishing returns from the present locations. Balance is thus achieved unintentionally by negative feedback rather than through conscious concern with excessive use. Market demands and other pressures that sedentarise and enlarge these communities, thus disrupting traditional residence and settlement patterns, coupled with new technologies such as outboard engines that cut travel times and machines to process crops, may upset these negative feedback cycles and cause indigenous communities to over-exploit their locale (ibid.).

Under such drastically changed conditions, affected indigenous communities also have to devise explicit conservation rules. It has been found that self-imposed conservation rules are more likely to emerge among indigenous communities than elsewhere. In India, for example, a 'forest/poverty/tribal inter-face' (Poffenberger et al. 1996:4) has been identified with respect to successful community forest management:

> Forest protection activities appear most common in areas that are characterised by significant concentrations of forest, poverty, and high tribal populations. Cultural and economic ties to the forest often lead tribals to play a leadership role in establishing controls over degrading forests, although low-caste and low-income groups are also active (ibid.).

And in a National Workshop on Joint Forest Mangement it was concluded:

> On the positive side, there are regions (especially hills, uplands and tribal regions, where most forests are located) in India where communities have shown a capacity for managing their land resources (Society for Promotion of Wasteland Development 1993:5).

Some of the decisive factors ensuring that self-imposed conservation rules are actually followed in indigenous communities are the small size of traditional communities 'where people know each other', the prevalence of customary law, traditional authority, and social control exerted and sanctions imposed by the community (ibid.; see also Posey and Dutfield 1996:44f).

**New Approaches in Development and Conservation: Towards a Genuine Partnership with Indigenous Peoples?**
Many indigenous peoples today find themselves confronted with conditions which have seriously disrupted their economies and socio-political systems and do not allow them to continue with their traditional resource use practices any more. Some of the articles in this volume bear testimony to the multitude of outside threats indigenous communities have to face these days. Ironically, many of the encroachments on indigenous territories happen in the name of 'development', are projects and programmes which pretend to be guided by the aim to make a 'more rational' use of the respective land and resources. However, the 'rationality' standing behind these kinds of 'development' is all too well-known: more profits and power for the already wealthy and powerful, and not, at least after closer scrutiny, sustainability

and concern for the majority of present and future generations. The World Council on Environment and Development considers the marginalisation of indigenous peoples as a clear indicator of a misguided development:

> In terms of sheer numbers, these isolated, vulnerable groups are small, but their marginalisation is a symptom of a style of development that tends to neglect both human and environmental considerations. Hence a more careful and sensitive consideration of their interests is a touchstone of sustainable development policy *(World Commission on Environment and Development 1987:116)*.

And the Commission demands:

> Their traditional rights should be recognised and they should be given a decisive voice in formulating policies about resource use in their areas *(Ibid. p. 12)*.

In the decade since the publishing of the WCED report, the important role indigenous peoples can play in sustainable development and conservation has increasingly been recognised. The Rio Declaration states this unambiguously in Principle 22:

> Indigenous people and their communities and other local communities have a vital role in environmental management and development because of their knowledge and traditional practices. States should recognise and duly support their identity, culture and interests and enable their effective participation in the achievement of sustainable development.

And decades of lobbying for the recognition of indigenous peoples' rights at the UN level has led at least a few European countries (Denmark, Norway, the Netherlands and the UK) to come up with a special policy on indigenous peoples for their international development work, which tries to put into practice the 'New Partnership' called for in the proclamation of the United Nation's Year of the Indigenous Peoples in 1993 (see de Kort's contribution in this volume).

More widely recognised, at least verbally, is the crucial role that accrues to indigenous peoples in conserving the world's threatened biodiversity. The stronger involvement of local people – whether indigenous or non-indigenous – in biodiversity conservation programmes, the reorientation of biodiversity conservation from 'protection from use to protection for use', as proclaimed by the leading conservation agencies such as the WWF and the IUCN, is basically the result of the failure of the conventional institutional conservation approach. This approach basically rests on the National Park concept, the so-called "Yellowstone model (see Kemf's contribution in this volume). The sobering lesson learned in decade long experiences with the conventional approach is summarised in a statment by Jeffrey Sayer of the IUCN:

> Legal protection is rarely sufficient to guarantee the continuing integrity of conservation areas. Local people, often with good reason, frequently see parks as government-imposed restrictions on their legitimate rights. Patrolling by guards, demarcation of boundaries and provision of tourist facilities will therefore not deter them from agricultural encroachment. Illegal hunting and gathering of forest products will be difficult to control. Laws which are resented by the majority of the population are difficult to enforce. In these situations, protected areas lose support and credibility, and their condition rapidly deteriorates *(1991: 1, cit. in: Colchester 1994:17f)*.

Indigenous peoples, having lived and actively contributed to the enhancement and preservation of the world's last refuges of high biological diversity, have so far been disproportionally affected by conventional conservation programmes. This occurs in spite of the fact that in many cases conservation and indigenous peoples' rights are all but incompatible. On the contrary, more often than not, there are considerable converging interests, and the results of indigenous peoples' assertion of their territorial rights may come close or be identical to what conventional approaches seek but more often fail to accomplish.

The categories of actions taken by traditional communities and their representative organisations in defending and consolidating their environmental interests sometimes resemble the mechanisms of institutional conservation but have different origins and purposes. They usually emerged from crisis of conflicts, negotiations over land or resource rights, controversies over resource use between traditional users and conservation agencies, campaigns against animal use by animal rights and protection groups, and resisting the impacts of industrial development (Poole 1992: 58).

## Collaborative Management and Participatory Development: Substantiating Partnership with Indigenous Peoples

Joint management or collaborative management for conservation is considered by many concerned conservationists the most promising – if not the only – way to protect the world's rapidly dwindling biodiversity. Indigenous peoples, having inhabited and used the world's areas of highest biodiversity for ages, are, one should assume, their natural allies.

As early as 1975, the IUCN passed a resolution at its 12th General Assembly in Kinshasa, Zaire,

> [. . .] recognising the value and importance of "traditional ways of life and skills of the people which enable them to live in harmony with their environment". The resolution recommended that governments "maintain and encourage traditional methods of living" and "devise means by which indigenous people may bring their lands into conservation areas without relinquishing their ownership, use or tenure rights". The same resolution also recommended against displacement and stated "nor should such reserves anywhere be proclaimed without adequate consultation" (International Alliance/IWGIA 1996:141f).

Although the reorientation of the prevailing conservation approach does not, in the first place, result from concerns for the local people affected by externally imposed conservation measures, some communities, and indigenous peoples in particular, may be able to take advantage of it.

In recent years, some governments have adopted collaborative management approaches in forestry, fishery, wildlife and protected area policies.[3] However, these co-management arrangements have hardly ever gone beyond the granting of rather limited usufruct rights to indigenous peoples. Even in some of the most enthusiastically acclaimed cases of conservation programmes which departed from the recognition of indigenous peoples' ownership rights to their territories, serious deficiencies were uncovered. Detailed research by Sally Weaver in Australia's Gurig and Kakadu National Parks, for example, showed that:

> [...] in the first place, recognition of ownership had been made conditional on the definition of the areas as national parks. Effective involvement of Aboriginal owners in management was neither achieved nor sought. Whereas Aborigines actually sought control of overall planning and policy decisions – rather than day-to-day

management – they were more often cast in the role of rangers, which they resented. Aboriginal authority, she found, was continually squeezed by a tendency for government and parks agencies to extend their political-bureaucratic power base *(Colchester 1994:37)*.

Granting land rights in many cases adds up to not much more than lip-services. As Colchester continues:

> In sum, it is clear that there remains an inherent reluctance of conservationists to relinquish or even share power over protected areas. Stung by the criticisms of their socially insensitive and politically blind approach, conservationists have been readily persuaded to admit that the needs of local people should be taken into account. They have been far more reluctant to recognize indigenous assertion, backed by international law, of their rights to own and control land and exercise their authority over their own domains (1994:38).

Cases of creating conservation areas with the full support of indigenous peoples remain rare. One of the few success stories is Wasur National Park established by the WWF in the south of West Papua, Indonesia. The strong support the WWF was able to gain among indigenous peoples rests on its persistent and unremitting endeavour to secure resource rights for the people within a legal framework which does not in any respect recognise indigenous peoples' land rights (see Kemf's contribution to this volume; Craven and Wardoyo 1993; Colchester 1994: 39).

In spite of the still considerable influence of more conservative factions within the WWF, above all in some of its national branches, and although, on the ground level, implementation of its protected area programmes in many countries leaves much to desire, WWF International is clearly on the forefront when it comes to recognition of indigenous peoples' rights in conservation programmes. In its recently adopted Statement of Principles on Indigenous Peoples and Conservation it is stated that the 'WWF fully endorses the provisions about indigenous peoples contained in the following international instruments: Agenda 21; Convention on Biological Diversity; ILO Convention 169; draft UN Declaration on the Rights of Indigenous Peoples" (WWF 1996: 4). And Parapgraph 8 reads:

> WWF recognises that indigenous peoples have the right to the lands, territories, and resources that they have traditionally owned or otherwise occupied or used, and that those rights must be

recognised and effectively protected, as laid out in the ILO Convention 169 *(ibid.)*.

However, Pragraph 9 hastens to add some qualifications which reintroduce the priority of national conservation and development objectives.

> WWF recognises the right of indigenous peoples to exert contol over their lands, territories, and resources, and establish on them the management and governance systems that best suit their cultures and social needs, whilst respecting national sovereignty and conforming to national conservation and development objectives (ibid., emphasis added).

Still, the WWF has taken a great leap forward towards establishing a true partnership with indigenous peoples in conservation, as compared to the IUCN, the world's leading and most influential conservation agency. Attempts by the International Alliance of Indigenous-Tribal Peoples of the Tropical Forest to convince the IUCN to revise their policy on indigenous peoples and conservation have been frustrated:

> Officials from the World Conservation Union, stressing the intergovernmental nature of the Union, have expressed reservations about the wisdom of indigenous peoples insisting on a right-based approach to conservation *(International Alliance 1996:142f)*.

This attitude finds its expression in the fact that the IUCN's list of Protected Areas Management Categories does not yet include Indigenous Territories or Communal Reserves. And still few are the governments which, like Colombia, have come to realise *'that securing indigenous land ownership is the best means of ensuring conservation'* (Colchester 1994: 39).

What makes the argument in favour of collaborative management so convincing is its pragmatism, its call for a partnership in conservation based on converging interests and compromise. The sharing of rights and duties – in most cases between the government and communities, which involves a de-facto devolution of central government power – is understood as the main precondition for establishing viable collaborative management regimes.

There is no doubt that this approach may be beneficial to many indigenous peoples. But these benefits have so far been rather limited, as the rights granted to indigenous peoples turned out to be mainly an instrument for pursuing largely externally defined goals. Factual evidence even justifies fears that collaborative resource management and participatory development programmes, which do not depart from a genuine recognition of indigenous rights to self-determination and territories, may prove to be nothing but another 'development bandwagon' (Saxena 1996) on which governments jump in order to comply with foreign donors' demands, or even a means for maintaining control over indigenous territories while maintaining 'political correctness' in a context of growing international concern for indigenous peoples' rights.

Somewhat similar problems exist with the participatory approach in development. Basically aimed at ensuring that the needs of the recipients are properly reflected and agreed-upon measures appropriately implemented, it undoubtedly reflects concern for the people. But whereas the current development practice is as much determined by the need for efficiency, the participatory approach is usually combined with a 'systems' or 'investigation' approach, which again reintroduces a top-down relationship between donors and the local people (for a more detailed discussion see Gray's contribution in this volume).

Indigenous peoples are well aware of the need for maintaining or re-establishing sustainable resource use and conservation measures on their territories. In many cases, they also need external assistance and are therefore ready to co-operate with governmental or non-governmental agencies. But, for them, the recognition of their right to self-determination and their territories is more than just a means for accomplishing this shared goal. And although these rights are undoubtedly the fundamental precondition for their cultural or even physical survival, indigenous peoples likewise reject an instrumentalistic and paternalistic conservation approach to their own situation. As the Indigenous Peoples Earth Charter states in paragraph 59:

> We value the efforts of protection of the Biodiversity but we reject to be included as part of an inert diversity which pretends to be maintained for scientific and folkloric purposes *(IWGIA 1992: 59)*.

An underlying instrumentality can even be found in apparently concerned reflections like the following, in which it is suggested that '... *indigenous peoples hold a distinct advantage over other rural social sectors'* in developing what the author calls *"vernacular approaches in biodiversity protection', '... because they have the possibility through ancestral land claims of regaining some measure of control over land and resources'* (Poole 1992: 56).

For indigenous peoples, the right to their territories and self-determination is a given and therefore non-negotiable. Consequently, it is something they do not feel they need to claim. As the Indigenous Peoples Earth Charter in paragraph 71 states:

> We must never use the term "land claims". It is the non-indigenous peoples which do not have any land. All the land is our land. It is non-indigenous peoples who are making claims to our land. We are not making claims to our land *(IWGIA 1992: 59f)*.

For indigenous peoples, the recognition of the rights to self-determination and to their territories are the bases of negotiations of any further sharing of rights and duties on which co-operation in development and conservation rests. Taking this demand as the point of departure in the respective policies and programmes is what substantiating partnership with indigenous peoples means.

## References

Archibold, Guillermo and Sheila Davey 1993. "Kuna Yala: protecting the San Blas of Panama"; in E. Kemf (ed.): *The Law of the Mother*. San Francisco: Sierra Club Book.

BalJe, William 1985. "Ka'apor Ritual Hunting". *Human Ecology* 13(4).

Berkes, Fikret 1989. "Co-management and the James Bay Agreement" in E. Pinkerton (ed.): *Co-operative Management of Local Fisheries: new directions for improved management and community development*. Vancouver: University of British Columbia Press.

Clarke, William C. 1977. "The Structure of Permanence: The Relevance of Self-subsistence Communities for World Ecosystem Management" in Bayliss-Smith, T.P./R.G. Feachem: *Subsistence and Survival. Rural Ecology in the Pacific*. London: Academic Press.

Colchester, Marcus 1994. "Salvaging Nature: Indigenous Peoples, Protected Areas and Biodiversity Conservation". UNRISD Discussion Paper 55. Geneva: United Nations Research Institute for Social Development.

Collins, N. Mark, J.A. Sayer, T.C. Whitmore 1991. *The Conservation Atlas of Forests. Asia and the Pacific*. London: Macmillan.

Craven, Ian and Wahyudi Wardoyo 1993. "Gardens in the Forest" in E. Kemf (ed.): *The Law of the Mother*. San Francisco: Sierra Club Book.

Doubleday, N.C. 1989. "Co-management of the Inuvialut Final Agreement" in E. Pinkerton (ed.): *Co-operative Management of Local Fisheries: new directions for improved management and community development*. Vancouver: University of British Columbia Press.

Hill, M.A. and A.J. Press 1993. "Kakadu National Park: An Australian Experience in Co-management"; in: David Western and R.Michael Wright (eds.) 1994. *Natural Connections. Perspectives in Community-based Conservation*. Washington, D.C./Covelo: Island Press.

International Alliance of Indigenous-Tribal Peoples of the Tropical Forest, IWGIA 1996. *Indigenous Peoples, Forest and Biodiversity. Indigenous Peoples and the Global Environmental Agenda*. IWGIA Document No. 82. Copenhagen: IWGIA.

IUCN/UNEP/WWF 1991. *Caring for the Earth. A Strategy for Sustainable Living*. Gland, Switzerland.

IWGIA 1992. Newsletter 4/92

IWGIA 1995. *The Indigenous World 1994-95*. Copenhagen: IWGIA.

IWGIA 1996. *The Indigenous World 1995-96*. Copenhagen: IWGIA.

Lewis, Henry T. 1989. "Ecological and Technological Knowledge of Fire: Aborigines versus Park Rangers in Northern Australia". *American Anthropologist* 91(4).

Metcalfe, Simon 1994. "The Zimbabwe Communal Areas Management Programme for Indigenous Resources" in David Western and R.Michael Wright (eds.) 1994. *Natural Connections. Perspectives in*

*Community-based Conservation*. Washington, D.C./Covelo: Island Press.

Poffenberger, Mark, et.al. 1996. "Grassroots Forest Protection: Eastern Indian Experiences". Asia Forest Network, Research Network Report No. 7. Berkeley: Center for Southeast Asia Studies, University of California.

Poffenberger, Mark, B. McGean (eds.) 1996. *Village Voices, Forest Choices. Joint Forest Management in India*. Delhi: Oxford University Press.

Poole, Peter J. 1992. "Indigenous Peoples and Biodiversity Protection" in Shelton H. Davis (ed.): *The Social Challenge of Biodiversity Conservation Projects. A Collection of Articles*. Washington D.C.: The World Bank, The Global Environmental Facility.

Posey, Darrell A., W. BalJe (eds.) 1989. "Resource Management in Amazonia: Indigenous and Folk Strategies". *Advances in Economic Botany*, Vol. 7. New York.

Posey, Darrell A., Graham Dutfield 1996. "Indigenous Peoples and Sustainability". Gland, Switzerland: IUCN (Draft).

Rambo, A. Terry 1985. "Primitive Polluters. Semang Impact on the Malaysian Tropical Rainforest Ecosystem". *Anthropological Papers* No. 76. Ann Arbor, Michigan: Museum of Anthropology, University of Michigan.

Reichel-Dolmatoff, G. 1976. "Cosmology as Ecological Analysis: A View from the Rainforest". *Man* 11(3).

Sahlins, Mashall 1974. "The Domestic Mode of Production: The Structure of Underproduction" in *Stone Age Economics*. London: Tavistock.

Sankhala, K.S., P. Jackson 1985. "People, Trees and Antelopes in the Indian Desert" in McNeely, J. A., D. Pitt, 1985. *Culture and Conservation: The Human Dimension in Environmental Planning*. London: Croom Helm.

Saxena, N.C. 1996. "Joint Forest Management in India. Empowering the people or another development bandwagon?" Bogor, Indonesia: Centre for International Forestry Research (Draft).

Society for Promotion of Wasteland Development 1993. "Joint Forest Management: Concept & Opportunities". Proceedings of the National Workshop held at Surajkund, August 1992. New Delhi.

Thomas, Steve 1992. "CAMPFIRE and Institution Building for Natural Resource Conservation and Utilization". Paper presented to Provincial Workshops on CAMPFIRE. Harare: Zimbabwe Trust.

United Nations 1992. "Report of the United Nations Conference on Environment and Development", Rio de Janeiro, 3 – 14 June 1992. A/CONF.151/26 (Vol. I), 12 August 1992.

Vester, Frederic 1984. *Neuland des Denkens. Vom technokratischen zum kybernetischen Zeitalter*. Munich: Deutscher Taschenbuch Verlag.

Wily, Liz 1995. "Collaborative Forest Management and Government: The Case of Mgori Forest", Tanzania. Report. Swedish International Development Agency.

World Commission on Environment and Development 1987. *Our Common Future*. Oxford: Oxford University Press.

**Notes**

1 Side dishes that go along with starchy staple food.

2 The expression is adopted from Rambo 1985.

3 On collaborative forest management see Wily 1995 for Tanzania; Poffenberger/McGean 1996 and Saxena 1996 for India; on fisheries and wildlife in Canada: Berkes 1989 (James Bay Agreement), Doubleday 1989 (Inuvialut Final Agreement); on wildlife in Zimbabwe: Thomas 1992, Metcalfe 1994; on protected areas: Archibold/Davey 1993 for Panama, Hill/Press 1994 for Australia.

Victoria Tauli-Corpuz

# THREE YEARS AFTER RIO: AN INDIGENOUS ASSESSMENT

## Introduction

3 years have passed since the historic Earth Summit in Rio was held and indeed, it is about time to take stock of what has been achieved since then. I am most grateful to the organisers of this conference for inviting me to provide an assessment from an indigenous person's perspective. I do not claim to speak on behalf of all indigenous peoples because I do not think anyone can do this. I can only speak on behalf of the organisations and networks I belong to.

I will start by reviewing the main achievements in Rio. I will then continue with what has happened to indigenous peoples within this 3 year period. I would also like to consider some major events which took place at the international arena which directly impact on indigenous peoples. This will answer the question 'what are the main opportunities or obstacles to achieving sustainability?' Finally, I will discuss the hopes and challenges for indigenous peoples as well as for those who are advocating our rights. What points should be discussed in international and multisectoral dialogues?

## Key Achievements of Rio

Agenda 21, the Rio Declaration on Environment and Development, and the Statement of Forest Principles are the final negotiated documents which were borne out of Rio. Except for a few chapters in Agenda 21, such as Chapter 16 (Environmentally Sound Management of Biotechnology), the rhetoric in these documents could be favourable for indigenous peoples. Principle 22 of the Rio Declaration states:

> Indigenous people and their communities and other local communities have a vital role in environmental management and development because of their knowledge and traditional practices. States should recognize and duly support their identity, culture, and interests and enable their effective participation in sustainable development.

Principle 10 states:

> Environmental issues are best handled with participation of all concerned citizens, at the relevant level. At the national level, each individual shall have appropriate access to information concerning the environment that is held by public authorities, including information on hazardous materials and activities in their communities, and the opportunity to participate in decision-making processes. States shall facilitate and encourage public awareness and participation by making information widely available. Effective access to judicial and administrative proceedings, including redress and remedy, shall be provided.

Principle 14 says:

> States should effectively cooperate to discourage or prevent the relocation and transfer to other States of activities and substances that cause severe environmental degradation or are found to be harmful to human health.

These are just 3 of the 27 Principles of the Rio Declaration, all of which are finely balanced to take into consideration the common but differentiated responsibilities of countries. It also acknowledged that unsustainable patterns of production and consumption should be reduced to achieve sustainable development (Principle 8). This is important because somehow it is an acceptance that the prevailing development paradigm is unsustainable and therefore certain elements should be altered.

Another key achievement for Rio is that it was able to integrate environment and development issues to a certain degree. I can still remember the euphoria felt by many of those within the NGO community who have followed the whole process. The fact that many of the issues which activists from the '60s have been talking about were affirmed by these documents which were signed on to by heads of governments is reason enough to be euphoric. However, on the whole, the Rio documents still do not question the basics of the dominant development model, and this is thus one of the major weaknesses of the documents. They still speak of how economic growth should be achieved and how trade liberalisation is going to be one of the ways to achieve growth.

One thing which is glaringly absent from the documents is the issue of mining. For many indigenous peoples, mining is one of the main economic activities in their communities which has resulted in massive environmental degradation and economic disasters. Mining is one of the most unsustainable activities in land and resource management, but in Chapter 10, entitled 'Integrated Approach to the Planning and Management of Land Resources', there was no reference at all to lands rich in minerals.

Agenda 21 included Chapter 26 (Recognizing and Strengthening the Role of Indigenous People), which is the result of lobbying efforts by indigenous peoples and advocates, both before and during the Rio Summit. This chapter has somehow reinforced our lobbying at the UN-Working Group on Indigenous Populations (UN-WGIP) which produced the final draft of the Declaration of the Rights of Indigenous Peoples. It has also helped strengthen our demands to have our rights to our ancestral territories and resources, as well as our right to self-determination, recognised. Chapter 26 has been constantly referred to in many of the resolutions passed by the UN from the General Assembly to the Working Groups. Many of the chapters of Agenda 21 also include at least one phrase referring to the role of indigenous peoples.

The formation of the UN-Commission on Sustainable Development (CSD), which is the body which will monitor and follow-up the Earth Summit, is also important. The yearly sessions and intersessional meetings of this body provided NGOs and major groups the chance to present their concerns and reports. The chapters which were addressed during the Commission on Sustainable Development 3rd Session (11-28 April 1995) were all very relevant for indigenous peoples. These were Chapters 2: Trade and Environment, 3: Combating Poverty, 4: Consumption Patterns, 5: Demographics and Sustainability, 8: Integrating Environment and Development in Decision-Making, 10: Land Management, 11: Combating Deforestation and Forestry Principles, 12: Combating Desertification, 13: Mountain Development, 14: Sustainable Agriculture, 15: Biodiversity, 16: Biotechnology, 23-32: Major Groups, 33: Finance, 34: Transfer of Technology, 35: Science and 40: Information for Decision-making.

In that CSD session the governments were supposed to report on how they have implemented these chapters. I was present at these sessions and the governments had little to say other than presenting a few case studies which were supposed to be success stories. What was absent were critiques on unsustainable programmes and policies of governments, UN agencies and other intergovernmental organisations like the World Bank. This is the area which NGOs and major groups tried to fill.

## What Happened During the Three Years after Rio?
Today, we would like to see whether such grand statements and declarations were able to bring about substantial positive changes to our situation. I will be very frank on this issue. I am afraid that many indigenous peoples will not have the confidence to say that positive changes did occur after Rio. In fact, I can safely say that for the majority of indigenous peoples in the world, they would not even know that there was such a thing as the Earth Summit.

The reality is that many of the world's available natural resources are found on indigenous peoples' lands. The reasons for this reality vary from country to country, but a key factor is the resistance offered by indigenous peoples against such extractive activities which usually end up devastating the precious ancestral territories. There is no hard data for me to quote, but if we take a look at the ongoing conflicts in the world today, many of these are conflicts over resources on indigenous peoples' lands. Many of the Third World countries who have not achieved a balance between agriculture and industry are simply relying on extracting their natural resources to trade with richer nations. These resources are needed to fuel economic growth, pay foreign debts, to line the pockets of corrupt politicians or to make the balance of trade and balance of payments positive.

Therefore, since resources are found on indigenous peoples' lands, the indigenous peoples have to sacrifice for the sake of national interests. This is the story of indigenous peoples from colonisation up to the present. The only difference between then and now is that the rhetoric acknowledging indigenous peoples' roles in sustainable development, importance of indigenous and traditional knowledge, etc. are found almost everywhere. They are found in Agenda 21 and World Bank documents. In fact, governments are all paying lip service to indigenous peoples and sustainable development. But the practice has remained basically the same. Why do I say this? What is my proof?

## More Aggressive Mineral and Oil Extractive Activities

In the Philippines, the government has just passed the Revised Mining Code, called the Philippine Mining Act of 1995. It aims to attract foreign mining investors to the country. This Mining Code allows for foreign investors to own 100% foreign equity, repatriate 100% of the profits they earn, lease mineral lands of not less than 81,000 hectares for 50-75 years, and they can make use of the most sophisticated technology (translated as strip mining) to recover their investments within a short period. A recent report states that the Philippines, next to South Africa, has the richest endowment of gold deposits. Even before the law was passed on 16 February, 1995, there were already 54 applications from foreign mining firms. Most of these are firms from the USA, Canada and Australia.

Most of the mineral lands in the Philippines are found in indigenous peoples territories. Since 1991 the indigenous peoples in Itogon, Benguet, in the Cordillera have been protesting against the strip mining operations of one of the oldest mining corporations, Benguet Corporation. This protest is still alive and the mining corporation has resorted to all sorts of dirty tricks to cow people into allowing their lands to be strip mined. In Southern Mindanao, there is a growing opposition against the expansion of Western Mining Corporation (WMC), which is one of the largest Australian mining firms. Some of the peoples which will be displaced by these operations are 3,000 B'laans and T'bolis, two groups of indigenous peoples found in southern Philippines.

Between June 1994 and February 1995, 22 civilians and 15 alleged guerillas were shot by the Indonesian army, aided by security forces employed by Freeport McMoran. Others were arbitrarily arrested, beaten and tortured, and forced to flee into the jungle. The villagers – members of the Amungme, Dani, and other West Papuan peoples – were demonstrating in opposition to the expansion of the current copper and gold mine at Grasberg, one of the biggest mines in the world. The Amungmes have lost more than 10,000 hectares of their customary lands since 1967 without any compensation. Freeport's Second Contract of Work on Block B covers 2.6 million hectares of the Central Ranges, and this will affect thousands of indigenous peoples. The

43

Indonesian government said that it would remove, by force if necessary, 2,000 indigenous peoples from the concession area.

The traditional economic base of the Ogoni people in Nigeria has been destroyed by the drilling of Shell Oil Company of over 900 million barrels of oil. Ogoni traditional lands are ruined beyond redemption, and the people continue to live in dire poverty.

Even in industrialised countries, indigenous peoples are not spared. In the state of Arizona in the USA, the Sacred Black Mesa, Dineh families are being forcibly displaced by continuing expansion of the open pit mines of the Black Mesa Peabody Coal Mines. The fragile desert ecosystem has deteriorated, water supply has become scarce, and the traditional livestock-based economy is destroyed.

In the Arctic circle in Alaska, the Gwich'in Athabasca peoples are currently resisting the plan of the US Congress to consider reopening the Arctic National Wildlife Refuge for oil and gas exploration. This will threaten the calving grounds of the Porcupine Caribou herd which provides the cultural and economic basis for the survival of the Gwich'in people in Alaska and Canada.

More than 70% of all uranium reserves in the US are beneath indigenous lands. Up to now uranium mining and milling continues. This has led to the contamination of Indian reservations through the 'tailings' or waste piles from the milling that blow radioactive dust throughout the land and into water supplies. Deaths due to cancer have increased among the Hopi, Navajo, Laguna, Acoma, Sioux, Cheyenne and Cree peoples because of this.

With trade liberalisation being led by the General Agreement on Tariffs and Trade (GATT)/World Trade Organisation (WTO), the Norwegian government is in the process of deliberating whether they will allow RTZ (Rio Tinto Zinc) to enter Samiland to mine. The Sámi in Norway are closely watching developments in these agreements and are demanding that they be part of any decision-making body.

The number of examples is endless, and they are all very recent developments, after 1992. With the ratification of the Uruguay Round of the GATT, and the setting up of the WTO, national laws, whether in the South or North, have to be harmonised to concur with the Trade Related Investment Measures (TRIMs) clauses. Mining has always been an area of investment which ensures tremendous profits, so indigenous peoples sitting on mineral rich lands should anticipate more aggressive incursions into their lands.

## Dam Building.

Dam building has been a major area for World Bank lending from the late 1940s to the 1980s. By mid-l980, however, dam construction had slowed down mainly because of protests from peoples who have been adversely affected by such dam projects. There seems to be a comeback, however, of dam construction. World Bank reports state that approximately 350,000 people may be displaced by dams funded by the Bank between 1994 and 1996. Evidence of aggressive dam construction can be seen in all parts of the world.

Governments of the Lower Mekong Basin, Kingdom of Cambodia, Kingdom of Thailand, the Socialist Republic of Vietnam and the Lao Peoples' Democratic Republic signed, last 5 April, 1995, the 'Cooperation in the Sustainable Development of the Mekong River Basin'. This is a plan that will build 200 hydroelectric dam projects along the 4,200 kilometre long Mekong River. This is the tenth largest river in the world and this river basin sustains the most biologically diverse fish and aquatic fauna populations in the world. This is also the centre of great cultural diversity as many of the indigenous peoples found in these four countries are inhabitants of the river basin. It is estimated that the projects will produce 60,000 megawatts of electricity.

The Kong-Chi-Mool project in Thailand, part of the larger project, has commenced in spite of the fact that the Environmental Assessment Report has been rejected as being very inadequate. This project has already destroyed extensive tracts of seasonally flooded forests and increased salinisation of farmland in northeast Thailand. One of the affected peoples here are the Akhas.

In Brazil, 400 Maaxi Indians in Carapara 11 were driven out of their villages to make way for the construction of the Cotingo River Hydroelectric Dam. The indigenous lands of Raposa-Serra do Sol were already delineated as such by the Federal government in 1992. In spite of this, however, the Maaxi Indians remain displaced.

The Bakun Dam in Malaysia which was once thought to be cancelled, has been revived again. It is a 230 metre high dam along the Balui River about 37 kilometres from the town of Belaga on Borneo's northern coast. If built, it will require the clearcutting of 80,000 hectares of rainforest, and forced displacement of 5,000 – 8,000 indigenous peoples from 15 communities.

In Nepal, the World Bank is funding the construction of the 201 MW Arun 111 Hydroelectric Project, with the cost of US$ 1082.3 million, double the national development budget of Nepal. There are 24 different ethnolinguistic groups found within the Arun Valley. Among these are the Rai and Limbu tribes who are still maintaining communal ownership of land.

Resistance to dam construction has always been a part of the struggle of indigenous peoples the world over. The main reason is the displacement caused by dam-building to indigenous peoples who have inhabited such lands since time immemorial. The legacy of 50 years of dam-building has shown that mega-hydroelectric dams are extremely unsustainable, yet loans and funds for such projects still continue. In June, 1994, NGOs came up with the Manibeli Declaration calling for a moratorium on World Bank funding of large dams.

### Recent Concerns

The most recent concerns which have occupied a significant amount of indigenous peoples' time and focus within the past year are those of intellectual property rights, bioprospecting, biopiracy and biotechnology. The role of GATT/WTO and regional economic agreements in ensuring the harmonisation of intellectual property rights in regimes all over the world has also been monitored.

While transnational corporations and governments are still pursuing classic extractive activities such as mining, oil exploration, logging, etc., they have also discovered that genetic and biological resources are also 'gold mines'. The science of biotechnology, particularly genetic engineering, has provided the impetus for the commodification and commercialisation of genetic resources. The Final Agreement of the Uruguay Round, particularly the Trade Related Intellectual Property Rights Clause (TRIPS) has provided the legal framework for this commercialisation. Even before GATT was concluded, however, Agenda 21 had chapters on biodiversity (Chapter 15 and Chapter 16). The negotiations for the Convention on Biological Diversity also started at that time.

Recognition of the importance of conserving biodiversity was stressed, but recommendations for its conservation ranged from setting up integrated protected area systems and valuating biodiversity. The roles of indigenous peoples in conserving this biodiversity was acknowledged and it was recommended that these roles be strengthened.

Transnational corporations and industrialised countries, however, primarily looked at biodiversity as raw material for the biotechnology industry. Thus, following the pattern of how ancestral lands and territories and resources of indigenous peoples were appropriated, legal frameworks to justify such appropriations are being put into place. The only difference is that Public Land Laws and Mining Codes were legislated at the national level, even before the colonisers left. This time the legal framework for the appropriation of genetic resources is being negotiated internationally and governments should harmonise their laws with the international agreements reached at the Uruguay Round. Regional Economic Agreements like NAFTA, APEC, etc. are following the same track, and it seems like what has not been achieved at the GATT/WTO will be opened up at the regional levels. The Biotechnology Chapter of Agenda 21 has been the victory for TNCs and the industrial world. Unlike other chapters which are promoting environmental protection, this chapter is blatantly promoting the biotechnology industry.

Indigenous peoples have sponsored, on their own or in coordination with other NGOs or UN agencies, discussions and conferences on intellectual property rights. Almost all of the conferences arrived at a common conclusion: the intellectual property rights regime of GATT/WTO is a western concept which is antithetical to the world view and practice of indigenous peoples. There is still confusion, however, on how to deal with this situation. Some indigenous peoples see that the biodiversity they have preserved through the years could be a source of income. Therefore, what they are aiming for is the more equitable sharing of benefits when this biodiversity is exploited. Others, however, feel that since they cannot have any control over the market and the whole economic system, they will always be at the losing end of any bargain over biological resources. Added to this is the fact that if we allow our biological and genetic resources to be commercialised and commodified, are we not in effect already reneging on our historical responsibility as responsible stewards of mother earth and all creation?

Thus, the situation is that on the one hand, we have Agenda 21, the Convention on Biological Diversity, Rio Declaration of Principles, etc. which are all acknowledging the contribution of indigenous peoples and farmers in the conservation of genetic resources. On the other hand, we have GATT/WTO TRIPS, which legitimise the patenting and commercialisation of genetic resources and life forms such as parts of animals, plants and micro-organisms. Hordes of biopirates (who come in the form of pharmaceutical and agribusiness corporations, geneticists, molecular biologists, lawyers, anthropologists, ethnobotanists, etc.) are now landing in our territories to appropriate our knowledge and our genetic resources. They tinker with the genetic resources and patent them. Thus, it will not be a surprise if one day we wake up and are told that our traditional medicinal plants, our indigenous seed varieties, and worst, our human genes, are now owned by Roche Pharmaceuticals, Monsanto, Cargill, or by the US Secretary of Commerce.

By now we are all familiar with the Human Genome Diversity Project which has been protested against by many indigenous peoples all over the world. The HGDP, for me, symbolises the ultimate colonisation of indigenous peoples and the destruction of values, traditions and the world views which have kept our communities intact and sustainable. If we are going to be pushed to commercialise and commodify our genetic resources, whether plant, animal, micro-organism or human, because we believe we have no options left, then we might as well forget our identity as indigenous peoples.

### Assessment and Conclusion
The picture presented, although still very incomplete, is sufficient evidence to claim that there have been no substantial positive

changes for indigenous peoples in the world, 3 years after Rio. In fact, in many areas the situation has deteriorated even further. The ongoing conflicts in indigenous peoples lands, which basically revolve around the conflict over land and resources, is proof enough to show that governments have not really internalised and implemented what they have signed in Rio. In a world where resources are rapidly being depleted, and corporations, governments and individuals are becoming more greedy for profits, such conflicts are expected to worsen.

With all the rhetoric about sustainable development by governments, businesses, inter-governmental bodies, and even environmental NGOs, there is no strong evidence to show that there is the political will to really implement Agenda 21. The most convincing reason for this is that the mainstream development paradigm which is now referred to as the neo-liberal economic, political and cultural system, is still the model being implemented by most governments and inter-governmental organisations. In a World Trade Organisation era, it will be expected that this neo-liberal system will be further entrenched. Indigenous peoples, at present, do not even have an effective international legal instrument in place which recognises and protects their rights. In the face of the increasing power of institutions like the WTO, World Bank, IMF and industrialised countries, what chances will there be for indigenous peoples who can not even have the UN pass the Declaration on their rights? In fact, the most recent development at the UN in relation to the draft Declaration on the Rights of Indigenous Peoples shows the kind of odds indigenous peoples are up against. After the UN-WGIP spent 12 years drafting the Declaration, it was submitted to the UN Commission on Human Rights for deliberation and approval. What happened was that it was decided to form an open-ended working group to further elaborate on the Declaration. This might take another 12 years.

### Where do the Hopes and Challenges Lie?
I apologise if what I presented is a gloomy picture. This does not mean, however, that we just should sit and twiddle our thumbs, because this is exactly what the status quo wants. Within these 3 years there are also positive developments upon which we can build our hopes. In spite of tremendous limitations, indigenous

49

peoples have shown that they can equally and effectively participate in lobbying international bodies and conferences. If we can further build up our capabilities to carry out lobbying and advocacy work, I believe we can achieve even more.

More importantly, however, we have also seen that many indigenous peoples have persisted in their resistance against detrimental development projects and policies. I strongly believe that the capacity of indigenous peoples to say no at the community levels should be reinforced many times over. Whatever achievements we achieve at the international level will be meaningless if our people at the local level have lost the will to assert their rights and demands. The challenge for us is to be able to withstand the aggressive moves of the neo-liberal system to harmonise us and impose their monoculture on us. We have to assert our right to be different and be respected for being such. The organising and educational work at the local levels should still be supported because it is there that our hope lies.

In the face of the odds we are confronted with, we also have to strengthen the dialogue with our indigenous counterparts, the NGOs, social movements and even governments and inter-governmental organisations. Indigenous peoples are actually on high moral ground because the alternatives which we can offer for a sustainable world are still viable. These may be on small-scale levels, but if we are given the chance to implement our indigenous visions and practice of sustainable development on larger scales, we are confident that we can do it. However, for us to be able to do this, the international community and governments should once and for all recognise that we have distinct rights as indigenous peoples. We look at the achievements in Rio and the Convention on Biological Diversity, aside from the other declarations which we presented, as building blocks towards recognition and respect for our rights. However, if the draft Declaration on the Rights of Indigenous Peoples is finally approved and ratified by governments, then we will have an additional legal instrument in our favour.

# II
# Land Rights,
# Self-determination
# and Resource Use

MARGERET FRIEL

# BUT ONE PART OF A WHOLE PICTURE OF SURVIVAL. RESOURCE MANAGEMENT IN AUSTRALIA FROM AN URBAN ABORIGINAL PERSPECTIVE

Friends, I am here on behalf of the National Committee to Defend Black Rights. I would like to thank you for enabling us to participate in this forum. Our organisation arose many years ago in response to the unacceptable numbers of Aboriginal people dying in police custody. The Committee has participated at local, national and international levels to ensure that the rights and interests of Aboriginal and Islander people are promoted and protected. In relation to this conference specifically, it is relevant to note the work of other members. The Committee was involved in the 1980s in the Nuclear Disarmament Coordinating Committee, responsible for organising observances of Hiroshima Day, and highlighting the attrocities committed at Maralinga in Australia when the British tested bombs in areas occupied by the Pitjantjantjatjara people. In 1990 a foundation member of the Committee, Ms. Helen Corbett, was the leader of the Australian delegation to the 6th General Assembly meeting. And more recently, Helen and two other indigenous Australians participated in, and were signatories to, the UNCED and Karioca meetings. I am here today to further develop the outcomes of those two meetings.

First, however, I should speak briefly about myself. I am a Jawoyn woman from the Northern Territory of Australia. There are between 800-1000 Jawoyn people in the Northern Territory. Some Jawoyn people retain greater ties to land than others. My mother was one of the many generations of stolen children, taken from her parents when she was about 6 years of age. She was not reunited with her family until she was some 50 years of age, about 20 years ago. I am a person who has grown up in the dominant ideology and who has reaped the benefits of many years of struggle by Aboriginal leaders and their constituencies. I have not learned grandmothers' law in the old fashion. Aboriginality, however, is not about remaining in a static society. Aboriginality is dynamic, both responsive and proactive. Aboriginality is, however, tied to the land, and the land will speak to those who have a right to hear and will listen, be it through ritual education or some other natural law. I come to you, therefore, as a well-educated western indigenous person with a particular intent. I wish to speak to you about the indigenous experience of resource management from an urban Aboriginal perspective.

Finally, I should also say that my people are a very interesting people. The Jawoyn people are the people that succeeded in stopping a major mining project on the basis of religious beliefs and in the next breath surrendered native title to another area of land on which now exists a gold mine, and many other exploration licences are current. The Jawoyn people are the first and only indigenous people in Australia who have surrendered native title. That is enough of an introduction.

## Philosophy

As a prefacing statement, I wish to state that I believe that the use of the term 'resource management' is one of the keys to the difference between indigenous peoples and others.

Peoples cannot simply be seen as managers of resources. We are part of a greater system of existence. Traditionally, indigenous peoples are the ones who have recognised and respected the impact of what other people call resources on the arrangement of our lives.

So why do we use the term resource management? We use it because situations of conflict about resources always arise. And that is the case whether we are talking about a mining company, trying to secure the enjoyment of fundamental human rights, or trying to assert our interest in a debate where non-indigenous peoples are more concerned about protection of fauna than about us.

Indigenous peoples are no longer the only humans interacting with particular areas of land, sea, air and other living life. More commonly, indigenous peoples, like the environment, have been subject to decisions and actions of conquering peoples whether they come under the flag of a treaty, cession or conquest. These

*'Indigenous peoples have always had a particular understanding and connection with particular areas of land': Ayers Rock, sacred site to the Australian Aborigines. Photo: IWGIA Archives*

peoples have brought with them their ideologies, their technologies (as distinct from ours, rather than as the only owners of technology) and their masses. They have altered the way most indigenous peoples live.

But indigenous resource management is still special. It is special for a number of reasons. Firstly, it is important because it recognises natural laws. The essential spirituality and soul of the earth is a living evolving thing. Indigenous peoples have always had a particular understanding and connection with particular areas of land whether they be Australian Aborigines, the Ainu from Japan, or the Sámi peoples. This connection has been maintained through access by individuals to ceremonial education or to seemingly inexplicable spiritual connections. Indigenous peoples have stood up many times as the human voices of the land.

Indigenous resource management is also about survival. It is about cultural maintenance and empowerment. All of those who have passed before us resisting the successive waves of invasions were the first fighters for the right to manage land and resources as determined by the laws governing our existence.

When we talk about indigenous resource management we refer to a time before the environmental movements of society as they currently exist. We pay homage to our grandmothers and grandfathers.

Resource management is not just about resources; it is about all the living things in our state of existence. I found it very difficult to even begin to think of how to address this convention on indigenous resource management not being a resource management expert nor an anthropologist. Nor am I a person who has lived in a remote community or had access to ritual education. I realised, however, that that is one of the keys to the problem. It is possible that the whole question of resource management may well be subject to the likelihood of being locked up in this fashion. The high order of it, the speciality of it, will mark it as a particular field in which only particular people engage. This marginalisation of the discourse has particular ramifications in terms of agendas and processes, and of course the outcomes. It is important for all of us to be able to participate to ensure that all world views are heard, considered and acted upon. We must recognise the value and power of education of many varieties as the key to future developments in terms of defining the field.

**Indigenous Resource Management in Australia: Strategies**

I cannot hope to talk to you about each and every aspect of indigenous resource management in a fashion representative of all indigenous Australians. What I would like to do, however, is to document a history of involvement in resource management questions since colonisation and to highlight two key issues that arise in this connection. After that, I would like to provide some directions for the future with reference to the two documents before us.

In Australia much has happened since colonisation. We have gone from outright plunder and pillage, to non-recognition of any enforceable interests in land and, finally, to a recognition of a variety of forms of interest in land and resources.

More specifically, most indigenous peoples have been removed from their own lands, and those that have not are subject to a range of legislative regimes when non-Aboriginal interests deem further encroachment necessary or desirable. It is a fact of Australian history that indigenous peoples have found it easier to be granted interest in areas of land that nobody else wants – and even this is a modern day approach. And that is not a problem when it is your own land. It has not been so easy to secure recognition of ownership of land when that land is rich in resources.

Indigenous strategies of resource management since colonisation can be characterised as a continued resistance to attempts to destroy Aboriginal society, culture and practices. Although we talk of the Aboriginal people of Australia as one nation, the reality is that the country was one with over 600 nations, each with an association to particular lands, dreamings and resource management strategies. Aboriginal people have used many tactics to resist the invasion because resource management is but one part of a whole picture of survival. The outcomes of government policies and practices were the decimation of Aboriginal populations, the degradation of land and the destruction of other life (including flora and fauna). The Aboriginal populations that exist today are testimony to the determination and struggles of our forbearers. The paths taken by our forebearers also demonstrate a commitment to hope in the face of exclusion and difference. We were not wanted as we were, nor were we fully accepted when we became like them. The sort of ideology that extends from the doctrine of terra nullius and is used constantly in resource management conflicts includes reference to the belief that Aboriginal peoples did not cultivate the land and would not know what hard work is, that we are lawless, descend from savages and so on. The clinging onto this history of difference and exclusion has had particular consequences for non-indigenous resource management. Aboriginal peoples have built their own frameworks for survival within the parameters of non-Aboriginal existence and continue to attempt to build upon those frameworks.

In recent times, the most easily identified coalitions or organisations working towards recognition of indigenous resource management practices have been land councils – representatives of indigenous peoples of particular areas of land. Some of them are established under legislative regimes, like those in the Northern Territory, and attract particular resources and revenue as a consequence. Others are independently established and have secured other types of funding sources. The preliminary question that concerned such organisations was ownership and control over land – the recognition of prior and continuing interests in land. They have also been involved in negotiation over the precise nature of that recognition, e.g. a grant of an inalienable freehold title, perpetual lease or freehold title and control over minerals. Other organisations have also been extensively involved in the purchase of land for indigenous peoples who have been removed from land and whose interests in land are not capable of being recognised under existing mechanisms. Such purchases range from purchases of individual houses to investment in larger areas of land and commercial development proposals. Not all lands are secret sacred places, so Aboriginal peoples have been involved in development activities.

Throughout this period there have also been other developments which will contribute in the long run to the whole area of resource management practices, within a holistic framework. They include demands for recognition of Aboriginal systems of knowledge in terms of customary law, education and health. Aboriginal cultural revival and maintenance is constantly under attack under many different guises. In some communities, Aboriginal children and youth are subject to two systems of education. Governments have, however, yet to recognise the validity of indigenous education for young people in remote communities in the same way as they afford recognition of Aboriginal Studies courses offered to urban indigenous youth and non-indigenous youth. In some cases, community schools have lost Education Department teaching staff because the indigenous community adhered to its traditional educational system. Such education includes knowledge of land and resources, relationships with such, Aboriginal law, health and medicinal practices, and ceremonial and ritual education and initiation.

All of these things – law, education, health and so on – are tied to the question of land ownership and resource management.

## Two Key Issues

I would like to move on to focus on two key issues related to land management, and it is interesting to observe that I am not the first person at this meeting to raise them. They are control over land and participation in negotiation.

I note the statement from Karioca that – All the land is our land. It is non-indigenous peoples who are making claims to our lands. We are not making claims to our land.

The reality is that non-indigenous peoples do not recognise our interests in land as they should. Instead, they force us to occupy our lives fighting and fighting. They have created whole industries of lawyers, anthropologists and so on, on this point alone. Participation in resource management questions only ever comes when we hold within our hands some bargaining point with governments be it an actual piece of paper or the threat of such a possibility.

At the same time, dispossessed indigenous peoples are usually the undisputed title holders in terms of poverty, ill health, poor education and incarceration to highlight just a few statistical indicators. What we continue to fail to remind the dispossessors is that they got rich and continue to get rich off our backs. Resource management is not simply about the megabucks from strategic investments. Resource management is also about the right to enjoyment of fundamental human rights. When we marginalise the parameters of this discourse, we remove the focus from the wider picture to a bird's-eye view. We also limit the participants on the playing field.

And so we come to the final issue that I wish to highlight, which is about participation in negotiation. The general approach of non-indigenous powers in terms of resource management is to talk to us about how they can have the largest piece of a pie that must be baked if not today, then as soon as you can be worn down to give in. When resource management is looked at in terms of doing business with people who have resources, we are talking about the last frontier, the last wave of invaders. They have taken all else before them and left any Aboriginal survivors in their wake. They have still failed to share the resources they have stolen, and depending on who you are they can deal with you in a variety of ways. If you do not already have a title that they recognise they can either usurp your authority (national interest) and pay your community compensation, or drag you through the court system for an extended period of time; in both cases you will have to establish your bona fides in terms of proving the legitimacy of your claims based on criterion they have established. Or they may treat with you. And to ensure that all is fair and above board you will need to secure the best advice available – meaning expert help – yet again. Alternatively, if you have a recognised secure interest in land they are still in a position to legislate it out of existence (e.g. in the national interest). All these activities are conducted at a relatively local or regional level. Some communities have been happy to engage in resource development activities such as this because the reality is that governments have not ensured the enjoyment of fundamental human rights arising from the equitable distribution of resources in Australian society.

## Conclusion
My message to this meeting therefore is twofold. Firstly, resource management needs to be seen in a much wider context with larger numbers of indigenous participants. Secondly, this is the type of focus that needs to be highlighted in international forums and negotiated upon in terms of development of international conventions and committments. To not do so is to participate in the extension of the colonial empires.

When you are engaged in international forums or forums involving resource management I want you to think of these things:

1) That aboriginal resource management involves both spirituality and survival.

2) That all indigenous peoples must be involved or be heard in the resource management field – not just indigenous peoples with control over land; and

3) That when we begin to talk about negotiations that we recognise the inheritance of inequities from our histories that contribute to an imbalance of power in negotiations, and we develop models to overcome the continued pillage and plunder approach to all living indigenous beings.

RIKHA HAVINI

# FROM VICTIMS TO VICTORS: DEVELOPMENT AGGRESSION AND INDIGENOUS MOBILISATION

After colonising and gaining territorial control over Africa in the 18th and 19th centuries, the West embarked onto their next splurge for colonies within the Asia-Pacific rim. In 1668, the French fableist La Fontaine wrote: 'Those who enjoy power always arrange matters so as to give their tyranny an appearance of justice.'

The indigenous peoples, were and are, without doubt, the victims of imperialist conquest seeking raw materials and natural resources. But now, the conquest has taken new forms such as foreign 'multinational corporations'. La Fontaine may have had these new forms in mind when he spoke of the great powers and privileges these nations were revelling in. He could have been referring to the great empires, then being built by the Spanish, British, Portuguese and Dutch. This process was continued by the Germans, Italians as well as the Japanese, at the height of colonial and imperial expansion by the West and Japan in the Third World during this period.

## Bougainville, the Solomon Islands Archipelago and Papua New Guinea
*Some historical settings*
One of our first contacts with the West and discovery of mineral resources and raw materials in the Solomons/Bougainville region as a whole goes back to 1568.

This is when the Spanish seaman Captain Alvara de Mendana became the first explorer to set foot on the Solomon Islands' shores. He thought that he had discovered the source of the mythical 'Biblical King Solomon's mines' there in the Solomons Archipelago. The region was therefore seen as a potential source of plunder, back then, principally for gold and any other interesting finds for the 'motherlands'. Mendana returned to the Solomons again in 1594 but took ill and died there. He is buried somewhere in the Archipelago.

A relatively long period of non-contact with the West on Bougainville was next punctuated with the visit of another European visitor, the French sailor Captain Louis de Bougainville in 1768. He made landfall and sailed north the length of Bougainville, making contact and trading with the people of Buka, Northern Bougainville. He named the big island *'Bougainville'* (the village or the town of the *Bougain)* after his family name. But he also blew the whistle to the West about his new discovery.

He entered into his log book an impressive description of the place and people, and made additions to his world map of the new island of 'Bougainville', and obviously where to find it. He also named the island where he first made local contact *'Bouka'*, now called Buka.

He had asked the locals he was bartering with what the name of this small island was; the gentleman nearest to him turned to his friend and asked, *'bouka?'*, meaning: *'what did this s..!*!*...man, say?'* The captain promptly entered into his logbook the new name 'Bouka'. Needless to say the island already had its local and original name of Ritana or Litana/Letana, before its colonial name.

### The German Rule in Melanesia from 1884 and their Colonial Developmental Policies
Some three decades later, from the 1800s onwards, Bougainville and the other regions faced yet another intrusion from British, Germans, Dutch and French 'invaders' as part of the next push of imperialism to colonise and control indigenous peoples within the Asia-Pacific rim.

Under Chancellor Otto von Bismarck the German Imperial government set foot in New Guinea, Bougainville and the Solomons in 1884. This was not to immediately establish administrative posts but rather for the purpose of economic exploitation of the region's raw materials in order to send them back to the Fatherland.

His argument was that Germany did not have enough manpower or even a navy to control any territory it would lay claim to. But he did not deny those Germans that were already in the field involved in various activities, to come under the protection of the Reich. He put forward the theory that 'nations have no friends, they only have interests', and that 'the flag follows trade – not the reverse and further that it should not cost the government much to keep the flag flying'.

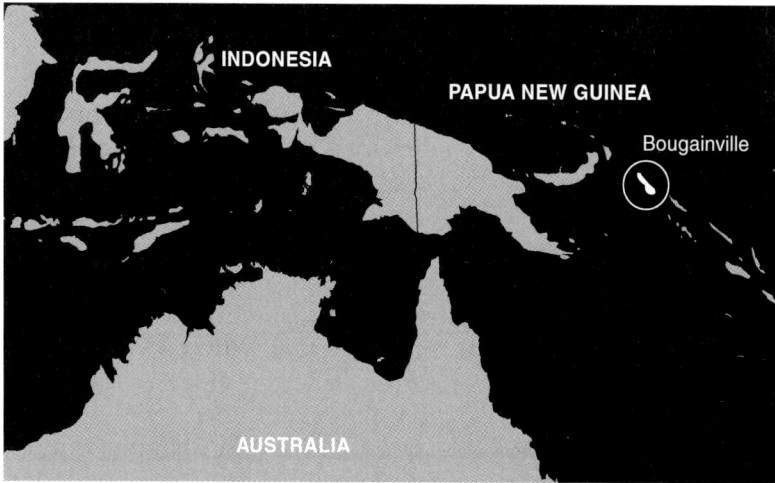

But because of the ensuing competition between the competing imperial governments, Germany later changed its notion of simple economic interests to that of territorial control as well. Bismarck used his gunboats to extend his control into the Solomons from Rabaul. The area of the Solomons Archipelago which now came under German control was Bougainville; while the rest went to Britain and became known as the British Solomon Islands Protectorate (BSIP).

The eastern seaboard of New Guinea all the way to Bougainville was immediately transformed into agricultural projects, by way of the establishment of huge coconut plantations. These plantations remain today but now in the hands of Australian multinational corporations. They are still not controlled by Bougainvilleans whose vast lands were simply taken by the Germans for their own exploitative economic programmes to establish these plantations. They also continued to barter with the locals buying copra and other raw materials which were constantly shipped back to Germany.

Any input into the local population by the German Imperial government was only to 'educate' the natives to better understand their white masters. This was to enable them to become efficient productive agents, working in their plantations as labourers or as trained policemen to help maintain the status quo, all for the 'Fatherland'.

## The Separation of Bougainville through Political Horse-trading by Germany and Britain

The contention between these colonial powers as to their properties and spheres of influence within the Pacific became such a serious business that it became necessary for them to settle their territories and boundaries. These negotiations between the two powers, initiated in 1886, began to sort out their spheres of influence within the Western Pacific once and for all. In this settlement, 'the Solomons south of Bougainville fell within the British sphere of control; while Bougainville remained with Germany, in exchange for territories Germany had in Samoa', where the government of Great Britain was the major 'real estate' proprietor and coloniser. It was not until 1899 that this Agreement was ratified between London and Berlin by a mere exchange of diplomatic notes. It was ultimately implemented in February 1900.

But Germany's control and all its holdings in the South Seas were short-lived; in 1918 she lost the First World War to the allied forces. She subsequently also lost the rest of her territories in the Pacific to the allied forces. German New Guinea and Bougainville fell into the hands of Britain and Australia, and later become a Mandated Territory under the League of Nations administered by Australia on behalf of Britain, along with its own Territory of Papua.

The right thing at this stage would have been to return Bougainville and its people back to the Solomons. Despite utterances of objections from our leaders, Bougainvilleans were just simply forced against their will to be part of this new 'unholy marriage', with the trust territory of New Guinea and Papua.

Bougainville is geographically a part of the Solomon Islands Archipelago. It is the biggest island lying north of the Solomons chain and lies a mere eight kilometres from the arbitrary sea border between the independent state of the Solomon Islands and Bougainville. The land area is about 9,300 square kilometres. The big island of Bougainville is 208 kilometres long and 96 kilometres wide. The mountains, some of which are still active volcanoes, rise up to 3000 metres in height, with a mountain range that forms the backbone from the north to the south.

Bougainville is also over 990 km away from the Papua New Guinea (PNG) capital Port Moresby. It is not part of the land mass of PNG and is separated by the Solomon Sea. The nearest land mass of PNG to Bougainville is its town of Rabaul in East New Britain Province, a distance of 322 kilometres.

The people of Bougainville and the Solomons are related to each other culturally and ethnically, and have visited and traded with each other since time immemorial. Indeed, even after the formal separation from each other through different colonial administrations and control, 'traditional border crossings' from Bougainville to the Solomons and vice versa, used as clan visitations for family reasons, still continue today. The people also have much darker skin than the people of Papua New Guinea.

The common lineage is through the matrilineal clan system, where the clan is traced through the 'Queen' of the clan who is also the titleholder and custodian of the tribal land. There are no resemblances whatsoever with the people of Papua New Guinea who themselves are a very culturally diverse grouping of people consisting of 800 different tribes and languages.

Another interruption in the lives of Bougainvilleans was the next occupation, this time by the Japanese Imperial Army which entrenched itself in southern Bougainville, followed in hot pursuit by the Americans and allied forces in 1942-43. The Americans landed in West Bougainville and there soon followed fierce fighting between the two forces. The people did not quite know why their land was once again occupied by foreigners and being used as a platform to fight their own wars away from their shores. Needless to say, hundreds of Bougainvilleans were also unnecessarily killed in the crossfire throughout Bougainville.

When the war suddenly ended by the dropping of the atomic bomb on Hiroshima, the warring parties just packed up and left, leaving behind a war ravaged Bougainville which soon reverted back to the Australians, then to the United Nations, along with Papua and New Guinea, as a trust territory.

The people of Bougainville were once again never asked by the Australian Colonial Administration whether they wanted to continue with that 'political marriage' to a people and place they were not related to. Did Australia indeed have any 'sovereign right' to manipulate the Bougainvillean's rights and their future destiny? This only supported Bougainvillean nationalism and dissent to develop and grow. At this stage, however, they were not yet in any position of strength to do anything about it.

While Australian 'colonialism' over the Trust Territory of New Guinea and Bougainville became complete at this stage, a free platform for resources and economic exploitation began in earnest both in New Guinea and in Bougainville. In New Guinea, major finds of alluvial gold were found in the Morobe province districts called Bulolo and Wau from 1926, as well as in the Papuan region. By 1932 the Bulolo Gold Dredging and Mining had developed into a booming enterprise for Australian mining interests, needless to say all gold being shipped out of New Guinea.

Economic imperialism from the Germans and the British only continues and gains strength with Australian colonialism in this new stage. Who are being denied their sovereignty and resources? Again, it is none other than the indigenous peoples of this region.

**An Australian 'Slave Trade' or 'Blackbirders'**
In the 19th century, after American whalers had occasionally come to trade, Australian slave traders, euphemistically called 'blackbirders', came to enslave not only Bougainvilleans but also Solomon Islanders and New Caledonians (now Ni-Vanuatuans). They were taken to do slave work in the sugar fields of Queensland and the coconut plantations in Fiji and Samoa. Solomon Islanders and Ni-Vanuatuans suffered more, but Bougainvilleans turned the labour recruitment around and became the 'skilled elite' working in other parts of the German Colony.

Head taxes first imposed by the Germans to draw the people into menial employment for cash caused trouble for Australians after World War II. This is when Bougainvilleans rejected the idea of colonial wages on Australian plantations and also rejected ideas of development imposed from above which demanded taxation.

The people, at this stage, began their own productive and efficient plantations of cash crops which led Bougainville to become the richest agricultural exporter in the Pacific within 40 years. To achieve this with their own resources the people had to undergo tremendous physical work, and they had to resist colonial oppression with physical force.

In time the economic base within Bougainville was combined with the development of an educational resource. Bougainvilleans have always been amongst the best educated in the colony, but in the struggle for independence the island attracted back a highly educated elite who applied their training to develop a unique village-based education system at the same time as they led the way in developing local autonomy in the PNG political system.

The localisation of the economy came about in the struggle against central control. An example of the most significant business projects which Bougainvilleans shared was the Bougainville Development Corporation, which localised enterprises whose development was controlled by Bougainville Copper Limited in turn funded by multinational capital driven by Australia. As the world at large developed its interests in the extractive industries on Bougainville, the local political leadership was to demand repeated negotiations of Bougainville's share in the economic benefits and the political power that was brought to bear to protect extraction.

The demand for self-determination was first nurtured on Bougainville as the people reclaimed their identity in the decades of struggle. The village people have shared in their struggle and directed its course in spite of the power and wealth used against them. The tyranny was concealed in the talk of justice for everybody except the villagers of Bougainville.

The attachment to traditional culture has strengthened the political struggle and provided the resources to mobilise in strength at the village level. Their identity as Bougainvilleans is more and more based on the affirmation of their culture as Solomon Islanders. Small-scale resistance to colonial rule was liable to bubble up for many decades of the twentieth century as the people struggled to determine their own form of development.

The localisation of leadership in the Catholic Church and the Methodist Church has been a central factor in the stronger development of a distinctive Bougainville cultural and political identity.

Land has been the most important factor as it is the *basis* of all Bougainville culture. Alienation from agricultural land was a problem but this paled in comparison to the grievances of landowners who were affected first by mine construction and then the destruction and devastation of the environment by Bougainville Copper.

The struggle outlined here shows how the people in the villages, in conjunction with their national leaders, struggled for a hundred years to bring things together: their world, their education, their economic development as well as their culture, religion and political institutions. The solutions were continually worked out in the villages where the state's proposals for development were brought to a halt by the barbaric intervention of the Papua New Guinea military, let loose on the people of Bougainville by the Papua New Guinea government.

They have torn apart the fabric of Bougainvillean society. This was achieved through the active support of the Australian government and, once again, the plan to set Conzinc Rio Tinto Australia's Bougainville Copper Limited on its feet has been announced.

**The Plunder**
*Conzinc Rio Tinto Australia (CRA), Mining, Bougainville Copper Mine: Victims and Indigenous Mobilisation.*

The 'mother of all plundering' on Bougainville really began with CRA, a subsidiary of RTZ. Conzinc Rio Tinto is one of the world's leading mining giants. CRA is the 'baby mining giant' within the Asia/Australasia and Pacific region. RTZ of London also owns 49% of CRA.

CRA in turn owns about 16 other major mining companies in Australia, of which Bougainville Copper is one of them. CRA has a 53% share in Bougainville Copper Limited (BCL) while the other 20% is owned by the Papua New Guinea government. Not even one equity share was offered to the people of Bougainville, and more specifically to the landowners whose land was expropriated for the CRA mine.

Australia's mining interests on Bougainville go back to 1929 when the Germans departed from Bougainville and New Guinea. This was Australia's general prospecting programme and activities, which had already commenced in New Guinea and Papua.

A Sydney prospector by the name of Jack Comb and his mate, sea captain Bob Palmer, went into Central Bougainville looking for gold at Kupei and Moroni just west of Kieta but northeast of the present mine at Panguna. They carried out patrols through the Panguna ridge and saw evidence of copper, but they were only interested in gold which they mined at the Kupei ridge.

Mining at Kupei was very small-scale as is evidenced by the remains of drilling equipment still visible today. The work finally ceased in the 1950s. But in 1961 a report was released by J. E. Thompson of the Australian Bureau of Mineral Resources that renewed interest in further mineral exploitation on Bougainville. He had investigated copper at the Panguna ridge and his report was coming out just as RTZ was diverting its interest for low grade copper in Australia.

In 1963 a prospecting authority was granted and a company geologist, Ken Philips, went to Bougainville in 1964. This prospecting licence virtually gave them the freedom to march all over the mountains of Kieta, and, in most cases, they arrived unannounced, upsetting the landowners who did not understand what was going on.

By May, 1965, a rich copper deposit was being drilled and RTZ soon became excited about its positive results. The mountains buzzing with activities only continued to compound the landowner's anxiety about what was happening to the once upon a time serene and undisturbed environment.

A bewildered people watched fearfully as their country was being transformed into one of the largest industrial development sites in the southern hemisphere ... a classic case of machine-made modernity being dumped rather unceremoniously into primitive communities still on the edge of the Stone Age.

What a shocking experience for a peaceful people still content with hunting and gathering to have to suddenly cope with the full brunt and impact of Western industrialisation pushed upon them. It tore at the very heart of their existence, i.e. their land and their ancestors', defiling the home of their ancestral spirits, their practices and culture.

An Australian journalist, John Ryan, who was closely following the events between Port Moresby and Bougainville during this period made the following observations:

The hundreds of Europeans flocking to Panguna knew exactly what they were doing and what lay ahead, but to the 10,000 Bougainville men in and around the valley almost everything they saw and heard was new, and a little frightening. In 1964 the prospectors had made their first mistake, and the blame belongs to the Australian government.

They had entered the Panguna and surrounding tribal land without clearly asking permission of the owners. This was the beginning of a surging wave of tribal resistance to try and keep their only heritage, their land, and to get rid of the Australians and Conzinc Rio Tinto.

The size and strength of the resisting groups vary from month to month, but the hard-core remains. The Moronei, Pakia, Guava and the neighbouring villages appealed to the government men at Kieta. The villages were desperately afraid of losing the land for which their ancestors had fought and died, or having to leave the mountains in which their protective tribal spirits lived.

Port Moresby, Canberra and Conzinc Rio Tinto were adamant that prospecting should continue despite the Panguna tribes. The company was at Panguna to make money for its shareholders, and the Australia government wanted it to stay in the hope of revolutionizing the Papua/New Guinea puny economy.

The landholders had to be brushed aside as politely as possible in the national interest. Some of the angry villagers began erecting Tambu signs ('keep out') and one group destroyed a company tent and some equipment.

He continues:

1965 and 1966 were nerve-racking years for the government and the company, with the ever-present danger of ambush and fighting. Equipment were damaged, helicopter pads were put out of action and the Kieta police detachment under Deputy District Commissioner Bill Brown was increased and drilled in riot fighting. Near one mountain village, Patrol Officer (i.e. colonial officer) John Gordon Kirby was greeting a Conzinc Rio Tinto helicopter when the village women with their babies in their arms rushed forward screaming "kill us, kill our children". They began piling tons of stockpiled cargo on the helicopter to keep it on the ground. Kieta's riot squad had to be called in but the incident ended without injury. There were other incidents in other areas as the hard-core of resistance broke out again.

## English Mining Legislation in Direct Conflict with Traditional Land Tenure Laws

CRA's 'legitimacy' on Bougainville was by way of the English/ Australian 1928 Mining Law which gave it the right and free run on the land to prospect. The landowners, the Nasioi tribe, were already cultivating this land for cash cropping, i.e. copra and cocoa. Permission to enter such tribal land was not required from the landowners.

In 1966 this mining law was modified, giving CRA an unlimited run of the field to a ceiling of 10,000 square miles around the deposit. Further confirmation of a viable deposit confirms the go-ahead to mine. But it only had two years of prospecting left and unless it was renewed by the PNG Government there would not be any more incentive to continue with the project. The company had already spent millions of dollars in confirming the viability of the deposit, and it was not about to lose this opportunity.

Another Agreement was therefore entered into, the 1967 Agreement, negotiated with the Australian authorities and CRA where the formal shareholdings were also declared: 53% to CRA and 20% to the Papua New Guinea government.

This agreement, which did not include the landholders, virtually gave CRA freedom to all resources on Bougainville. The other obligation from the PNG Government was to also give land to the company to build a company mining town and port facilities for CRA.

The next victims of this draconian legislation were the coastal people of Rorovana who owned the prime land at Loloho, most suitable and ideal for a port. In a confrontation with the riot police and the colonial officers from Port Moresby, the people fought tooth and nail to prevent their land from being taken from them. The unarmed villagers, men, women and children, were confronted by armed police carrying rifles, batons, shields and gas masks. They were fired upon with tear-gas and charged with batons, all for doing nothing more than protesting the handing over of their land to a multinational mining company. Women threw themselves in front of company bulldozers prepared to sacrifice their lives for their ancestral land.

A newspaper editorial in *The Australian*, August 1969, was so disgusted by the assault that it wrote:

The use of tear-gas and clubs this week to enforce alien laws on the uncomprehending people was a damning indictment of the administration of the Papua New Guinea – which is to say of Canberra.

Another journalist on the scene during the bitter fighting between the people and the Australian PNG riot police force wrote: 'Mothers put babies on the survey pegs to stop the pegs from being hammered in; a village leader publicly threatened to cut his throat in protest.'

Their young leader, Raphael Bele, emphasised the importance of land within his culture in his reply to Sir Maurice, Chairman of CRA when he tried to negotiate for the land to build his company port:

If someone wants my land and I do not want them to have it, he will have to kill me or I will kill them …To Bougainvilleans, land is like the skin on the back of your hand. You inherit it, and it is your duty to pass it on to your children in as good a condition as, or better than, that in which you received it. You would not expect us to sell our skin, would you?…

## A High Court Challenge

This fight went as far as a challenge in a lawsuit in the Australian High Court, by plaintiff Mr Teori Tau, who was arrested in September, 1968, for supposedly assaulting a surveyor on his traditional land.

The legal council for the Bougainvilleans argued the point that 'the minerals belong to the landowners'. He argued that

it had always been so, even before World War I, when Bougainville was a colony of Germany. The Australian Administration after it had taken over the mandate from the League of Nations, had not itself acquired the minerals.

And since the Australian Constitution expressly provided that 'there could be no acquisition of a person's property, except on the condition that just terms of compensation were payable', and

since no compensation for minerals had been paid, THE COPPER IN THE GROUND AT PANGUNA BELONG TO THE OWNERS OF THE LAND. Therefore the Mining Ordinance of Papua New Guinea giving permission to the company were invalid…

But in August, 1969, the seven judges that heard this case decided in favour of Australia thus legitimatising the mining leases on Bougainville. The High Court of Australia used a *1963 High Court Ruling* that

under the Constitution, Australia had the power to administer Territories, and that their power in the Territories was quite self-contained. Thus the terms which applied to the taking of land in Australian States did not have to be applied to the Territory of Papua New Guinea.

The landowners of Rorovana and Panguna were so outraged at this decision that they decided to send their two leaders, Raphael Bele and Paul Lapun, to Australia to issue an injunction to stop the mine. The people were even prepared to go as far as the United Nations if need be.

Needless to say, this move made the company and the governments very worried. Combined with very clever manipulation by the governments, and using 'agents' such as the semi-religious group the Moral Rearmament, government lawyers, economists etc. as middlemen, the two men were 'hijacked' in Australia and their course of action completely re-routed and changed. The two leaders were worried about the Administration's aggressive push for mining and their deployment of well-armed riot police. Not wanting any bloodshed, the leaders, uneducated and unwise in the politics of Western business dealing, conceded blindly into the hands of the 'Moral Rearmament' negotiators. They insisted that a peaceful agreement with the mining company would be beneficial to Bougainville's future. They skillfully followed up from behind, gently prodding and patronising the leaders in their reluctant decision to give in to CRA's assuring proposals.

### Agreement and Deal – that was only a Band-Aid Solution
An Agreement was signed in September, 1969, whereby the people of Rorovana would have

…140 acres of their land leased for 42 years, renewable for another 42 years, BCL would then immediately pay $30,000 and another $7,000 annually. That this amount be reviewed every 7 years, that the landowners would be offered 7,000 ordinary shares in BCL at the issuing price; the company to have the right of occupation of the land and to do whatever was necessary with it.

This agreement then set a pattern by which all other deals were agreed with by the landowners and the company from Rorovana to Panguna, west of the mine and the Jaba River where the tailings dumping would eventually affect those areas to the detriment of their environment, flora and fauna.

Moroni village and her people, sitting on that deposit in the Panguna valley, would later be moved so that an open-cut mine could be sunk. And, unbelievably, some twenty years later it would measure 4,000 feet across and 2,000 feet in depth.

## Dissent Grows, Mobilisation Follows and the Mine is Shut in 1989

In 1972 BCL exported its first copper concentrate and gold to Japan, Germany, Chile and China. It also enjoyed a three year tax holiday during these years when the price of metal was very high. The provision to renegotiate the Agreement after 7 years and the time thereafter was unfortunately never stricly adhered to. Beside the fact that the landowners never fully had a comprehensive understanding from the beginning, the absolute destruction, degradation and pollution of their environment, land, sea and air was yet to follow.

After 17 years of trying to negotiate with CRA and the government of PNG for better terms within the Agreement (the Bougainville Copper Agreement of 1967), for more efficient methods of environmental control, and with no cooperation from the Papua New Guinea and CRA, the Panguna Landowners Association saw no other avenue but to mobilise. They started with demonstrations, petitions, submissions and meetings but without avail.

When they saw that these actions would not bear a positive outcome, they resorted, after being tested to the nth degree, to the only thing that would command a distinct and serious change of attitude by CRA and that was to shut down the Bougainville Copper Mine.

The landowners used militant methods to achieve their goal, including blowing down power pylons supplying power to the mine from the coast. This immediately ceased operations in the mine. The PNG Government responded by sending its Defence

Force to Bougainville, thereby declaring an all out war against the people of Bougainville.

The mine was closed in March, 1989, and what has ensued since has been a protracted seven year war with the PNGDF and the Bougainville Revolutionary Army (BRA). The people of Bougainville are known throughout the world as the only indigenous people that have shut down a mine owned by one of world's mining giants, Conzinc Rio Tinto.

## The Conflict between State-enforced Development and the Challenge of the Indivisibility and Universality of Fundamental Rights of the Bill of Human Rights

The conflict between state-enforced development and the indigenous peoples of the Asia-Pacific region has led to naked and blatant exploitation of their natural resources, be it timber, fisheries or mineral wealth. In some instances, such exploitation has now been going on for scores of years, especially where indigenous peoples have come under repressive and dictatorial regimes, a common phenomenon within Asia-Pacific.

The concerns of the indigenous peoples of this region where more than two thirds of the world's indigenous peoples reside are focused on the way in which some of these governments have been dictatorial in their developmental policies.

A new threat from such governments has been their unwillingness to recognise and apply the Covenant on Economic, Social and Cultural Rights and the Covenant on Civil and Political Rights of the International Bill of Human Rights as a total package. For these fundamental rights are 'universal' and 'indivisible', and cannot be applied without each other.

The United Nation Declaration on the *Right to Development*, which was adopted by the General Assembly in 1986, recognises that:

> Development is a comprehensive economic, social, cultural and political process, which aims at the constant improvement of the well-being of the entire population and of all the individuals on the basis of their active, free and meaningful participation in development and in the fair distribution of benefits resulting therefrom.

Article 1 states:

> The right to development is an inalienable human right by virtue of which every human person and all peoples are entitled to participate in, and enjoy economic, social, cultural and political development.

Article 6.3 states:

> All human rights and fundamental freedoms are indivisible and interdependent; equal attention and urgent consideration should be given to the implementation, promotion and protection of civil, political, economic, social and cultural rights.

'Development' is a fundamental right as enshrined in the Right to Development as adopted by the General Assembly's declaration. It is a 'social contract' between the governed and the governors, the state and nation (i.e. its citizens). Governments ultimately have the responsibility of delivering development (i.e., services) to their people, based on civil and political as well as economic, social and cultural rights, as a total package.

But most governments (e.g. India, Pakistan, Malaysia, Philippines, Indonesia, Papua New Guinea, etc.) within the Asia-Pacific region choose to be selective in their application of human rights. For instance, they prioritise 'economic rights' over other rights.

They assert that in order to provide adequate social benefits they must be allowed the right to exploit their country's natural resources, etc., the excuse often used is 'on behalf of their communities'. And most of the time these kinds of governmental policies are backed by stringent legislation, often discriminatory and disadvantageous to its citizens.

In one sense they could have also learnt directly from the examples set by their Western counterparts, who for decades, emphasised economic rights over other rights by way of their 18th and 19th century economic imperialism, as practised by the early colonisers: Britain, Germany and others in the Asia-Pacific.

At the United Nations these governments are often to be heard arguing very strongly for the notion that the rights of the 'community' come first, before the rights of the individual.

In our region this has contributed directly to severe exploitation, increased poverty and consequently blatant disregard for the other fundamental human rights of their people. Enforced development by these governments has therefore become more exploitative, destructive in nature and less responsive to the needs of their people, rather than providing for their welfare.

Our view (the indigenous peoples) is that one can not talk about human rights in a limited way as just civil and political rights or as economic, social and cultural rights. We abide by the United Nations Universal Declaration of Human Rights that *all* human rights are indivisible, universal and interdependent.

Development must be holistic, balanced and sustainable. It must not be dictated from the top downwards. Furthermore, it must involve all citizens in such a way that full participation is maximised and equal opportunities provided and distribution.

Indigenous peoples have always been faithful custodians of their land and resources. Thus, skilled sustainable knowledge to manage land and the environment is a scientific method that they have perfected and practised for centuries.

## Conclusion
*'When Injustice Becomes Law, Resistance Becomes Duty'*
When people are deprived of their rights, then it is natural to resist. And when injustice is purported to become law, then resistance is justified, and it becomes their duty.

1. Governments of Asia and the Pacific in their quest to 'develop' and 'catch up' with the rest of the developing world, have endorsed aggressive developmental policies, e.g. compulsory acquisition and land re-allocation, exploitation of indigenous and landowners' timber resources, mineral wealth, etc., sometimes backed up militarily, or by military governments.

Thus the people have been made landless, poor and have been denied access to health care, education, etc., due to a lack of it. Naturally, resistance from the people becomes their only form of expression. But this has also often been met with extreme repressive actions from their governments through their armed forces.

2. The military which has been used to enforce dictatorial rule by such governments is yet another enigma and area of concern for the indigenous peoples of the Asia-Pacific region. They are

sometimes funded with up to two thirds of the national budget in order to keep governments in power. Militarisation has therefore become the biggest threat to democracy, peace and development of the indigenous peoples of the Asia-Pacific region. It has deprived civil society of its political freedom, denied the right to liberation, self-determination and freedom from fear and expression. The line between military rule and democracy in our region is increasingly becoming blurred these days. Militarism poses an ever threatening picture of gross violations of the rights of indigenous people.

3. The big picture of exploitation of their resources is bound to continue leading to increased poverty and inequality. The gap between the 'haves' and the 'have nots' can only continue to widen under these circumstances, negating the notion that *all* have the right to development, which must be holistic, equitable and sustainable, as prescribed by the Right to Development of the United Nations General Assembly.

4. The Bougainville Case: the people of Bougainville have been in the same flight path of exploitation, plundering and defrocking of their sovereignty as all the world's indigenous peoples, from northern Europe, to the Americas, Canada to the Pacific, the Asian mainland, Australia, New Zealand and Africa. Bougainvillean sovereign rights over their land and natural resources were 'stampeded' by antiquated English/Australian colonial legislation, the 1928 Mining Ordinance. It gave CRA a free run on indigenous-owned natural resources, which were declared to belong to the colonising authority (the state) in a 1968 Australian High Court decision in the case: Teori Tau (plaintiff) v. The Commonwealth of Australia (defendant), which ruled in favour of the state and CRA.

Given prospecting rights on Bougainville, CRA set loose and plundered the island, not only resulting in monetary exploitation of Bougainvilleans but also in the devastation of their environment, flora and fauna. Their sacred grounds, the land of their ancestors, are gone forever, captive in the 'jaws' of modernisation and development.

The struggle outlined here shows how the people in the villages, in conjunction with their national leaders, struggled for a hundred years to bring things together – their world, their economic development as well as their culture, religion and their political institutions. Faced with the might of the state, the power of the multi-nation and their aggressive 'development policies', and with no solution to their grievances in sight, the only option left to Bougainvilleans was to mobilise and face the aggressors head on. The 'militant element' of the landowners literally went bush and waged their war on the establishment by blowing down a few pylons carrying power to the mine resulting in the Australian CRA Bougainville Copper mine closing in May 1989.

For over 20 years of operation the mine has caused massive pollution to the Jaba river system, which has carried the copper tailings with its chemical poison all the way to the west coast, turning a jungle river into the size of a mountain glacier, a glacier of poisonous sludge tailings which killed all the adjacent flora and fauna.

Papua New Guinea's economy was born on behalf of the rich Bougainville copper mine. They still largely depend upon an annual financial budget from Australia, but they have also since then come to depend more frequently on the World Bank. The Papua New Guinea military continue to try and reopen the mine for CRA. But the war on Bougainville has torn down the mainstay of Papua New Guinea's foreign earnings because of the lost income and the high cost of war. The Prime Minister, Sir Julius Chan, has had to accept the necessity to negotiate with the World Bank and IMF for a financial aid package. Chan's rescue plans include the reopening of the Bougainville mine. He expects the mineral wealth on Bougainville to generate an equal part of PNG's repayment. It is said that the Panguna mine still has an estimated '496 million tons of low-grade copper and gold to be mined'.

PNG's persistence to defeat the Bougainville Revolutionary Army and restart the mine is a strategy which reflects the pressure put on them by the IMF and World Bank.

The Bougainvillean people have until now paid a high price for their resistance. A land, sea and air blockade has been imposed on Bougainville. Close to 10,000 Bougainvilleans, men, women and children, will have died so far, both from lack of medicine and from the war. The choice has been a hard one.

But after a century of social, cultural, economic and political exploitation and subjugation by outsiders, our people decisively acted to stop further exploitation. And we join hand in hand with other indigenous peoples of the world as we continue to claim our 'right to self-determination', the right to conduct our own public affairs and manage our own economic and social needs in a civil society where all peoples of the world should happily coexist together.

BEN NAANEN

# OIL-PRODUCING MINORITIES AND THE RESTRUCTURING OF NIGERIAN FEDERALISM: THE CASE OF THE OGONI PEOPLE

On 4 January, 1993, about 200,000 of Ogoni's estimated 500,000 people participated in a peaceful protest march that took place at four different centres in Ogoni. Greenpeace sent a camera crew. The World Rain Forest Action Group sent an observer from London. The rally, organised by the Movement for the Survival of Ogoni People (MOSOP) and given widespread coverage by the Nigerian media (e.g. *Daily Sunray* G/11/93, 11/1/93, *The Guardian* on Sunday 17/1/93, *Newswatch* 25/1/93 cover story) and to some extent the Western environmental press, marked the effective launching of the Ogoni movement. Ogoni has since become not just a national issue but to some degree an international one as well, as will be seen in the course of the present discussion. What are the origins of this movement? How does it relate to the national question? What does it hope to achieve? What is the potential impact of the movement on the Nigerian state and economy? These are the main question which this paper attempts to address.

If one has the luxury of time one can remotely trace the movement back to the late 19th century when the Ogoni began resisting colonial incorporation. Most ethnic groups in the Niger Delta had signed the so-called treaties of protection with British agents after the Berlin treaty of 1885. These treaties provided the basis of colonial occupation. The Ogoni refused to sign any treaty (CO 554/1121/5907: Memorandum on the Protection Treaties with the Chiefdoms of the Rivers Province...). The Ogoni, reported by early colonial sources as having 'always borne a reputation for hostility and independence' (NAI: CSO 28032 (1932), Intelligence Report on the Ogoni Tribe...), waged a determined struggle against colonial conquest until they were finally subdued on 17 January 1890 (NAE: CSE 35/1/21). They were subsequently incorporated as part of the Opobo Division of Calabar Province.

Their first organised political protest under the colonial state took place in the 1940s when they won their demand in 1947 to be constituted into a separate administrative division of their own. Ethnic nationalism had by then begun to gain ground in Nigeria and the Ogoni joined the other Delta groups in the present Rivers state to press for the creation of a separate Rivers province, granted in 1948. This was followed by agitation for the creation of Rivers state, achieved in 1967. The Ogoni, like the rest of the Delta minorities, had complained consistently about their alleged domination and discrimination under the Eastern Regional government. That struggle is better documented elsewhere (Saro-Wiwa, 1968; 1982; 1989).

As seen already, the gains of having a separate state were soon undone by the imposition of a centralised state which established a new kind of domination. Of immediate local concern, however, was the ethnic tension that arose in the Rivers state, resulting from alleged domination by certain numerically greater ethnic group in the state. In 1974 certain sections of the state, including Ogoni, signed a petition for the creation of a Port Harcourt state out of the Rivers state. That effort has continued and even dovetails with the present Ogoni movement in certain important ways. Although it can by no means be rightly claimed that the Ogoni have not benefitted from state creation in any way, their economic and political situation has not shown any appreciable improvement over the years. On the contrary, their economic situation has clearly deteriorated.

From the brief introduction so far, it is possible to see the Ogoni as persistent agitators. If this is so, it can only be because of the enormity of their problem. Ogoni's fundamental problem is that of being a minority within minorities in a nation-state where ethnic domination takes the form of a ruthless, winner-takes-all zero-sum game. This is a great historical burden which their peculiar ethnicity has placed on them. To avoid liquidation as a group requires constant struggle against tremendous odds. Their land, moreover, is rich in oil and natural gas – natural assets which are difficult for such a small group to defend and control for their own use in a large multiethnic polity. The Ogoni trace their current tribulations to the existence in their land of these natural resources.

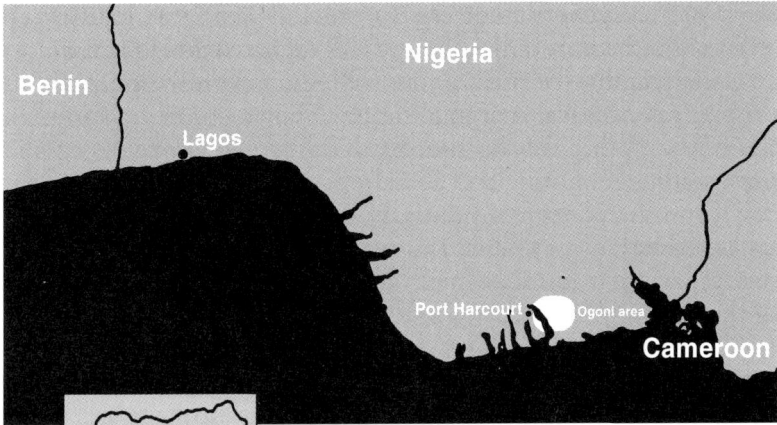

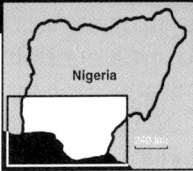

The Ogoni's pursuit of economic and political empowerment through the use of formal channels such as the political parties when these were allowed to exist, petition to military authorities and agitating for a separate state were all yielding little tangible result. In 1983, for instance, an Ogoniman, Kemte Giadom, was elected governorship candidate for Rivers state on the platform of the two leading parties in the state. He lost. The party, and indeed most Ogoni people have somewhat remained convinced that he was cheated out of victory by the ruling party. Fiascos of this kind only seem to have reinforced the growing feeling in Ogoni that an alternative strategy was necessary for a successful prosecution of the Ogoni cause. There arose the conviction that the problem was structural. As long as the existing political structure and constitution continued to exist there was little that even an Ogoni governor could do to change the situation in a fundamental way.

The new thinking, spearheaded by Ken Saro-Wiwa, a prolific writer and businessman who had accummulated a sizeable fortune through real estate and trading, was beginning to take root by the late 1980s. The first major event of the new orientation was the formation in 1990 of the Movement for the Survival of Ogoni People (MOSOP) as the vanguard organisation for the social mobilisation of Ogoni people. In 1990 Ogoni people, under the leadership of MOSOP, formulated and submitted to the Nigerian government the Ogoni Bill of Rights (OBR). To appreciate the substance of the OBR, discussed below, requires an understanding of the Ogoni problem. A critical aspect of this problem is political marginalisation. This is crucial in terms of the ethnic politics of the country. As observed already, access to the existing economic and social opportunity structure depended upon the control of political power. Although Ogoni representatives sat in the federal and regional legislative chambers, the paucity of their number made their impact on the government of the day negligible.

The Ogonis complained of being denied access to economic and social opportunities such as scholarships, jobs, significant positions in the public service, development projects, etc. They were so upset about the Eastern Regional Government that their chiefs made it clear to the visiting Nigerian governor in 1956 that they were not willing to be a part of the soon to be self-governing Eastern Nigeria (Saro-Wiwa, Genocide: 22). Their political views, for instance voting against the regional NCNC by voting for the Action Group and their advocacy of a separate Rivers state, did not endear them to the Eastern Regional Government, and there is evidence that they were often targets of victimisation, which greatly increased during the civil war, assuming the sinister dimension of the death of many Ogoni people (Saro-Wiwa, Darkling Plain; Genocide).

There was euphoria following the creation of Rivers state in 1967, which only became a reality with the end of the civil war in January 1970. As noted, it was not long before the Ogoni and other groups in the state began complaining of internal discrimination. While the control of power at the national level was being used against them like the other minorities, they were also suffering as an internal minority. The most poignant indication of the extent of Ogoni's deprivation, in spite of the enormous contribution to the Nigerian economy through oil, is the fact that Ogoni till date has no electricity, no pipe-borne water, and most communities remain barely accessible by road. This is a situation which has generated great anger and frustration among the people.

A new dimension was added to the existing problem of marginalisation with the commercial exploitation of oil in Ogoni beginning in 1958, Nigeria's first and largest oil field before the 1970s. By 1972 Ogoni had six oil fields making a combined daily production of 200,000 barrels per day. The oil companies were granted mining leases which Ogoni people were scarcely aware of by the colonial administration which vested ownership of all minerals in the crown. The post-colonial Nigerian government retained this policy through a petroleum decree, broadened from the 1970s by a land use decree. What this legislation meant, in effect, was that not only did the mineral under the soil belong to the state but also any land deemed to be of economic interest to the state, which of course all oil-bearing land is. On the basis of the legislation, the federal government collected mining rents, royalties and petroleum taxes, conceding nothing to the land-owners and putting virtually nothing back into the oil-producing communities.

This deprivation was to be aggravated by the ecological conse-quences of the oil industry. At the time oil production started in Nigeria, the country knew very little of the oil industry. It was therefore not unexpected that Shell, like any other multinational company whose sole motive is profit, had free rein to the environment. Pollution caused by uninterrupted gas flaring and frequent oil spills has since become endemic. Evidence of envi-ronmental disaster is conspicuous throughout Ogoni as vast areas of terrestrial and aquatic vegetation are destroyed by oil spills. Marine life for which the vegetation provided a life sup-port system, have gone with the vegetation. While the environ-ment was undergoing this steady degradation, substantial parts of the land were being gobbled up by pipelines which are laid on land surface, not buried.

To appreciate the social effect on the area of this environmen-tal degradation and land use one has to have some idea of the demography and economy of Ogoniland. With a mainly rural population of 500,000 concentrated within 404 square miles of territory, Ogoni's population density is overwhelming. This po-pulation is heaviest in the Gokana area, precisely the very area where oil exploitation has had the most damaging impact. This population has historically depended on a peasant farming and fishing economy. The destruction of the aquatic culture and the available limited farmland through oil spills has caused grave

*Bearing the costs of oil production...: Environmental destruction in Ogoni land. Photo: Anne Hege Simonsen*

economic distress in Ogoni. The most conspicuous aspects of life in contemporary Ogoni are poverty, malnutrition and diseases.

The death rate is high even by Third World standards. Corroborating this description of the overall situation in Ogoni, from the environmental to the socio-economic, with hard statistical data is not an easy task in a situation where the government is notoriously short on relevant data. Moreover, it is neither in the interest of the government nor the oil companies to commission relevant studies to furnish the desired statistical data. Till date, one is not aware of the existence of any scientific social or economic study of the effects of oil production in Ogoni, except one very recent health study commissioned by MOSOP. However, even the most fleeting casual contact with Ogoni will readily reveal the extent of devastation and misery. A visitor to Ogoni may be hard put to accuse an Ogoni public figure of exaggeration when he stated:

> The Ogoni case is that of genocide being committed in the dying years of the twentieth century by multinational oil companies,

*... while being denied the benefits: Ogoni communities still suffer from poverty, malnutrition, diseases and lack of basic infrastructure. Photo: Anne Hege Simonsen*

under the supervision of the government of the Federal Republic of Nigeria...The once beautiful Ogoni countryside is no more a source of fresh air and green vegetation. All one sees and feels around is death. Death is everywhere in Ogoni. Ogoni languages are dying; Ogoni culture is dying; Ogoni people, Ogoni animals, Ogoni fish are dying because of 33 years of hazardous environmental pollution and resulting food scarcity (G.B. Leton, OBR: 7-8).

Ogoni represents a kind of socio-economic paradox that will be difficult for an outsider without knowledge of the Nigerian power game to understand. Ogoni is simultaneously the poorest and most industrialised part of Nigeria. It has one of the world's largest fertiliser plants and the only one of its kind in Nigeria; two out of the countries four oil refineries; a major petrochemical plant; the fourth largest ocean port in the country; and several oil-servicing companies located within a few kilometres of each other in addition to six oil fields. Yet the level of unemployment in Ogoni is difficult to fathom. Nor are Ogoni people able to benefit from the lucrative business opportunities that these enterprises offer. The main reason for this grave is that all the big enterprises are state-owned and their employment and general business pattern closely correlate with the pattern of power control in the country. In frustration, the unemployed youth have, on several occassions, gone on the rampage, which has always been broken by the deployment of troops. Another popular pattern of response is mass seasonal migrations to the Cameroons where the migrants are engaged predominantly in fishing. In certain communities the emigration is as high as fifty per cent of the active population. Commenting on the Ogoni situation, the official government paper, *Daily Times*, stated:

Ogoniland is a good example of where one must keep a safe distance even as he points it out as the goose that lays the golden egg for Nigeria. Ogoni is the pioneer in the oil industry in Nigeria: first oil field, first refinery (now two), first petrochemical industry, first and most viable fertiliser industry, a maze of oil pipelines; all concentrated in one tiny land of 500,000 inhabitants. It is a very manageable and easy-to-develop community. [But] in terms of thoughtless pillaging, plundering, pluming, and pumping away of gasoline, acid rain and petroleum fumes and flares all over their lives, Ogonis can be easily overrun. We must look our conscience in the eyes, point the accusing finger at ourselves as the predatory, rapacious, even sadistic society which just takes without giving..." (*Daily Times* editorial, September 1993).

It is against this background that one can appreciate the present Ogoni movement and the content of OBR. Among its several declarations, the document states that 'In over 30 years of mining, the Ogoni nationality has provided the Nigerian nation with a total revenue estimated at over 30 billion dollars ... That in return for the above contribution, the Ogoni people have received nothing.' It further states that the people have no representation whatsoever in all institutions of the federal government of Nigeria, no pipe-borne water, no electricity, no job in federal state, public sector or private sector companies, no federal economic or social project (p. 10).

Ogoni people believe this state of affairs has been primarily caused by their political powerlessness and proceed to demand in the OBR political autonomy 'to participate in the affairs of the Republic as a distinct and separate unit by whatever name called, provided that this autonomy guarantees ...' among other conditions political control of Ogoni affairs by Ogoni people, the right to the control and use of a fair proportion of Ogoni economic resources for Ogoni development; adequate representation as of right in all Nigerian national institutions, and the right to protect the Ogoni environment and ecology from further degradation (p. 11). The document concludes by authorising MOSOP to make representation to the United Nations Commission on Human Rights, the Commonwealth Secretariat, The African Commission on Human and People's Rights and the European Community, pointing out the violation by the Nigerian state of the political, economic and cultural rights of Ogoni people, and that the Nigerian constitution does not protect the rights of Ogoni people as an ethnic minority (p.13). MOSOP followed up the OBR with a demand notice to the oil companies operating in Ogoni asking for the payment of oil royalties worth 6 billion dollars and another payment of 4 billion dollars as reparation for ecological destruction.

## MOSOP Strategies
Given the revolutionary nature of the demands which touch upon the constitutional basis of the Nigerian state and time-

honoured policy of the oil companies, it was obvious right from the beginning that neither the Nigerian government nor the oil companies would rush to appease the Ogoni people. In fact, it was rightly expected that they would ignore the request and instead take measures to exterminate the Ogoni movement. Therefore, a coherent strategy had to be worked out in pursuit of the demands. First, the whole Ogoni population has to be socially mobilised, to eradicate the spirit of despondency and fatalism which decades of exploitation and psychological torment has imposed on them. The people have to be made to know their rights and realise that these rights will not be conceded to them without a struggle. The struggle has to be a non-violent one in the tradition of the 1960s American civil rights movement. It was obvious that armed struggle will get nowhere except perhaps to bring about the extermination of Ogoni since such a small group can by no means withstand the military power of the Nigerian state and alienate potential supporters across the country. Second, the Ogoni case has to be made an international concern since it involves fundamental issues of human rights and the environment.

**Social Mobilisation**

The Ogoni leadership made sustained efforts to mobilise the people from 1989. For a people who had apparently lost confidence in themselves and faith in the ability of the Nigerian state and the rest of the world to deliver justice, the initial response to the efforts was at best one of indifference. The adoption of the OBR and its publication in several national newspapers in 1991 and the general publicity it generated began cutting a swath in the people's apathy. The subsequent presentation of the Ogoni case by Saro-Wiwa before the United Nations Commission on Human Rights in Geneva in May 1992 – which was widely reported by the Nigerian media – marked an important turning point in building the people's confidence. The momentum that was now building up was steadily reinforced and by December, 1992, when the grounds were being prepared for the big push, an air of expectation had engulfed most of Ogoniland. The date carefully chosen for that big push was the 4th of January 1993. There was to be a massive demonstration by the Ogoni people as a protest against the way they have been treated by Shell and the Nigerian government. The rally was also intended to mark in Ogoni the inauguration of the United Nations International Year of the World's Indigenous People.

In spite of the initial opposition of the national security services, the success of the demonstration was beyond MOSOP's expectations. The people had been gradually and meticulously worked up with a series of activities during the Christmas holidays, including a memorial service and a visit to the grave of Ogoni's first nationalist, Paul Birabi, who has had something of a mythical character in Ogoni history. Fiery speeches were made in defence of a struggle that had practically taken off. What happened next is better described by one of the several national news magazines and newspapers which gave the demonstration generous coverage:

> The rally was billed for 10 a.m. on Monday January 4, 1993, but as early as 6.00 a.m., Bori, the traditional headquarters of the Ogoni people of Rivers state, had come alive with streams of young men and women chanting war songs. They barricaded all entrances to the town. Vehicles were not allowed into the town. Those inside were not allowed out either. All markets, schools and offices were closed and no one went to the farms. By 9.00 a.m the whole town had completely been enveloped by protesters carrying pacards with inscriptions like "No oil right no peace", "UN Save Ogoni", "Assasins go home", "Shell leave Ogoniland". An estimated 100,000 people [in Bori alone] took part in the demonstration that spread to all the (six) kingdoms of Ogoni … At the rally, a burnt Nigerian flag was hoisted on a pole to demonstrate their disenchantment with the federal government" (*Newswatch* 25/1/93).

The demonstration surprisingly ended peacefully in line with MOSOP's philosophy of non-violent struggle. Henceforth, national attention was focused on this new political experiment that had begun and its potential outcome. The pride and confidence generated by the success of the demonstration among Ogoni people enabled the mobilisation process to assume a momentum of its own. The people had woken up and no longer needed much persuasion to fight for their rights. Ogoni would, perhaps, never be the same again. The following March, a vigil of all churches in Ogoni, including non-Christians, was organised. This was followed by the launching of an Ogoni Survival Fund (ONOSUF). Meanwhile, rallies were being regularly organised in all the six kingdoms of Ogoni.

A high point in the struggle came with the Ogoni boycott of the 12 June, 1993, Nigerian presidential election. The boycott, the first of its kind in Nigeria, made national and international news. The presidential candidates of the two political parties, the Social Democratic Party and the National Republican Convention, made frantic efforts to make the Ogoni change their mind in the weeks preceding the election, but it was too late. Once MOSOP Steering Committee took the crucial vote at a stormy meeting on 1 June, in which the pro-boycott group won, there was no going back. The principal argument was that Ogoni people should not give legitimacy to a president who will swear to uphold a constitution that dispossessed Ogoni people of their natural rights. The boycott was consistent with the methods of non-violent resistance which MOSOP had adopted.

**The International Dimension**

The local campaign has been pursued simultaneously with the international campaign. In fact, the latter has substantially aided the former. Mention has already been made of the contribution made by the representation of Ogoni at the United Nations Human Rights Commission in Geneva in May 1992. Ogoni's case similarly received critical attention when presented by the Ogoni delegation at the summer 1993 United Nations human rights conference in Vienna. At its 43rd session held in Geneva in August 1993, the United Nations Committee on the Elimination of Racial Discrimination appointed a special rapporteur on Ogoni after the Ogoni delegation's presentation of its case (UN Information Service, press release RD 400, 10/8/93).

A critical factor in Ogoni's international campaign has been the admission of Ogoni in January 1993 to the membership of The Hague-based Unrepresented Nations and Peoples Organisation (UNPO). The organisation has become a crucial organ for rallying international support for the Ogoni cause, especially through publicity. The international human rights movements and environmental organisations have been particularly generous in their support. Amnesty International has several times reported and mobilised action against human rights violations, including extrajudicial executions, in Ogoni (e.g. AI, Urgent Action appeal 19/5/93; for a summary of human rights reports on Ogoni see Anti-Racism's Information Service's 'Analytical country summary' focusing on Nigeria, summer 1993). Greenpeace has similarly championed the environmental aspect of the campaign, resulting in considerable publicity of the Ogoni situation in the ecology media (e.g., *Cultural Survival Quarterly,* 'Ogoni Protest, "Agent of Death" in Nigeria', summer 1993). The publicity given the Ogoni case in the general international press has been significant. There is hardly a Western country in which the Ogoni case has not been reported. English language publications that can be mentioned quickly include *Newsweek, The Guardian, The Times, The Sunday Times, The Independent,* and the *New York Times.* Ogoni groups in the United States and Great Britain have also been mobilising support through publicity and petitions to governments.

So far, what is the effect of the Ogoni campaign on the Ogoni demand and the national question? Ogoni people do not seem to expect magic. They appear to be aware that the achievement of the objectives of the kind of struggle they have embarked upon will necessarily take some time, especially since the issues involved are fundamental and structural in nature. The most important achievement yet has been the raising of national and international awareness of the Ogoni case. The case has become an important national issue, seen as a test case of the government's attitude toward ethnic minorities. It has accordingly drawn widespread support from both the secular and the clergy. The church perceives it mainly as an issue of social justice. The Catholic archbishop of Lagos, Olabunmi Okojie, one of the nation's most outspoken social critics, issued a statement on behalf of the church. He noted that the Ogoni situation has

> plunged the country into international disgrace ... We feel that the Ogoni people have a right to protect their environment and have a right to survive ... They have an inalienable right to make use of their land first for their personal development before any other consideration (*Daily Times,* July 3, 1993).

*The Catholic Herald* (September 1993) reflecting the position of the church, observed:

> Try and empathize the abysmal plight of the Ogoni people. Not less than 200,000 barrels of best grade oil is lifted, every day, from their land which, at $18 per barrel, conservative rate, earns this country

not less than $3,600,000 ... every day. Yet they do not have electric light, no school – where large sums of money are provided for [northern] who are, apparently being forced to read; they have no hospital – they take their sick people to Port Harcourt, usually getting there with them as corpses or people close to death, because it is very far away and the road is miserably bad. They have no pipe-borne water, they have been denied most of their farms, and their river has been polluted and poisoned.

The Government of Nigeria has admitted at a number of meetings with MOSOP that Ogoni has a case. But the government does not seem to know how to approach the problem since it is rooted in the very structures of domination that have coerced the nation together. While some of MOSOP's key demands such as an Ogoni state are less difficult to concede, given the way the military has created states in the past, the others are not so easy to deal with. For instance, would the Nigerian government, dominated as ever by the majority groups, concede the Ogoni demand that oil royalties be paid to the landowners instead of the central government? Or can the government accept MOSOP's proposal for national restructuring which recommends a return to the parliamentary system and a system of ethnic confederations in place of the present surplus-appropriating centralised command system? These are some of the critical questions that have placed MOSOP at the forefront of the campaign for a national conference, at which these issues can be resolved. Indeed, the Ogoni case is frequently used as a justification for a national conference by its advocates. To that extent, Ogoni has become integral to the national question.

In the meantime, the general social mobilisation of Ogoni people means that Shell may not be able to resume full operation in Ogoni, nor can the gas and oil pipeline projects that are important to the national economy be possibly completed without a resolution of the Ogoni crisis. The people appear determined to use people's power to resist further degradation of their environment and the confiscation of their land. The longer the crisis is allowed to continue, the greater the risk of the spread of the Ogoni type of non-violent revolution to other oil-producing communities which are anxiously waiting for the outcome of the Ogoni case. The additional danger, however, is that these groups, lacking the kind of leadership that Ogoni has in MOSOP, may find it difficult to control the protest and keep it non-violent.

## State Response

Government response to the Ogoni struggle has so far been a combination of carrot and stick, although mostly of stick. While inviting MOSOP to argue its case and, in fact, appealing for 'cooperation' (without doing anything to earn that 'cooperation') as the Interim government did at the end of August 1993, it has at the same time taken stern measures that can be interpreted as being aimed at breaking the Ogoni resistance. The leadership of MOSOP has frequently been harrassed by the security forces and jailed without trial. Saro-Wiwa, for instance, was jailed at least four times in 1993. The latest detentions occured at the end of 1993. These leaders have several times been prevented from travelling through seizure of their passports. The security services also not infrequently prevent MOSOP from carrying out its activities, particularly demonstrations. At the end of April, 1993, the Federal Military government promulgated a Treason and Treasonable Offences Decree which made demand for autonomy a capital crime. The law, generally believed to be aimed at MOSOP, was only repealed after widespread international condemnation.

Shell, for its part, has been held responsible by MOSOP for a good measure of the violence and deaths that have since occured. In April, 1993, troops hired by Shell to accompany its American multinational pipeline contractor, Wilbros, opened fire on peaceful protesters, killing one person and seriously injuring several others (Amnesty International 19/5/93; *The News* magazine 17/5/93, cover story). Several more deaths have since taken place under similar circumstances.

There have been other more gruesome circumstances in which Ogoni people have accused Shell and the government of complicity, but for which there is little direct evidence. From July 1993, for instance, there occured a horrendous communal conflict between Ogoni and one of its neighbours. The conflict resulted in the death of several hundred Ogoni people and the destruction of eight Ogoni towns and villages, producing a refugee population of about 20,000 (*The Guardian* 9/8/93, *News-*

*week* 20/9/93). Since the neighbour's attacks that precipitated the conflict were totally unprovoked, according to Ogoni sources, and given the professional logistics and sophistication of the weaponry used throughout the duration of the conflict, the Ogoni people concluded that the government and Shell were behind it. The latest assault occured in mid-December, 1993, during which three satellite communities occupied mostly by Ogoni people in Port Harcourt, the capital of Rivers State, were completely destroyed. The police failed to intervene in the two-day orgy of continuous violence that resulted in the death of over 60 Ogoni people, mostly women and children (*Tell* magazine, 31/1/93, *The African Guardian* 31/1/93).

The conflicts have been seen by the Ogoni as a kind of proxy war used by the state and Shell in their efforts to break the Ogoni resistance (*The Guardian* 9/18/93). Shell has consistently denied the allegation. The federal government has also denied the claim during meetings with MOSOP. It is not impossible that most of the security and military crackdowns against Ogoni were masterminded by the Rivers state government, whose chief executive, until November 1993, was a former employee of Shell.

## Conclusion

The discussion has attempted to show how political centralisation and ethnic domination in Nigeria have created tensions whose resolution has engendered strong demands for a national conference. The prevailing opinion in Nigeria is that to survive as a nation-state, the country must restructure its political relations, vesting a substantial degree of autonomy in the component units. The paper has also endeavoured to demonstrate how the impoverishment of the oil-producing minorities who sustain the national economy – resulting from the transfer of resources from these communities through the use of political power which is sanctioned by the existing constitutional structure of the country – has led these minorites to be among the most vocal advocates of restructuring. The struggle by the Ogoni people, which symbolises the frustrations of these oil-producing minorities with the existing system, is an indication of what can develop into a widespread movement with predictable consequences for the Nigerian state and economy if the demands of Ogoni and the rest of the oil minorities are ignored. The conclusion that can now be drawn is that political restructuring and the practical recognition of the need for social justice in the oil-

MARCUS COLCHESTER

# INDIGENOUS PEOPLES AND THE POLITICAL ECONOMY OF LOGGING: THE CASE OF GUYANA AND SURINAME[1]

I would like to broaden the context of the discussion about indigenous peoples and look at some of the political and economic forces that are working against their interests by looking at the particular case of logging in the Guyanas.

### Indigenous aspirations and 'sustainable development'

Before going into detail, I would like to make sure that we start from a common understanding of indigenous aspirations. We are talking here about a political struggle. Indigenous peoples want control of their own destinies, expressed as a demand for self-determination, for local control. This must be the starting point in any discussion about indigenous peoples. The indigenous movement is a political movement – something that environmentalists seem very wary of accepting.

Economically, indigenous peoples are not seeking to prevent development or reject development if by that we mean improvements in their material well-being. But they want such 'progress' to be achieved on the basis of their own efforts and with them retaining control of their lands and natural resources. So their vision is to assure that there is subsistence first and generated surplus for the market only thereafter.

I think it is important to note that these kinds of views of the role of people in development have been accepted by proponents of what is called 'sustainable development'. Let's look at a couple of quotes which are quite revealing. They are from the book *Our Common Future* (WCED 1987), now out of date. Nevertheless, they are important statements which still bear scrutiny. The first states that sustainable development:

> …requires a political system that secures effective participation in decision making. This is best secured by decentralising the management of resources upon which local communities depend. Giving these communities an effective say over these resources…

101

And then in terms of indigenous peoples themselves, the same document stated that 'they should be given a decisive voice in formulating policies about resource development in their areas'.

So this is the moral highground that Vicki Tauli-Corpuz referred to (see her contribution in this volume). The concept of sustainable development fits very well with indigenous peoples' agenda, if this is what we mean by sustainable development. These quotes also underscore the political nature of sustainable development: that it is acheived by a reallocation of power.

Unfortunately, this is not the concept of sustainable development that was adumbrated at Rio. For me, this is why the Rio-Conference failed, because it did not afford more power to local communities; on the contrary, it focused power in the state.

Thus, if we look at the problems which confront indigenous peoples we will at the same time obtain a clear notion of the forces that are making sustainable development impossible. There are several questions we have to ask when we are studying the situation in specific countries:

- What are the forces that deny local communities a voice in decision-making?
- How do they seek to disqualify indigenous institutions from having a voice?
- Who seeks to expropriate their lands and resources?
- Who gains form this expropriation?
- How are these economic forces organised politically to achieve their ends?
- What are indigenous peoples doing about it to reassert their own vision?
- How are they reorganising to confront their new problems?

### The Situation in Guyana and Suriname

The broad economy that developed in northern South America was very similar in both countries. Of course both countries were inhabited by indigenous peoples before the European invasion. There were sporadic contacts with the coastal groups during the 16th century. But colonisation did not really start until the 17th century with the build-up of the sugar-economy. This economy was built on slavery. Initially they were indigenous slaves. This triggered a whole series of slave-wars throughout the

interior. Indigenous peoples tried to capture each other and bring them down to the coast to serve on the estates. But this form of labour was not very productive. Unfortunatly, indigenous peoples died from Western diseases. Thus, American indigenous slaves were replaced by indigenous people from Africa.

By the end of the 18th century the coastal areas in both countries were dominated by sugar plantations. And the indigenous peoples were scattered in the remoter forests, largely in the interior. What was unique in Suriname was the emergence of new societies in the interior. These were societies of so-called Maroon peoples. They were runaway-slaves, African people who escaped from the plantations and recreated whole new societies in the South American rainforests. Whether we call them 'indigenous' or 'tribal' is something we can dispute and indeed they do dispute this in Suriname.

Hence, we had a British-Dutch dominated coastal-economy that was export oriented, mainly sugar. Mining then became the big issue in these countries. In many ways it was the mining of bauxite and, to a lesser extent, gold that determined the way these countries evolved. Sugar and mining were the main determinants of the political economy of these countries. Indeed, there was talk in the 1920s of selling Suriname to the US because

Suriname was their main source of aluminium. 65% of the aluminium used in World War II in the US came from Suriname. Therefore, the US had to station soldiers down there in order to maintain their interest. Bauxite, then, was the determining force in Suriname and to a slightly lesser extend in Guyana.

The economy was, accordingly, primarily based along the coast. The interior peoples were relatively unaffected. They were essentially left out, and in Guyana the British government's policy was very paternalistic. They did not provide land rights, but they accepted the creation of reservations.

In Suriname there were no land rights, but the Dutch government had defined the interior as being the domain of the Maroon-peoples and other indigenous peoples and signed treaties with them after several vicious wars. In a general sense the interior was essentially left undisturbed.

In both countries rule was carried out through created indigenous chieftaincies, not traditional organisations. Captaincies were created in the communities. They were supposed to assert the authority of the colonial state at the village level.

**Logging in Guyana**
At independence in the late 1960s there were only about 800,000 people living in a large area of 21 million hectares in Guyana. The politics of the country developed basically on the coast. Again, the indigenous peoples were more or less out of the picture. It was a competition largely defined along racial lines, between the Indians who had replaced the black slaves as the main labour force on the coastal plantations and the black peoples. Thus, there was a kind of racial tension underlying the politics of that time.

This is not the proper forum to go into detail as to how Guyana fell under the control of a quasi-socialist dictatorship, but basically what happened was that the country tried to define a cooperative form of socialism, which degenerated into croneyism and fraudulent manipulation of democratic processes which eventually fell to pieces economically and generated a huge national debt.

Since the end of that regime – with the country in very serious debt – there has been an attempt to revive the economy through the intervention of the international financial institutions. The World Bank, the IMF and the Inter-American Development Bank have come in with a more or less coherent package in their mind of how to rescue this country. The basic structural adjustment package included, of course, the encouragement of foreign direct investment in the country. Minimal attention was paid in this macroeconomic restructuring to the interests of the local people or the environment.

### The Situation of the Indigenous Peoples in the Interior

Firstly, by then they had obtained land rights. One of the conditions of Independence was that they should be given rights to their land. And in some areas they had been given such rights. But the politics of the country were complicated by the fact that the western area is claimed by Venezuela. The Guyanan state felt that it needed to particulary develop this western part in order to show that it was using it, that it was part of its domain. Therefore, they emphasised mining in the north-west and hydropower development in the Upper Mazaruni. And that meant that the communities of the Upper Mazaruni were denied rights to land, and the communities of the north-west were also denied rights, while the others more or less got some kind of title.

### The Beginning of Logging Operations

Initially, there was not much logging. It was a butchering of the coastal forest that was occurring. They were just taking out the best logs to serve a market mainly in England. Some very unsuccessful efforts were made to build up the logging-industry with loans from the European Community and the World Bank. They were not successful because of this political system of croneyism, patronage and state control. As a result, the logging loans did not increase production.

By 1989 only about 2.4 million hectares of forests in the north of the country were under exploitation. A very small amount of timber was coming out, about 94,000 cubic metres per year. And that was not being properly managed; there was no real control of what was going on whatsoever. But that year was when the notion of encouraging structural adjustment and opening up to foreign direct investment began. And thus the logging boom suddenly got under way.

I think it is interesting to note that the market existed before this logging boom. It was political changes and the macroeconomic prescriptions which then triggered the boom. The market by itself was not enough to determine what happened in the country.

The prescription that the development agencies had was to open up the forests and maybe increase the area under exploitation from 2.4 to 3.6 million hectares. And there were NGOs like The Rainforest Movement which said that this was ridiculous, they could not even manage the 2.4 million hectares. They were advised to first build up their capacity to manage and then increase the area to be logged if that was really necessary. But this kind of advice was ignored and within a few years practically the whole of the interior forests were allotted as logging concessions to domestic and foreign companies. This led to an outburst of protest.

The companies that were benefitting from this development were mainly foreign companies. They were given extraordinarily generous terms to come into the country as part of the strategy of encouraging foreign direct investment. For example, the Barama Company Limited, which is owned by a Malaysian and South Korean consortium, was given a 25 year license, renewable for a further 25 years. The area is 1.7 million hectares in size, and they are allowed to export raw logs and sawn lumber. They are allowed to take up to 300,000 cubic metres in the first year (compared to 94,000 for the whole country only a few years earlier) and 1,200,000 cubic metres after ten years.

But what shocked many people when they later found out about this was the tax concessions that this company was granted. A ten year tax holiday, including income tax, corporation tax, withholding tax, consumption tax, property tax, exemption on import duties on just about everything – including machinery, fuel, building materials, office equipment and medical supplies – was offered. They were only going to pay export taxes on one species: greenheart, which, in fact, hardly grows in that area. Moreover, royalty payments were fixed in Guyanese dollars, so as the currency declined, the amount they were paying to the exchequer became derisory. The entire agreement was apparently a gift.

They were also permitted to hold external, foreign currency accounts. They were allowed to employ at least 15% foreign workers or more if they wished. And if there were any disagreements with the government the 'International Centre for the Settlement of Investment Disputes' in Washington, DC would oversee the case. In which case the company 'shall be deemed a national of a state other than Guyana'.

As the British government has later admitted: 'The terms and conditions of these concessions do need to be re-negotiated by the new government.' But, unfortunately, new deals are now being made of the same kind. Currently, after this concession was granted, they are in the middle of negotiating another concession in an indigenous area. More concessions are being negotiated for in the south, as much as another 4-6 million hectares are on the verge of being handed out. This would constitute nearly all of the accessible forests because much of these areas is either savannah or very mountainous.

Most of the involved companies are Asian companies from Singapore, Korea, Malaysia, Indonesia and so on. Some of them are from Canada and Great Britain as well.

At present, the environmental threats are visibly very severe. To be brief, I will only point out that the Forestry Commission has only about 5 foresters to handle approximately 9 million hectares of forest under concessions. It is clearly a ridiculous situation. And they admit that it is a very difficult situation that they confront. The fact is that they were not even able to control the small area that was given out in concessions earlier.

### The Social Implications of Logging

The controversies focus particularly on that concession in the North-West. There were campaigns right from the beginning to say that this concession should never be granted because the indigenous communities in the area had not got land rights. This was never believed. Everybody said 'rubbish', 'you don't know what you're talking about, all these people have got land rights, you don't have to worry about them'.

Therefore, The Rainforest Movement carried out a study last year. We walked through the forest for about a week to see who was living in the concession area. And, of course, it is true, some of the areas have been given titles and some of the indigenous peoples are, therefore, to some extent secure. But the vast majority of the area and its communities are completely left out by these considerations. The communities consist primarily of Carib-people, Karinas, as they are called in Venezuela. It is an outrage. This area is not an indigenous titled area but a sort of reservation. Hence, they do not have any rights.

**The Handing Away of Resources**
Institutionally, the appropriate mechanism for handing out concessions is that the Forestry Commission should be looking at the concessions and deciding on them. However, at the time that these concessions were handed out, there was no head in the Forestry Commission. The previous one had resigned in disgust at the way the forests were being dealt with, and he was not replaced. The Forestry Commission was meant to be answerable to a Natural Resources Agency. It too did not have a head. The previous head of the Natural Resources Agency was indeed the one who negotiated the contract with the Barama Company Limited. When the government changed, he left the Agency and went to work as a consultant for the Company.

Thus, we had a headless set of institutions that were meant to be controlling what was going on in the forests. And, in fact, what was happening was that the brother-in-law of the President was the chairman of the Board of the Forestry Commission, and he was the one who was cutting the deals without even telling the Deputy Commissioner of Forests what was going on. What we discovered was that the logging companies were very closely linked with the political elite. They were paying for them to go on tours around South-East Asia to drum up further investment. Of course, what we know from the record of these companies in Papua New Guinea and the Solomon Islands is that they are very prone to bribery and the like. Moreover, their practice in the field is very very damaging to forests and local communities.

So what we have here is a situation which is called 'the capture theory' of institutions, whereby the institutions that are meant to be controlling resource extraction are in fact being controlled by the industries that are benefitting from that extraction.

## The Indigenous Peoples' Response

The Amerindian Peoples' Association was one of the main national organisations that emerged during this period. The political liberalisation also allowed that emergence. That is the other side of the package of reform. And, of course, their demands were for land, to have a voice in development. Much of their effort in the early years was focused on this issue of the takeover of indigenous lands by logging. They campaigned to have this concession rejected; they were not listened to. They threatened to call for a boycott of timber and nobody listened. They called for the boycott on timber and the government immediatly promised a comission of enquiry to look into the indigenous peoples' situation. After two years had elapsed nothing happened. The government never bothered to form the comission of enquiry or to go and study the situation.

But the denunciations from indigenous peoples did lead to a lot of press and a general solidarity within the country. A lot of resentment was generated within the general population about the way the national heritage was being sold off cheap. Hence, indigenous peoples were able to tap into a quite strong nationalist sentiment which rejected this kind of overseas exploitation.

Additionally, there was mobilisation to put pressure on aid agencies to change their policies and to demand a freeze on the hand-out of concessions as a condition of further investment in the country. Various institutions agreed: the British government agreed in the middle of negotiating a contract with the government; the World Bank's environmental experts agreed as well. And the freeze did indeed begin to hold after the scandals were revealed in the press.

There is an interesting situation in the World Bank now, a kind of schizophrenia. On the one hand, there are the economists who are pushing for economic liberalisation, and on the other hand, there are environmentalists saying: 'Well, you know we've got to be prudent; we've got to have natural resource management and we've got to get national parks; we've got to respect indigenous rights.' The argument also focuses on the re-negotiation of this contract. Should they re-negotiate the contract, give better terms to the country or not. Economists are claiming that if 'we do that, we put off further investors'. Environmentalists, are countering by making it clear that 'we've got to make sure the country benefits from the existing areas under concession and not allow the opening up of further areas.'

However, it must be pointed out that indigenous peoples are not united in all this. A number of the communities are also selling timber to foreign companies. In addition, there is an argument within the indigenous movement about the ethics of this and whether indeed indigenous peoples on their lands should be subject to certain restrictions in the sale of timber.

This is the current situation in Guyana, a very interesting legal dilemma. Once the indigenous peoples get titles to their lands they are outside of the jurisdiction of the Forestry Commission and, in fact, do have the right to sell timber and cut it as they wish.

### Logging in Suriname

In neighbouring Suriname we find a somewhat similar situation but a very different political context, at least ostensibly.

The country is also being tempted to sell off its timber. Only a few years ago mainstream conservation organisations were stating, with some confidence, that 'there is probably a better chance of conserving large tracts of undisturbed rainforest wilderness in Suriname than virtually anywhere else on earth' (Mittermeier et al. 1990:12). But this no longer seems likely.

The political situation in Suriname is very different from that in Guyana and the economy has been somewhat different. Since gaining independence from the Dutch in 1975 they were guaranteed about 1.5 million dollars in what are called treaty funds – a continuing aid programme over the coming years, so that up to 40% of their foreign exchange was from Dutch development assistance. And the rest, as explained above, came from bauxite and aluminium.

What developed along the coast was an economy wholly dependent on these foreign deals: aid and bauxite. Over 90% of the population is urban. A vastly oversized bureaucracy developed. 40% of employable adults were in state employment. This created a huge middle class, wholly or largely dependent on imports. The job of the political parties in all this was really just to compete for access to the aid and to develop patronage networks for parcelling out foreign development assistance. The interests of the interior communities were completely irrelevant to the political economy of the country as a whole.

There was a military coup in 1980, a kind of rejection of this dependency on the north. But it was not very well conceptualised. The country went completely bankrupt because development assistance was frozen and there was mismanagement of the economy as well as declining prices of bauxite and so on. The country refused to carry out structural adjustment programmes and was consequently denied aid.

This created problems in the interior with people even more cut off than ever. The trickle of aid monies that had been getting through to the communities was cut off, and a civil war started in the interior with the Maroon people demanding greater autonomy and control of what was going on. That only ended in 1992 when they were promised land, as they had not received any land rights yet, except in so far as their treaties did recognise territorial rights in the 18th century.

The logging companies were moving in quickly. One company from Indonesia tried to get rights to log the whole southern part of the country, 5 to 6 million hectares of loggable forests. A look at the maps will show how the concession overlaps indigenous territories and, as a consequence, communities living there.

Actually, they found that there was a law which stated that to obtain a concession of more than 100,000 hectares it was necessary to go to the Parliament. But they got around this by creating 63 companies and applying for a concession for each of them. However, this led to much condemnation in the press, and they had to withdraw the ploy. In the end they obtained a small concession of 150,000 hectares, which itself has led to conflict with one or two communities in the west of the country. The rest of their timber derived from indigenous areas.

The indigenous peoples do not have land rights, but they are being accorded what they call woodcutting licenses. They are only given any recognision of rights if they are going to cut wood, and they are allowed to enter into contracts with other parties to cut the wood. Actually, they do not have to cut the wood, but that is the basic idea of giving them these licenses. This encourages them to get involved in the timber trade. And because the indigenous peoples' communities do not have any legal personality, these contracts are vested in the captains. This creates a temptation for the captains to negotiate deals with outsiders at the expense of the local communities. This turned our to be the case. Moreover, conflict within the communities about this selling of timber to outside companies developed.

At the moment companies have had to reduce some of their demands. There are three main concessions presently being negotiated with a Malaysian company and two Indonesian companies. They may in fact be the same one. This is the same company that wanted the 'whole log'. There is also a Chinese company trying to enter the area, a Canadian company, as well as about six other companies queueing up for concessions in the interior. That is where a large number of the Maroon peoples and the Wayana people, an indigenous people, also live.

At present, these concessions are again being negotiated in a rather unclear way. The first Musa concession was handed out without the head of the Forest Service even knowing about it. In fact, he admitted he had learned about the concession in the newspapers after it had been handed out.

We are truly surprised by the way the government feels it can ignore indigenous interests, considering that a six year civil war with the communities in the interior recently ended.

Where are the foreign assistance agencies in all this? They feel that they can not engage with the government until it says that it will carry out structural adjustment. The government will not carry out the structural adjustment because it faces elections in the near future. And the electorate supporting the political party are the middle class that enjoys these jobs in the oversized bureaucracy. These jobs would also be the first to go in any structural adjustment. Thus, structural adjustment actually means the political elite cutting its own throat, and they will obviously not do that. Therefore, there is no structural adjustment at the moment in Suriname, but there is still a push for foreign investment.

The indigenous peoples, in this instance, have founded a coalition with NGOs in the country: environmental organisations, human rights groups and development NGOs. And they have been able to call for a freeze on the hand-out of concessions and land rights which have gained a lot of press coverage as well as recruited the energy of international campaigning organisations. They have taken their concerns to the international community to the extent that there has been quite a response from international financial institutions which have visited Suriname to see how they can resolve these issues. In the absence of structural adjustment it is difficult to see how they can engage in dialogue.

**Lessons to Learn From these two Situations**
The first thing we see in these examples is that the development prescriptions of the international financial institutions like the World Bank, etc. are being made without considering the interests of local communities. They do not see a connection between macroeconomic prescriptions and the local reality.

One would be tempted to conclude from the Guyanese experience that indeed structural adjustment is the problem. This is what is provoking this increasing penetration of the interior by the private sector. Basically, they are being given a free rein to log and mine. Meanwhile, the State's capacity to regulate is reduced as part of the necessary cut-backs in the government's finances. This has caused an extremely difficult situation to ensue. Foreign direct investment is the panacea of the World Bank at the moment.

But if we look at Suriname, we see that there is no structural adjustment there, just the same problems. In fact, there have even been bread riots without structural adjustment. We can see that structural adjustment is not the only problem. It is really just this encouragement of liberalisation of the economy and opening it up to trade. Structural adjustment, one way or the other, does not matter. The point is that foreign companies are interested in implementing changes and there are people who collaborate within the country.

The dominant force that is being given access by the development model are the transnational companies. What we have seen by these examples is that in the case of mining they are largely from the North: Canada, Britain, the USA, the Netherlands, etc. In the case of logging, they are mainly from the South: Malaysia, Indonesia, Korea, etc. They may come with a commercial culture of their own, which may pose a particular threat to the decision-making processes, but it is not particularly more pernicious than the influence of the northern mining companies. In fact, to speak of Asian companies as being 'southern' is really illusory these days because most of these companies are on stock exchanges and are receiving heavy investments from northern enterprises, life insurance agencies, etc. Thus, we all may well have stakes in these logging companies without knowing it.

The north-south relationship does not have much relevance to these transnationals; the problem is that they are unaccountable. They do come with their own political culture, however, that does determine the way events play out at the local level. The point about the transnationals is, of course, that their interests are not identical with the governments of the countries from which they come. And that is something we have to hold on to.

Now, if we descend a level and look at the national elites, the active political class are key players. They are selling off their country's heritage, ostensibly in the interest of the local people: the coastal and urban groups, who are the majority of the population. We see their politics largely defined by their own factions, but many of their decisions have actually been made to favour their own pockets, rather than the interests of the nation as a whole. So again, let us hold on to that fact: the interests of the political elite are not identical with those of other citizens. We also see, unfortunately, that – largely because of legal injustices – the indigenous elite themselves are selling off timber without benefitting their own communities, and that is leading to disputes. The result is divide and rule all the way down from the top.

**What are the Solutions?**
The only obvious response is, if it is divide and rule all the way down, then we have to create solidarity against this all the way up. We have to take advantage of the fact that there are those coincidences of interests and we are not dealing with monolithic institutions. Of course, there are the demands from the communities which we must hang on to. The principal demands are for rights to their land and for legal personality of their community institutions. They should further be vested with control and rights over their territories at the village level, not at the individual level. Political changes are clearly necessary in terms of democratising and opening up decision-making to wider participation.

Indigenous organisations need support. They are asking for support, they are getting support, but they could do with a lot more. Indigenous peoples have been able to form alliances within their own countries. They have been able to attract other interest groups: conservationists, human right groups and so on. And they have been able to attract international support.

What are the possibilities for the indigenous people's movement of creating greater solidarity with other sectors of civil society who are also being marginalised to a greater or lesser extent by the same kinds of forces? Alone, indigenous peoples are doomed to be further and further marginalised. They must develop these broader alliances so that they can develop a greater political mass. I do not believe that you can change the world by changing people's way of thinking. Changes have to come from political mobilisation.

One of the lessons for the development agencies is that their macroeconomic policies have very direct effects on the ground level. Development agencies must look at these issues in the future. They must work with the communities right from the beginning, even in policies that seem so remote from reality, for example, dealing with balance of payments problems. Actually, they are fiddling with local people's lives.

These agencies need to recognise the political nature of their interventions. Their development prescriptions favour the interests of certain interest groups within the country, and they need to understand who they are empowering and who they are disempowering by their interventions. They obviously do not sufficiently understand this and, if they do, then they are being very dishonest in their work.

But a question for us is, to what extent is the conditionality that the local people are demanding really a solution for their problems. They are demanding that aid agencies place conditions on their own governments not to do certain things. They are therefore, in a sense, empowering these agencies over their own governments, creating further dependency which is part of the origin of their problem.

That is a major question which, perhaps, has no general answer.

## Note

1 This contribution is not based on a written paper, but represents a slightly edited, transcribed version of Marcus Colchester's oral presentation taped during the conference.

Lorenz G. Löffler

# LAND RIGHTS AS INSTRUMENTS OF SOCIAL TRANSFORMATION: THE CASE OF THE CHITTAGONG HILL TRACTS (BANGLADESH)

In the Universal Declaration of Human Rights of 1948 no mention whatsoever is made of a right to own land, and nothing like land rights is mentioned in the subsequent International Covenant on Economic, Social and Cultural Rights of 1966. Today, one may deplore this omission, but it was not by negligence that land rights have not been mentioned. Human rights were meant to apply universally, but no socialist state would, at the time when the declaration and the subsequent covenant were drafted, accept anything which could be construed as legalising individual or group rights in landed property.

Landowners exploiting landless labourers had not only excited the wrath of socialists following Marx. The founding father of modern economics, Adam Smith, argued against the worst plague of modern society called rent, that is income based on landed property and collected from those who were reduced to a mere labour force. Still it was left to Marx to draw the logical consequence: once you identify the exploitation of labourers turned landless by powerful landlords as the primary source of capital accumulation and the rise of private landownership as the main reason of social inequality, the ideal of an egalitarian society cannot be achieved unless any form of private landed property is permanently abolished.

However, the only institution able to enforce this abolition is the (socialist) state, and this implies that the state in fact arrogates to itself all land rights. Thus, the final abolishment of land rights will depend on the final abolishment of the state - provided only the stateless people will then be able to prevent the resurrection of the plight. Today, it seems futile to hope that this state of affairs will be realised, yet it is worth remembering that it existed and even survived, though in somewhat modified form, until recently.

There were stateless people whose land belonged to them as they belonged to the land, people who, in accommodating to modern concepts, now claim to have participated in common ownership, while still refusing to extend the notion of private property to land. I shall not try to be more precise in this respect, since the modern states and their judiciary who have the power to transform those feelings of belonging into modern legal concepts may take any anthropologist's attempt to rephrase the old concepts as proof that these people's claims cannot be substantiated.

Still, people who can argue with their government about their original rights are comparatively well off in comparison with those in developing countries where the promulgation of land rights is nothing but a legal camouflage of the process called primary accumulation by Marx, a process which others may approve of as modernisation and which might also be analysed as social transformation. Under whatever terminological disguise it appears, it means enforced destruction of a traditional, comparatively egalitarian social order and the establishment of a ruthless class society with a few powerful people keen to enrich themselves on the one hand, and many powerless expropriated people turned from self-sufficient farmers into a superfluous labour force fending for daily survival on the other hand. I have no remedy to offer against this process, on the contrary I tend to conceive of it as inevitable; nevertheless my moral engagement is on the side of the victims of this process.

In the case to be discussed here the victims are the indigenous peoples of the Chittagong Hill Tracts (CHT), an area now under the rule of Bangladesh. Bangladesh owes its existence as a state to the liberation war of 1971 supported by India. Before that time it was known as the Eastern Wing of Pakistan which came into existence due to the division of British India in 1947. At that time Muslims formed less than 4% of the population of the CHT, and according to the principles of the division people expected to be allotted to India, but the would-be Indian government bartered this tribal area away against some advantages on India's western border.

The British had established their rule in Chittagong in 1769 and availed themselves of the administrative system of the pre-

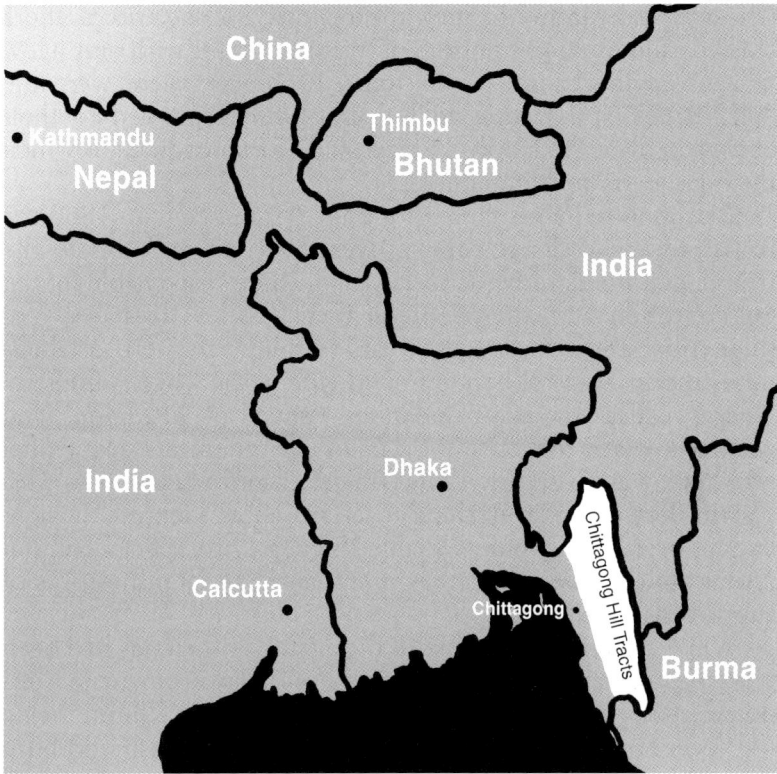

ceding Muslim rulers. These had established a kind a tributary
relationship with the tribal people living in the hills to the East of
Chittagong (subsequently known as the Chittagong Hill Tracts) by
allowing them access to the plains markets only against yearly
tributes of cotton to be collected and paid by certain tribal
representatives. For two of them this business proved rather
profitable. These 'rajas' controlled the two major inroads into the
CHT and established themselves as landlords in the plains bor-
dering the hills. For collecting the tribute they relied on their
agents living in the hill villages, but the system did not extend all
over the hills. Though the British referred to them as tribal rajas
and though the Chakma Raja had his bases among the Chakma
in the central and northern part of the hills and the Bohmong
Raja among the Marma in the southern part, by far not all
Chakma and Marma accepted them as their rulers, and though

Chakma and Marma formed the majority of the tribals, there existed (and exists) a minority of ten other tribes with only a few villages paying tribute to the rajas. Moreover, there were the 'wild tribes' still farther to the east who responded to their exclusion from the markets in the plains by sporadic raids which the rajas were unable to check.

Disappointed with the performance of the rajas, in 1860 the British assumed direct control over the CHT and turned the rajas into administrative officers called Chiefs responsible for the tax collection with the people in their 'Circles' irrespective of their tribal affiliation. In the years to follow the territorial administration was refined by subdividing the circles into tax villages, called 'mouzas', under the control of 'headmen' who were to replace the old tax collectors of the rajas. Again, tribal affiliation was no criterion for fixing the mouza boundaries. This system, however, did nothing to efface tribal identities which, backed by mutually unintelligible languages and special cultural norms, indeed survived rather unimpaired all later attempts of suppression until today.

While the tribute payable to the agents of the rajas had been reinterpreted as a capitation tax, the new government tax imposed by the British became known as 'jhum tax', 'jhum' being the local (Bengali) term for a swidden field, a slash-and-burn cultivation. The fact that widows and households not living by farming were exempt from this tax may have been a reason to call it 'jhum tax' – contemporary authors, however, insisted that it had nothing to do with land rights. Already before 1860 the Chakma Raja had started to auction the position of a tax collector and the practice continued into the beginnings of British rule. In 1876, W.W. Hunter in his voluminous compendium *A Statistical Account of Bengal* (vol.6, p.91) writes: 'The rights of the headman that were ... frequently put up for sale under the authority of British officers were rights affecting human beings ... they had no connection with any form of land tenure'. Thirty years later the tax business had been brought under control and the headmen had assumed the role of loyal magistrates. In 1909 the Superintendent of the Hill Tracts insisted: 'This tax is tribute to the state, it in no way partakes of the notion of rent or bears any relation to the land cultivated' (Hutchinson 1909:93).

Nevertheless, this tax could be interpreted as a tax payable to the state for the right to make a field, and this is the view taken, nearly fifty years later by the Pakistani Board of Revenue: 'Revenue [i.e. the jhum tax] is assessed on the jhum field, not on the household' (Bessaignet 1958:38). Without any change in the law regarding this tax, it now definitely 'partakes of the nature of rent'. The change in the nature of interpretation may seem trivial, but it becomes fundamental when phrased in other terms. While under the British administration the right to jhum accrued to every indigenous person in the hills by birth, under Pakistani state proprietorship this right is granted in exchange for the tax paid, and if the state decides not to renew the contract, the farmers who can not claim any ownership of the land have to go.

But this is not the fault of the Pakistani regime. Already in 1880-83 the British declared one fifth of the area of the CHT off limits to swidden farmers, viz as 'reserved forests'. In 1870 they outlawed swidden farming in the plains district. And 70 years before they took over the administration of the hills, in 1792, they abolished the 'cotton tax', replacing it with a cash payment, rephrased in 1909 by the very Superintendent Hutchinson, who at the same time asserted that the jhum tax in no way partook of the notion of rent, as a settlement in the name of the Chakma Raja, 'a settlement ... known as Jum Bangu or right to Jum under a chief'.

One hundred years later the then ruling Chakma Rani demanded a new settlement in her name for the Chakma Circle, but this time the British had good reason to assume that the clever Rani intended to transform her subjects into landless tenants, and they refused on the grounds that the jhum land in the CHT could not be rented. As a matter of fact the British refrained from interfering with the hill peasants' rights as long as this policy served their own ends, but they never stated unambiguously that the indigenous rights to jhum were inviolable.

The hill farmers on the other side had no reason to demand such a guarantee. The British had curbed the exploitative power of the rajas, and their tax collectors had replaced it by the jhum tax and for the rest did not interfere with their traditional way of life. Having no idea of European concepts of land rights, how could they demand more? And they also felt no reason to complain about the export tax levied by the administration on timber and bamboo leaving the hills. In their view the tax in the last instance would be paid by the plains people who bought these goods, and the less they bought, the better, as it prevented too rapid a sale of their resources.

As for the hill people, they had free access to timber and bamboo as long as it was growing on their village territory. 'Village territory' this time does not mean 'mouza' (the tax village), but the hamlet, the borders of which were left undefined by the administration but were well-known to its inhabitants. Nobody was free to use the resources of this type of village territory as he pleased, but the right to use them did not depend on paying a tax.

Rather, it depended on two types of consent: that of the villagers themselves and that of the guardian spirits. If you wanted to cut a field in a certain spot, you had to make sure that a family who had used that plot in former years did not claim priority rights, and even if they did not, you had to make sure that the spirits did not object. You had to inform them about your plans by putting up a certain sign in that plot, and they would let you know their decision in sending you certain dreams. If they accepted, you had to show them your gratitude and gain their support for a good harvest by presenting them offerings on several occasions during the agricultural year. One may object that similar conceptions are compatible with animism, but not with Hinduism or Buddhism, professed by the majority of the tribal population. In the world of the traditional hill farmer this made no difference. Whatever their religion, all hill farmers were convinced that by not propitiating the spirits you could expect misfortune. But even if you did pay homage, you could not really rely on their support. In a sense the spirits resembled the worldly powers outside the village who might swoop down on you to extract money however innocent you were. The decisions of these superior powers were just beyond your reach. But before you had to submit, you could try to evade the evil by withdrawing. Hill peasants moved their villages when plagued by too many diseases, and they moved again when pressed too heavy by tax collectors. Hill people did not like to move, but they preferred to move when difficulties arose, and they were free to move as they possessed no landed property.

This very freedom was definitely not in the interest of those who wanted to subject these people to their rule. The British tried – with some success in densely populated areas – to induce the people to take to plow cultivation and thereby to become owners of permanent fields. However, most areas in the CHT are unfit for plow cultivation, while swidden cultivation is the most suitable way to make a living provided that fallow periods can be maintained long enough to restore soil fertility. Swidden areas too can be privatised, but the swidden farmers I came to know in the CHT resented it, as in their view privatisation would inevitably break up their egalitarian society and lead to the formation of landowners on the one side and landless labourers on the other, replicating the very situation they could observe in the plains district and to which they attributed the ruthlessness and crookedness of the Bengalis whose morals they loathed.

Even if not able to grasp the truth of this rather 'Marxist' analysis, the fundamental difference in the moral system of the hill people and the plains people did not fail to impress the British administrators. No wonder they preferred the honest and amiable way of the 'simple' hill people to the fraudulent craftiness of the cunning plains people. And they also realised that the former were prone to become an easy prey of the latter. As a consequence, at the beginning of this century the CHT were declared an excluded area, and both the application of the judicial system of the plains and the influx of plains people, especially of traders and businessmen, were severely restricted.

Although some of the restrictions were lifted even before the end of the British era, the special status of the CHT survived into Pakistan times, until it disappeared without notice in the new constitution of 1964. Since then political representatives of the hill people have been demanding – so far without much success – the restitution of a kind of autonomy for the CHT. One of the consequences of the abolition of the special status was that land rights in the CHT had to be adjusted to national law. This could easily be done in all instances where land had been taken under permanent cultivation (plow land and gardens) as it was already differently taxed and more than often registered as private land. Surviving restrictions on sale and mortgage were lifted.

Areas of permanent cultivation had developed near rivers and on bumpy land mostly in the central and northern regions where the hill were less steep than in the south. In the centre, however, most of these lands went under water in 1964 after the construction of a huge hydroelectric dam. The flooding led to the displacement of one quarter of the whole indigenous population of the CHT. The annulment of the special status of the CHT brought no privileges to the owners of landed property; many of them did not even receive a nominal compensation (the Pakistani government blamed this on the Bengali administration), and only one fifth of the amount of territory now under water was offered for rehabilitation by opening up part of the reserved forest area for resettlement. This situation led to the first mass exodus of Chakma to India, where more than 20,000 of them were finally relocated in the northeastern border area, a thousand miles away from their place of origin. Others just moved uphill, resuming swidden cultivation in places where, due to heavily increased population density, fallow periods had to be shortened in such a way that crop failures became unavoidable.

Again, in 1964, the Pakistan government asked FORESTAL, a Canadian advisory group of natural scientists, for their opinion on the prospects of further land use in the CHT. The report, published in 1966, clearly stated that the population of the CHT had passed the limit up to which jhum cultivation could be considered a well-adapted solution and argued that new ways of earning one's livelihood had to be introduced if the ecological balance was to be kept. Their recommendations centred on horticulture which the experts thought would bring hitherto unknown prosperity to the inhabitants now under danger of pauperisation, provided that some provisions were taken. One of these was that a family turning from subsistence oriented swidden cultivation to market oriented horticulture should be provided with at least 10 if not 20 acres for planting cash-crops. The government 'experts' reduced these figures down to 5 acres. Another provision was that the cash-crop farmers should build up their own cooperative marketing organisation. Yet until today all trade between the hills and the plains has been monopolised by Bengali middlemen in collusion with wholesale traders in the plains, ensuring minimal prizes for the producers and maximal profits for the traders. Hill farmers who dare to bypass this monopoly are beaten up and robbed.

Fruit growers had to face an additional problem: as no facilities were provided for canning their products and the monopoly traders kept the prices in the plains more than ten times above those in the hills, large quantities of fruit to be consumed within a few weeks once a year could neither be absorbed by the plains market nor feed their producers for the rest of the year. Moreover, horticulture proved less well adapted to the soils of the CHT than the experts had imagined. Gardens became less and less productive due to soil erosion. No wonder many people preferred to stick to, augment their meagre income by, or return to their traditional methods of swidden cultivation. If they had been provided with 20 acres this would have been possible, with 5 five acres they were bound to give up and become landless labourers.

Before these developments materialised, the political situation had changed. When the Pakistani experts had finished drafting the new land regulation for the CHT, Pakistani rule came to an end. While Bangladesh became independent, armed anarchy reigned for some time in the hills. Not everyone in the hills welcomed Bangladesh. Illiterate hill peasants less effected by the modernisation process had experienced the Pakistani military regime as benevolent insofar as it had allowed them, by the 'basic democracies' order for the first time to elect their own representatives. Courts controlled by the military had, also for the first time, curbed exploitation by Bengali moneylenders and policemen.

On the other hand, a growing number of young people of the Chakma and Marma had entered higher education, some had even been admitted to the universities in the Bengali centres. Here they had come into contact with and absorbed modern ideas of socialist origin which at that time became the credo of the movement for independence. Together with their Bengali compatriots they fought against the Pakistani neocolonialism and capitalist exploitation, while at home they did not miss the opportunity to attack the remnants of former feudalism personified by the Rajas whom the British had turned into Chiefs and as such had become servants of the Pakistani regime. Above all, however, they hoped that an independent Bangladesh would also restore some kind of independence to them, at least in the form of the autonomous status which the CHT had lost under Pakistani rule. In this their expectations were not very different from those of the 'reactionaries' in the CHT who hoped that the Pakistani government would reward them for not participating in the Bengali upheaval.

However, all expectations were thwarted by the new 'socialist' regime of the founding father of Bangladesh who saw no reason to privilege the unreliable tribal minority by allowing them to humiliate the triumphant Bengali majority by again restricting their rights in the CHT. Tribal identities were remnants of the colonial past, the CHT should be open for all Bangladeshi people of whatever creed. The breaking down of old barriers would, no doubt, also benefit the tribals, as it would bring them into the national mainstream from which they had been artfully excluded by the British who were intent on keeping them backward and setting them against their compatriots in the plains. The Pakistanis, aware of the antagonism, had been reluctant to leave the administration of the CHT to representatives of the Muslim Bengali; now that every available position was allotted to them, Bengali traders poured into the centres to be urbanised, and Bengali presence soon dominated the area around the artificial lake created by the dam. Swidden farmers without deeds confirming them as proprietors of the land were told to move in order to make room for another government project advocated by the FORESTAL plan, viz the transformation of the hills judged unfit for permanent gardening into rubber plantations.

Since neither hillmen nor settlers knew how to do this, the government relied on the wisdom of its well-to-do citizens, far-sighted entrepreneurs and its own officers in the CHT by offering them thousands of acres to be acquired against a small fee with the prospect of investing in rubber. To comply with the wishes of the government, the crafty businessmen started by cutting down all trees and bamboo. By selling them they more than compensated their investment. Subsequently, some of them just rented their domain to the former inhabitants, thereby establishing themselves as absentee landlords. Less fortunate were those who relied on the government subsidies and really started planting rubber trees.

As these trees shed their leaves to regrow them only after the monsoon has set in, the soil is rapidly washed away by the rains and the rubber plantation starts to resemble mangrove forests. Hill people whom I asked about this phenomenon clearly stated that they regarded the government plans as a dangerous error. Similar experiments with teak plantations had already proved abortive in Pakistani times. Still, government experts repeat their conviction that every corner of the CHT could be planted with rubber and teak, and their endeavours in this respect are well received by international donor institutions since these plans which are contributing not only to the further eviction of hill peasants but also to the final deforestation of the CHT, are propagated under the green label of 'reforestation of the CHT'.

As hill people did not qualify as thrifty managers of horticultural plantations, the government in 1979 decided to speed up the process of modernisation by resettling hundreds of thousands of landless Bengali peasants in the hills. This, to be sure, could not be done without ousting a considerable part of the tribal population from their ancestral villages and land. The indigenous intellectuals who once were willing to support the poor, exploited Bengali masses in their fight against postcolonial and capitalist exploitation, now found their own people in growing numbers expropriated by these poor masses. The Shanti Bahini ('Peace Forces') who had their origin in the war of liberation resurged as an armed resistance force against the Bengali intrusion.

The government responded by stepping up the number of military and paramilitary 'security' forces and by having them trained in antiguerrilla warfare, by handing out arms to the settlers and by forcefully relocating the indigenous population in cluster villages under army control. Every action of the Shanti Bahini was followed by punitive measures, including burning down indigenous villages which might have supported the 'Peace Forces', and torturing, raping, mutilating and killing men, women and children. Another mass exodus of one fourth of the indigenous population of the CHT was the consequence. Several of them returned and fled a second time. More than 50,000 refugees are still living under miserable conditions in relief camps in the Indian state of Tripura.

The activities of the Shanti Bahini have served the government as a pretext to spread military camps all over the CHT. The army controls all vital aspects of civilian life, including the supply of daily commodities like rice, salt, kerosene and medicine. The so-called CHT Development Board is chaired by the highest military commander of Chittagong. This board decides on the allocation of any development aid for the CHT and even controls the admittance to higher education. Tribal people, especially those under constant surveillance in the cluster villages, have become quite accustomed to the fact that whatever they want to do, they will have to apply for a permit or a licence and will have to pay for it. For the military the occupation of the CHT has developed into big business. Whether it be natural resources, jobs or human rights, everything is for sale.

The most effective means of control is to outlaw activities which are essential for survival and then tolerate them against any kind of payment. The grossest act in this respect was an executive order totally prohibiting swidden cultivation on which probably still more than half of the indigenous population had to rely for survival. Instead of the jhum tax you now had to pay a substantial fine for your illegal use of state property, with the amount of the fine depending on the goodwill of the officer. During my visit to the central Hill Tracts in 1991, I was told that the prosecution of offenders was 'lenient'. After the downfall of the military dictatorship in Bangladesh this order has been repealed. There have also been some attempts to save the last remnants of reserved forests from being completely sold off by the military.

In general, however, the new government did nothing to curb the power of the so-called security forces. Under the threat of being driven from their land, be it for making room for settlers or for transforming it into a rubber plantation, most swidden cultivators consented to have it registered as their private or collective property. The legal framework for this procedure had been prepared during the last year of the Pakistani rule and enacted with some amendments by Bangladesh. The people had been informed about this possibility, but the details remained unknown since the government officers responsible for the registration denied the right to consult the text of the law even to educated hillmen.

All you had to do is to approach the headman of your mouza in order to get the confirmation that nobody (including yourself) had a claim on or was actually using this land which you were willing to acquire. I repeat: in order to become a legal owner of your land, you have to prove (and to pay for the testimony) that nobody but the state has any right to this land. This document must then be presented to the land registration officer who will decide, as he sees fit, how much you have to pay for the deed. This will take some months, and, as a rule, this payment will amount to more than a peasant is able to pay without getting heavily indebted. But what can you do? You may even be lucky if the deed for the same plot is not sold twice or thrice – due to the bad services of your headman. But what the civil administration finally has sold you may in short time prove of little worth should the military decide that you have to quit for reasons of security. You may, on paper, still own your plot, but you are no longer allowed to use it.

The military may help you survive by paying you food-for-work rations, and your work will more often than not consist in clearing any growth from the hills. For security reasons the military likes bare hills. If you have done your job well, the monsoon rains will also come to the help of the military and, by washing away the soil, ensure bare hills in the years to come. People will no longer be able to live on these hills, hence nobody needs to worry about land rights anymore.

Still, this process leaves us with a paradox to be resolved: why does the government threaten people into accepting land rights which they do not want, while at the same time expropriating them? The answer is simple. governments of developing countries have to care for their reputation when they want their regime to be financed by foreign aid. In order to gain in reputation they should at least pretend to abide by their own laws. Driving people from their land by mere force may be easy, but nowadays calls for some justification. Otherwise, people resenting expulsion and putting up some resistance may even be supported by unfriendly neighbouring states, and what seemed easy may become costly. The times when these costs could be more than retrieved by decrying those who resisted as communists are unfortunately gone.

In glaring contrast to these measures, granting land rights to people who never had such rights is an act of supreme benevolence. Any objections? The fact that the people have to get indebted for receiving this grant is, should it become known, surely not the fault of the law, but of corrupt officers. And who, besides a few individuals concerned, is going to point out that, in the long run, no family can make a living on a mere five acres of eroded hill land? As a matter of fact, nobody is forbidden to acquire more land, all he needs to do is to buy it – provided that he has the necessary means to do so. The best way is to lend money to some hill peasant who needs it in order to avail himself of the grant, lend him some more money to help him survive in the years to come and then ask him to cede his land to you to cancel his debts. As litigations are extremely costly, he will do so without any resistance. Hill people are, as is well-known, honest people.

By granting land rights to the hill people the state serves in the best possible way the interests of the well-to-do classes it represents. It sets in motion a fully legal process which in short time will bestow them with all earnings and possessions of the formerly free hill peasants. It might seem reasonable to keep this bonded labour and the corresponding resources alive as long as possible, but the peaceful times of moneylenders are gone – modern investments are made in a capitalist setting. Investments should have an immediate return, and they do, provided that you do not care what becomes of the resources.

This is what I meant by social transformation. Marx called it primary accumulation. Nowadays it is more profitable as it is liberally supported with billions of dollars called development aid. It is a gruesome process which might also be called modernisation. It is, however, even worse once we include the exploitation of natural resources: it is irreversible destruction.

Land rights in this connection only serve as a legal camouflage of the process. Stateless peoples had land rights. But these rights should not be confounded with rights to landed property. They did not serve capitalist accumulation but communal survival.

They could be violated and transgressed, but they could also be defended and redressed by the community. If defence failed, people could still think and behave in terms of their rights, but they lacked the sovereignty to redress them. Once the people are overpowered by a state their rights continue to exist only insofar as the state is willing to care for them. The state may recognise them, modify them, cancel them or replace them. There is no limit as to what can be done with the former rights of now powerless people. If they try to resist without being given the right to resist, they may end up dead. To turn the autocratic state into a democratic state may be seen as a way out, but it is of no help if the people concerned form a minority and the majority decides that the minority should be wiped out. To be sure, this decision would be in violation of the Universal Declaration of Human Rights, but until now the appropriate instruments of forcing the states to respect them are still missing. Rights have not ceased to be the rights of those in power. And land rights are no exception.

# III
# Biodiversity Conservation and Indigenous Peoples: Competing Approaches

Jonathan Kamomon Ole Lekuruon

# BIODIVERSITY CONSERVATION: WHOSE MAJOR CONCERN?

## Introduction

Biodiversity and indigenous knowledge are disappearing at a tremendous rate. However, I would say the famous Convention on Biological Diversity is an echo of the loud cry of indigenous peoples, whose land, culture and life are being crumbled at the expense of the Western market. Large-scale commercial farming and forest technology replace indigenous forests. At the same time, biodiversity in totality owes to a large extent its existence to indigenous cultures and knowledge, customs and taboos. The UN, UNEP and other international lobby groups have the voice and the power and therefore feel concerned over the distraction of peoples and cultures that totally depend on the diversity of the ecosystem. But can they influence, affect or implement policies and laws that are environmentally and culturally sensitive to the indigenous ways of living? No! Can indigenous peoples implement the articles of the conventions without the local support and bilateral support of the international community? No! It therefore follows that biodiversity conservation is our common concern. My major worry is that the past bids to help the indigenous peoples have not gone beyond study and policy formulations; would there be a change?; would articles 8(j) and 10(c) be implemented?; would the convention be respected?

Unless the notion about indigenous inability is dropped, I fear the convention will be yet another manipulative strategy to cower the commoners and satisfy their psychological well-being, while their material and physical beings will forever live in distress. Avoid, therefore, sympathetic approaches to our situation, in our struggle toward self-determination. We must be involved in all preliminary discussions, policy formulation and implementations of the same that affect our lives; you cannot do without us.

**Bitter Fruits of a Hard Labour: Our Sacrifice to Conserve the Environment and Wildlife at the Expense of our Lives and Property**

Indigenous people in general and the Maasai in particular are people of the environment who have co-existed with nature in the past with ease and satisfaction but at present with difficulties. Their cultures and taboos/customs have been a security to the diversity of the ecosystem. During the onset of colonialism and thereafter, the Maasai were slowly deprived of their land and the genetic resources which form part of their natural life situation. The new laws introduced ownership of the biodiversity. The Maasai were not told that this and that is a national asset. There was no consultation with the people and no benefits albeit the fact that co-existence continued. Land alienation and the creation of game parks has put pressure on the pastoralists by depriving their pastoral economy. In the 19th century the colonial government in Kenya formed the 1902 Social District Ordinance that created the Maasai reserves allegedly to 'preserve the Maasai', an act that influenced the marginalisation of the Maasai to date. Furthermore, the 1904 and 1911 purported agreements between the Maasai and the British were the first land loss strategy of that kind, combining trickery, legalism and force.

Game parks were created in the 1940s with subsequent expansions to date. The colonial and the post-colonial government in Kenya put animal first and man last, forgetting that it is we who have preserved this priceless heritage. The effects of the game parks were tremendous, while the laws governing were equally disastrous. Our pastures have been reduced to plots which we still share with overflow of wildlife from the parks, and the law on the park is 'shoot on sight'. We suffer from intermittent animal attacks, diseases and, to top it off, the accruing benefits of tourism are far from us.

The Maasai people still follow a traditional way of life. Despite the wealth gained from tourism in the Maasai Mara reserve, the Maasai still live in poverty. In the case of an animal killing a person, a compensation of 30,000 KSh may be had after a long struggle, and if a person kills an elephant you can expect seven years in jail if not death. So we are reaping bitter fruits of death for what we helped to conserve through our cultural mechanism. Most of the game reserves, at least in Kenya and Tanzania,

*The Maasai have still strong roots in their traditions: Warriors dancing. Photo: Frans Welman*

are situated in the former Maasai grazing lands and up to now the wildlife still owes their existence to the Maasai taboos, customs and low population. Therefore, in essence, indigenous occupation of the game parks is an asset to conservation, and policies must be developed to protect and benefit the indigenous peoples in as far as wildlife is concerned.

## The State Concept

Tourism has remained a large foreign currency earner for Kenya, and as such the government is putting all the efforts it can to improve the quality of the tourism industry. These include tight security for the tourists, prosecution of poachers, improving infrastructure, the introduction of revenue sharing, granting wildlife user rights, controlling problem animals, etc. This is well done, however, our past experience undermines all the well-intentioned policies of today and therefore threatens our future prospects. Through the same well-intentioned policies we have lost all the best parts of our land; we are slowly losing our cultural heritage and we will soon lose our future. In this case our problem is not what policy is formulated but by whom, how and for whom. If revenue sharing is estimated at 25% of the money collected, we end up getting 5%. Where does the rest go? If life compensation is 30,000, we end up getting 25,000 or nothing at all. In any case, this is a mockery of humanity and the sanctity of human life. Human life, irrespective of colour, race and sex, must be treated with due respect. The alienation of land for conservation purposes is yet another oversight, as land is incompensatable as far as we are concerned. Our cultural traits have kept the land, forests and other resources intact because of our sustainable utilisation of them, and in turn we are told to accept, for the benefit of tourism, logging, commercial agriculture and other modern upcoming industries, at the expense of our economy (pastoralism), culture and future generations who will grow up to ask, 'where is our common heritage?'

In short, while we conserve for life and perpetuity, others do so for money and leisure. And we are told that it is time we leave our barbaric and archaic ways of living and enter into the mainstream of national and international development, money, economy and so on. Modernity or development, without us and our culture, will create a limping society that lives in a cultural and ideological vacuum where development is not likely to thrive anyway.

### Conservation and Development: The Turn of Events
It is common knowledge that the Maasai have only been passive recipients of local and international sympathy. As a result, they have adopted a cat-like attitude to the approach of issues affecting them. They have always depended upon missionaries, governments and national and international NGOs to help them combat illiteracy, diseases, famine and poverty in general. In most cases they have received the contrary and are therefore manipulated, exploited and forced into changes that leave them paupers.

In Kenya, for example, the Maasai lost their land en masse during colonialism and have continued to lose it in the name of conservation, agriculture and game parks and are therefore left with arid and semi-arid tracts while struggling for survival with

*Maintaining indigenous resource management systems can benefit biodiversity. Most of East Africa's biodiversity rich areas are found on Maasai land. Boy herding cattle in the Usangu plains, Tanzania. Photo: Jens Dahl*

wildlife. With respect to education, it seems surprising, but it is true that about 90% of the population still remains illiterate despite 32 years of independence, reconstruction and development. Their economy is in shambles; traditionally the Maasai are pastoralists by occupation and semi-nomadic in their mode of existence. Their economic base is not regarded as an economic entity. They are forced into sedentary life which is not economically viable with regard to the land occupied. Maybe this is the fulfilment of Sir Charles Eliot's prophecy that there can be no doubt that the Maasai and many others must go under.

However, there is a turn of events as manifested in my research paper 'The Maasai Moran: which way forward?' It is a dedication to the Ilkerin project and begins:

> This paper is dedicated to the Ilkerin project, an eye opener, the hope of a people whom the colonial imperialists said ...they must go under ... but through whose struggle to influence change is a manifestation of a blissful future to the Maasai...

So, what we are discussing here today may be seen as the successive stages of that hope, to keep the ball rolling and give credit to Ilkerin as a model of community based development, at least in Maasailand.

## The Loita Maasai Model

According to the 1989 census, the Maasai population was estimated at 377,089, about 1.76 per cent of the country's population. The Loita section is one of the smallest sections of the wider Maasai community. They live in the southern part of Kenya and northern part of Tanzania. Those in Kenya number about 17,000 which is about 4.5% of the total Maasai population. They occupy two administrative locations namely Morijo and Entasikira within Osupiko Division of Narok District.

The Loitans continue to maintain their traditional occupation and rich cultural heritage. Their land is still intact and managed under customary laws and practices. Despite being 128 km from the nearest urban centre, the Ilkerin project has made Loita a model in development and culture, at least among the Maasai, in Kenya and Tanzania.

The Ilkerin project was begun in 1968 and launched in 1973 in order to help the Loita Maasai manage their desired change and development. Since then, the policy has been 'let's develop but without losing our cultural identity in development'. The Loita Maasai are at least ahead of their counterparts. The two locations are divided into sub-centres, each with a primary school, a dispensary, a moran (youth) class, a beekeeping project, a dairy separator, a youth shop, a women's shop, women's activities and well-established committees. The project is run by a board representing the six sub-centres and includes a government official and a church representative.

## The Loita Naimina Enkiyio Conservation Trust

The Loita Naimina Enkiyio (Karsayia) is a unique forest located 300 km southwest of Nairobi. It is a sacred, spiritual and religious enclave venerated by all the Maasai people who are indigenous to this area. Based on a sophisticated social and ethnocultural organisation, the Loita Maasai have evolved a refined pastoral economy where the 400 km$^2$ forest remains well-preserved. This is manifested by the undisturbed forest ecosystem that shelters a rich variety of animals, birds and generally a rich biological diversity. The importance of this forest goes beyond the conservation of Kenya's remaining natural heritage. Besides its cultural and spiritual use, it provides an all-around water source to livestock and people even beyond Loita.

The Narok county council, a local government authority in the area, plans to alienate the forest for the purpose of developing tourism in the area. This is in disregard of the people's wishes and use of the area, as well as without their consultation. This act drew sharp criticism and an immediate response by the Loita traditional local leadership, including the elected and appointed leaders. We owe thanks to Chapter 26 of Agenda 21 of the United Nations conference on the environment and development which gave credibility to our rejection of the alienation of our land and which gave us the legality to own, manage and sustainably utilise, as before, our indigenous natural forest.

In this case, therefore, the Loita council of elders comprising all the chiefs of all age groups, clans, chairmen of sub-centres, project leaders, youth leaders, women leaders and elected and appointed government officials met and made a declaration to defend the forest by all means. However, they decided to form a legally constituted structure on the basis of our traditional social organisation to oversee the retention, management and sustainable use of this sacred forest. Without a doubt, the Loita people, through their past efforts and activities, have displayed an unchangeable track record of caring and conserving the forest resources of Karjayia outside the framework of official government. In May 1993 Loita formed the Loita Naimina Enkiyio Conservation Trust and pointed the way forward in the current global concern of promoting community based conservation strategies.

**Suggestions**
The problems of indigenous people that we are attempting to solve, in relation to the environment, arose as a result of numerous misconceptions, lack of awareness and lack of commitment to the plight of the same.

To look for solutions is a beginning of the process, while implementation and maintenance of a particular solution is the core of the process.

Therefore, biodiversity, being our common concern, is our common future. Thus, we should shake hands in preventing its distruction and maintaining it by giving credit where it is due.

It is time that articles 8(j) and 10(c) of the Convention on Biological Diversity are honoured and given the attention they deserve. However, who is to blame for the continued destruction of the diversity of the ecosystem?

In pursuit of Agenda 21 of the Rio de Janero Conference, indigenous peoples, through the Maasai whom I represent today, should be given an absolute right to self-determination. We are not interested in being like other people in as far as our culture and organisational structures are concerned.

In our bid to marry our culture with modernity, we strive to ensure our cultural survival and at the same time remain in the limelight of the modern world, in as far as education and awareness is concerned. Therefore, we are in need of an empowerment that maintains our dignity and not a model based on hand-outs. The United Nations and indigenous lobby groups should now go beyond policy formulations and corrections and beyond the sovereignty of nation-states to ensure that lands belonging to indigenous people are protected for the interest of the nation-state, its people, the rightful owners and for perpetuity.

Finally, I also advocate closer involvement of indigenous youth in meetings and consultations in a bid to sustain the motions and development of their people while also breeding a nature of understanding and tolerance.

### References
Ole Lekuruon, Jonathan Kamomon 1991. The Maasai Moran. Which Way Toward UNPL. Embu

EUCLIDES PENA ISMARE

# REFLECTION ON INDIGENOUS PEOPLES, NATURAL RESOURCES AND THE BIOPACIFIC PROJECT

The millennium that we are approaching indicates new times in which the cruel looks of the *conquistadores* will be exposed from behind their masks as, from the centres of international power, they proclaim the Pacific region a strategic zone. The conquest will not in any way be less destructive today than it was 500 years ago. These times forebode the advent of a threatening era for Afrochocoan, Embera, Kuna and Wounaan communities.

We, the indigenous peoples of Colombia, are present at this conference in order to make known our problems and the efforts we have expended in order to resolve them. We wish to share our thoughts and conceptions of our future, just as we hope that the discussions in this forum will in turn enrich us.

## Some General Information about Colombia

Colombia is a country situated in the north-western corner of South America, forming part of the natural bridge of the Americas. We are one of the most biodiverse countries in the world, as much in biological and mineral riches as in ethnic diversity.

In Colombia, 87 different indigenous peoples live together with black communities and a mestizo majority. Indigenous peoples represent 6% of the total population.

We live in one of the countries which forms part of the so-called Third World and as such, our economic progress is characterised by being a supplier of foodstuffs and raw materials for the large European and American industries. From the time of the colonisation up till today, we have handed over our gold, platinum, oil, cinchona bark, ivory palm, rubber, emeralds, bananas, coffee, etc.

Within this context and following the dictates of international bodies such as the World Bank, our model of development has, since 1950 and till the beginning of this decade, been orientated towards a process of import substitution based on coffee trade, with the aim of creating an industrial base. This model was called a 'protectionist model'. Due to the changes experienced in global political economics and the internal problems of our country at the beginning of this decade, a transition towards a new economic model was initiated. This was characterised by liberalising international trade practices, the modernisation of the state and the reconversion of the productive apparatus, a process designated 'economic Liberalisation'.

Supporters of economic liberalisation argue for our society's need to create new democratic niches, initiate a peace process and put a stop to administrative corruption and drug trafficking. Politically speaking, this process has led to the negotiation and integration of some armed movements into society and the drawing up of a constitutional charter in 1991 in which we, the indigenous peoples of Colombia, were lauded for our active participation. We achieved formal recognition of our rights as an ethnic group as well as the elaboration and creation of mechanisms that protect the right to a thriving, healthy environment.

In the field of administration, a process of decentralisation seeking to strengthen regions has taken place, including the creation of institutions such as the Ministry of Environmental Affairs.

As concerns the economy, subsidies to some productive sectors have been done away with, most state-owned companies have been privatised and taxes have been lowered, allowing free import.

In the social sector, labour laws that minimise the rights of workers have been drawn up and a law and order decree has been passed allowing secret judges and witnesses to take part in trials concerning drug trafficking crimes and crimes committed against the state.

Although we acknowledge that this process has included some benefits and important measures, it is not possible to disregard the fact that we continue to remain one of the most violent countries in the world, where the human rights of individuals and peoples are completely disregarded. The indigenous communities have especially suffered the persecution and destruction of communities and leaders such as the case of Caloto, located in the Department of Cauca, where twenty Paez indi-

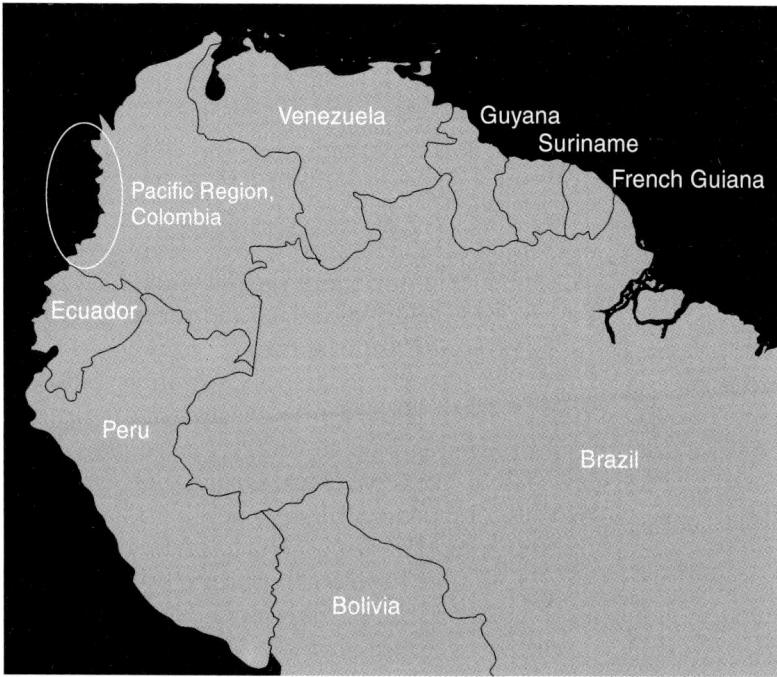

genes were assassinated, an event which seriously compromised members of the National Police. Also, the repeated assassination of the leaders of the Zenue indigenous people of the San Andrés de Sotavento reservation in the Department of Cordoba, the assassination of the traditional authorities of the Arhuaco people in the Cesar Department (Sierra Nevada) and the assassination of Zenue indigenes in Uraba Antioqueño are events that involve the military, landowners and paramilitary.

This kind of policy has resulted in thousands of unemployed workers as a result of modernisation and privatisation processes. Earlier, the state was the largest employer, but over the last five years about 80,000 workers have been laid off. At the same time, the few social security programmes that existed have been stopped and instability in the labour market has become constant; along with it all, this process has put an end to the role of unions.

Economically, no industrial expostulation has been made and our country finds itself inundated by foreign goods that are about to put an end to our small industrial base. This process has only served to consolidate the large economic conglomerations which exist in the country (Santo Domingo, Ardila Lule, Sarmiento, Angulo, etc.) and to whitewash the dollars coming from drug trafficking; all in all, the liberalisation has served only to make the rich, richer and the poor, poorer.

**The Truth about the Rights of the Indigenous Peoples of Colombia**
The constitutional rights that our communities gained in recent regulations have been significantly reduced and violated such as in the case of indigenous territorial entities, conceived in the national constitution as autonomous, administrative, political entities which would serve to pay respect to the ethnic and cultural diversity of indigenous people. Indigenous organisations such as The National Indigenous Organisation of Colombia, ONIC (of which OREWA is an affiliate), began consultations between the communities that, as a result, came up with a proposal for a set of regulations and a structureof the indigenous territorial entities. This has not been taken into consideration by the national government. The national government in turn presented to the Congress of the Republic a bill which is ignorant of the truth about our situation and designed so that it will be impossible to constitute indigenous territorial entities in Colombia.

The same events occurred as concerns another constitutional right which indigenous communities have: receiving budgetary transfers. They have only served to reduce and rid the state of their responsibility towards our communities.

Ironically, the constitution does acknowledge our territories, but since its promulgation it has stopped calling them indigenous reservations because political will does not exist, and because they are the territories most sought after by large national and international corporations (due to their vast natural resources). This means that our rights only exist formally and are not fulfilled because there is a lack of political will, a supposed lack of resources. And because there is a lack of a sense of pluralism and tolerance on the part of society and the government, it is impossible to make them a reality.

We believe that the titling of indigenous territories, creation of indigenous territorial entities and just and equitable participation in the everyday income of the nation are important foundations for the development not only of indigenous peoples but also of the country as a whole in order to preserve biodiversity, natural resources and the environment.

For many years indigenous organisations have denounced the actions of the state since its contradictory policies have been the source of major environmental, social and cultural problems, exemplified in the case of fumigation with glyphosphate and other herbicides to fight the cultivation of coca and poppies. This causes our trees to defoliate and destroys our crops. Another example is the construction of a large hydroelectric plant in Urra that affects the territories of the Embera peoples from the Verde and Esmeralda rivers area in the Department of Cordoba. Similar events occurred with the Salvajina Dam in the Department of Cauca which affected the Paez peoples, oil exploration which is cornering in the indigenous peoples from the Colombian Amazon and expanding to the Pacific, gold exploitation in the Naquen mountain range and the construction of the by-passes of the Pan-American Highway (Pereira-Animas-Tribuga and Medellin-Urrao-Palo de Letras or Tapon del Darien). These by-passes not only cross our territories, dividing them, but also put an end to our traditional flora and fauna sanctuaries.

**Survival in the Colombian Pacific Coast, another Threat to Indigenous Communities**
On the Colombian Pacific Coast, the Embera, Wounaan, Tule, Eperara Siapidara and Awa indigenous peoples and the black communities live together. The coastal region of the Colombian Pacific is the area situated between the borders of Panama to the north and Ecuador to the south, running approximately 1,300 kilometres. To the east the border is the western spurs of the western mountain range. Its continental expanse is approximately 71,000 square kilometres which corresponds to 6.2% of the national territory. It is the region with the highest level of rainfall in the country and more than three fourths of it are covered by tropical rainforest.

According to the estimates of the National Statistics Department, DANE, approximately 40% of its inhabitants are located in five urban centres, which in order of size are: Buenaventura,

Tumaco, Quibdo, Guapi and Istmina. These, in spite of their dense population, do not have an infrastructure adequate to provide most needed services.

About 80% of the basic needs of the inhabitants in this region are not satisfied, there is a life quality index of 50,1 and the per capita income is US$ 500 per year. Public services do not exist in the region, the infant mortality rate exceeds 150 per 1000, illiteracy lies at an average of 37% and 60% of the population live in absolute poverty.

Therefore, it is necessary to contrast this situation to the richness of the territory which is considered to have one of the highest concentrations of biodiversity in the world, where 20-25% of the species found there are endemic to the region and where there are 7 million hectares of tropical rainforest of which at least 5 million have not been touched. It is a territory from which, in 1991, more than 100 metric tons of gold were extracted and where 159,000 hectares of forest are felled annually.

We, the indigenous peoples, have created cultural systems in the Pacific that historically have proven an efficient guarantee for our survival and ethnic affirmation in spite of the described situation: an immense paradox of endangered life in the midst of incalculable richness. Our adaptive system with its harmonious relationship to the forest and traditional use of the territory has been the pillar in the continuation of our culture and lives.

### The Indigenous Communities and their Organising Process, the OREWA.

We want a place in this world where differences exist side by side and where these differences are considered part of our richness; a place where respect for life, a peaceful resolution of conflicts and authentic participation are the fundamental pillars of our existence.

For many years we, the Embera, Wounaan and Tule indigenous communities, who live in the territory corresponding to the Department of Choco (Colombia), have fought for the protection of our territories in an attempt to defend our life and culture. For this reason, we have organised ourselves in OREWA in order to be able to claim our territorial, cultural, social, economic and political rights as ethnic groups. The result has been a model of inter-ethnic unity.

We have been working for 15 years, and our fundamental objectives have been the acknowledgement of ownership of our territories, the protection and conservation of natural resources and the environment, respect and acknowledgement of our culture, to work towards an education that acknowledges our cultural identity, to establish an internal, social control of our communities through what we call 'indigenous justice' in order to bring social and cultural life together among our peoples, and to see traditional medicine as a form of cultural affirmation and also as a vision of the future of our communities. We work towards these issues to create a developmental alternative that respects cultural and biological diversity and guarantees the life of our peoples and the sharing of life with all other sectors of the Colombian population.

**Natural Resources and the Environment.**
During these years of struggle we have had to enter into major battles in order to defend the principles that we established in our organisation. One of the most serious problems we have had to confront is that of the exploitation of natural resources, especially timber, gold and platinum. This exploitation has damaged our ecosystem and our culture. It has dried out springs and contaminated rivers to the point of destroying one of the most important rivers in the region, the San Juan. The exploitation also imposes new economic models which are beginning to ruin the natural and social cycles that our communities have maintained, changing an economy based on extractive industries into one of the ways of robbing the peoples of the Pacific, not only in terms of physical resources, but also socio-culturally.

It is for these reasons that we are undertaking a battle in defence of our rights, claiming ownership of our territories and demanding that the Colombian state implement existing national legislation, both environmental and as concerns indigenous peoples in the country.

In these battles, several indigenous leaders have been assassinated. Among them is Enrique Arce who was assassinated in 1980 for defending indigenous territories from foreigners who sought to exploit gold from the Andagueda River. Similarly, many indigenous leaders from Jurado have died defending the territories from brute timber exploitation.

We, the indigenous peoples, are the prime defenders of natural resources and the environment because they are important elements in our lives; without them, we would not have been able to culturally resist for so many years because our spirituality and our *raison d'être* are explained through them, through the knowledge that our peoples have accumulated over thousands of years.

Therefore, we seek a binding denunciation of companies, firms or individuals who exploit and embezzle our natural resources. We demand that the Colombian state implement a coherent policy in matters of natural resources and the environment and respect for cultural and biological diversity. We further call on the state to legislate for the benefit of all sectors of the population and not only safeguard the interests of the few. For this we seek international solidarity so that human rights organisations, development organisations and the World Bank show interest in indigenous and impoverished parts of the country. Development should not be at the expense of peoples, their cultures and their lives.

**Territory is the Foundation of our Life**
For centuries we have owed our existence and survival to the equilibrious relationship that we have had with nature which has been the source for itinerant agriculture and activities such as hunting, fishing and the production of handicrafts, canoes, houses and working tools. This relationship has always been founded in the traditional methods and know-how of our ancestors; it is a product of our adaptation to the environment that we live in, where our own culture constantly recreates itself. The fact is that the guiding principle of our planning for the fulfilment of our needs is in line with our cosmovision and an ordering of the territory suitable for a respectful management of territory and natural resources that make our self-subsistence and the equilibrium of the ecosystem possible.

> The indigenous people were placed upon the face of the earth, our Mother, by the creator. We cannot be separated from our lands and territories. *(Land Charter of the Indigenous Peoples, 1992, No. 31)*

The only way to obtain an income in the Pacific region is by indiscriminate exploitation of natural resources, a development which is generating changes in the ability of the fragile soil to renew itself due to the loss of rich, wild flora and fauna native to these rainforests. This loss is caused by erosion, drought and soil infertility. The general situation in turn provokes a chain of cultural and socio-economic consequences which affect our communities because of changes in lifestyle, conflicts with other groups of human beings and forced migration.

It is for these reasons that the indigenous organisations of Colombia today, more than ever, claim that territory is the foundation of the lives of our peoples. It is a struggle to defend the culture that we the indigenous peoples still possess. In this battle we have learned to use the legal tools that Colombian laws provide us with and it is in this way that the Indigenous Organi-sation of Antioquia, OIA, accused the Compañía Maderas (Lum ber Company) of Darien-Pizano and the Corporation for the De-velopment of Choco CODECHOCO (responsible for watching over natural resources in the region) of exploiting the forest in a manner which harms and threatens the fundamental rights of the Embera-Katio indigenous communities in Chagerado in the Murindo municipality, Department of Antioquia.

The Constitutional Court of Colombia ruled in favour of the community, basing their decision on the fact that the close relationship existing between the ecosystem and the way of life of indigenous communities which inhabit the tropical rainfor-ests means that the act of deforestation constitutes a danger to the life and cultural, and social and economic integrity of these communities.

The National Indigenous Organisation of Colombia, ONIC, acting as guardian, lodged a formal complaint against the Co-lombian Oil Company, ECOPETROL, for their oil exploration activities carried out in territories of the Nukak-Maku indig-enous peoples who are the last nomadic peoples inhabiting the Colombian Amazon. The Colombian legal system ruled in fa-vour of these communities.

The Embera Wounaan of Choco Regional Organisation, ORE-WA, mobilised the indigenous peoples of Embera who were affected by the construction of the Animas-Tribuga branch of the Pan-American highway, supported by the fact that not all legal requirements for building this highway had been fulfilled with respect to the environment and indigenous peoples. This highway affects not only the rich forests of the tropical rainforest, but also the cultural diversity of its peoples. The state sees itself obligated through INDERENA to expedite resolution 0477 of 14 August, 1992, in which construction is to be suspended if legal requirements are not fulfilled and the just demands of indigenous peoples not considered. This act led the Ministry of Public Works to agree to acknowledge the rights of indigenous communities to participate in these kinds of state plans and programmes, a participation that we should clearly be entitled to. And at the moment, this particular construction is at a standstill.

These are some examples of the actions taken by indigenous communities resulting from our process of organisation to protect our culture, life and environment.

> Earlier, there were cars in the highway zone, but they were further away and it was possible to live without problems. Each family had a farm on ample territories, worked in unity and produced quality maize, palm, yams and avocados; there was good fishing and people hunted paca, boars.
>
> After they constructed the highway, the white man came and began to cheat the Indian, to exploit the timber. They fished with dynamite, they ruthlessly cleared areas and razed the forest, killing the animals; they ruined the soil. That is why it is now so difficult to cultivate, hunt and fish in the highway area and why the people are unable to properly nourish themselves when they grow old. (Testimony of an indigenous woman living by the highway).

### Environmental Policy and the True Situation of our Peoples

The Colombian government prides itself on being a state that promotes the protection of the environment through a set of laws and a Ministry. It also prides itself on including an environmental policy in its development plans which include the Natural Resources Management Plan (known as PAFC) and the Biopacific Plan (GEF).

But this programmatic and legal base is far from reality, as these policies are fundamentally directed towards regions where the state's presence is very weak and it is correspondingly difficult to manage the institutions. In these areas, the pressure and power of economic sectors interested in the unchecked exploitation of natural resources in order to achieve maximum profit continues virtually unrestricted.

This situation renders extremely vulnerable the population of these territories rich in natural resources, not only because of the marginalised situation in which they live but also because of their cultural characteristics. In short, a climate of tension and disquiet, where the losers are the involved communities, is being created.

Today, in the face of climatic changes on the planet, desertification, the loss of biodiversity, etc., the industrialised countries demand that the weak countries, which possess large nature reserves, preserve these reservations as they consider them the patrimony of all of humanity. That is why our riches are so important. But we wish to affirm that this wealth is important in the way in which conservation and the alternative development of the tropical rainforest are interconnected and overseen by the native population. This should be carried out through programmes and resources which help protect their economic and cultural lives in such a way that the population who live there will be acknowledged as the proper owners of the territory and their traditional knowledge recognised. Finally, the benefits of intellectual property rights and access to genetic resources should also be acknowledged.

### The Biopacific Project and Indigenous Peoples
The Biopacific Project has declared that its general, strategic objective is to maintain and strengthen the importance of biodiversity options through:

1. The integral protection of relevant ecosystems due to their variety and variability;

2. The sustainable use of ecosystems that have formed in the permanent habitat of the predominant ethnic groups; and

3. The regulation and vigilance of economic activities and infrastructural construction which impacts undesirably on the natural environment.

As mentioned earlier, we, the indigenous communities, advocate preservation of biodiversity, but we understand that this will only succeed if territorial rights of indigenous and black communities are accepted as a precondition to all other preservation strategies which must be carried out in coordination with our peoples. If this does not happen, we face the risk of losing the possibility of preserving one of the richest biodiverse areas on the planet, with the consequence that our culture will be condemned to eradication.

We also consider the resultant information as the heritage of our communities and, for that reason, the Biopacific Project ought to guarantee acknowledgement of our intellectual property rights and the usage of said information since we do not wish the events of other research studies to be repeated; the results of these studies now rest in the world's major research centres without there being any control over the use and the utility that will possibly derive from the recompilation of thousands of years of our communities' knowledge.

We believe that it is important to study and validate the alternatives of sustainable economic development for our communities. We further believe that our knowledge should be accepted as valid in the construction of a new development strategy based on conservation and sustainable use of biodiversity.

That is why we are worried about the lack of clarity pertaining to intellectual property rights as concerns the destiny and use of information which is a result of research undertaken by this project. This is a discussion that has yet to be resolved at the international level. But at the same time, we observe that in its plans, to be more exact in relation to the areas protected under the system of collective ownership, indigenous reservations and Law No. 70 from 1993 (The Law of Black Communities), the project does not possess a decided and consistent attitude towards helping this process. The future of biodiversity in the region is dependent on the project's having a clear nature conservation strategy which includes an understanding of the ownership of territory and its management.

It is impossible to foresee how the entrance of capital is going to be faced. There is pressure for 'development' in this region which, as stated earlier, provokes severe environmental and socio-cultural effects which incontestably affect biodiversity.

If part of the general strategic objective is 'the sustainable progress of the ecosystems which have been formed in permanent habitats of the predominant ethnic groups', then there should be more effective work carried out in the organisational processes of the indigenous, black and mestizo communities as concerns their objectives and expectations, the establishment of indigenous territorial entities, the titling of reservations, land titling in the black communities, the use, control and administration of natural resources, etc. Disassociation from the social, political, cultural and economic dynamics of the region does not contribute to the project having influence on the political decisions that are defined in the context of the region's development.

To be absent from the legislative process which is advancing across the country and which deals with territorial decree is to ignore that not only is it one of the principal interests of the indigenous movement, it is also the inclusion of the environmental component in the functions of the territorial entities of the country. It is crucial to support the indigenous communities of the Pacific as they determine how to control and administrate these resources as well as to establish additional guarantees to ensure that indigenous peoples are a part of the process to protect the region's biodiversity.

Much time and energy have been spent on workshops and seminars which have not contributed to developing public awareness when speaking of biodiversity. We do not think that the Biopacific Project can be managed through the criteria of political intriguers and patronage in the approval of projects and assignment of personnel, becoming a game for both traditional politicians of the region and recent arrivals at the national political scene. They should work in harmony with the organised, serious representative social movements of the region who have proposals for concrete work which will benefit the population and consequently biodiversity. They should not work with small sectors that are not representative and which while claiming to defend the communities, both black and indigenous, only contribute to the breaking up of the project and do not clearly uphold the work and objectives of the social movement or the Biopacific Project.

To sum up the latter, we reiterate that:

1. The Biopacific Project should assume a clear and concrete working method to support collective ownership regulations, indigenous reservations and the titling of black communities so that this process is stimulated in the region as quickly as possible within the framework of indigenous legislation and the most recent legislation of the black communities.

2. The discussions that are taking place at the international level concerning intellectual property rights and access to genetic resources should count on an expanded debate to include involved communities, and the project should guarantee that the serious, responsible and representative organisational processes of indigenous, black and mestizo communities will be a part of these discussions to guarantee that communities' rights be respected.

The fulfilment of legislation covering the rights of peoples at both national and international level will include 'consultation' as the way to guarantee the communities that they can take an active part in the decisions dealing with their territories and even more, in the decisions taken about intellectual property rights which will define not only the rights of Colombia but also the rights of communities possessing traditional knowledge.

3. The project should take a stand concerning the process of territorial regulation. Support should be shown for indigenous communities of the Colombian Pacific Coast in the definition of indigenous territorial entities as a guarantee for management and use of the territory which protects biodiversity in the specifying of local development plans.

4. The participation of communities in the structure of the regional and national project so that they are present in discussions and analyses of the role of the project in the Pacific will more decisively involve the population, ensuring that the project will have greater impact in the region.

PRASERT TRAKANSUPHAKON

# THE WISDOM OF THE KAREN IN NATURAL RESOURCE CONSERVATION

Northern Thailand, especially the mountainous area, is a place where hilltribes have lived and practised their traditional agriculture for centuries. Regarding the 'hilltribes', the majority of the public thinks that they are some sort of 'Forest Destruction Agency', only because their ways of life are different from those living in the lowlands. The agricultural system among the hilltribes is characterised as 'slash and burn' farming. But is it fair to make a judgement before we have a thorough understanding of their agricultural system and way of life?

At present, the concept of 'forest and environment conservation' is widespread. The government declared a ban on commercial use of the forests in 1989, imposing strict control on the utilisation of forest areas. Such controls have had adverse effects on the lives of the majority of hilltribes. Many hilltribe populations were evicted from their land and some were arrested on charges of 'encroaching on reserved forests'. Large areas in the mountains became off-limits for the purpose of residence and cultivation and, thus, the right to new family settlement was de facto abolished. The hilltribes felt that they were not properly consulted or advised about such important decisions. With wonder and fear, they are considered by outsiders as the 'enemies of the forest', though in fact they are the 'friends' and 'guardians' of nature and forest.

This article documents the wisdom in environmental conservation of one of the hilltribes, the Karen, particularly focusing on cultural aspects. It explores the beliefs, thoughts and means of protecting and conserving the natural environment. It aims at providing a better understanding of the hilltribes to concerned individuals and organisations. It will also help to 'repair' the conventional image of the hilltribes who are actually the true allies of the forest and its creatures.

## The Karen Concept of Conservation

The Karen's rule regarding living with nature is well explained by the expression 'Au Ti Kertaw Ti, Au Kaw Kertaw Kaw', meaning 'Live with the water, care for the river. Live with the forest, care for the jungle'. This rule is regarded as most important in directing the relationship between humans and nature. The word Kaw in the Karen language means land and includes all the natural beings on it. It also means that all nature's creatures and humans have to live together in harmony as they depend on each other for their survival. This rule has been strictly followed by all the Karen for generations. Thus, they are one of the hilltribes which take great care of the forest and maintain the balance of nature.

## Land Ownership

Land ownership among the Karen can be divided into three types: community ownership, ownership shared by the village community and individuals, and private ownership.

## Community Ownership

### 1) The village border line

The village border line, or *Kaw Ser* in the Karen language, means the limit of the land area of each village. The village border lines usually utilise local geography; e.g. a river or a hill. At the border line, there are normally physical signs posted, called *ta leaw*.

Though border lines exist between villages, members of the same tribe can cross them and enter each other's village's territories for the purpose of hunting and collecting forest products under the condition that such activities will not cause deterioration of the natural resources.

### 2) Community forest

Each Karen village holds a community forest for its own utilisation and protection. The community forest is located near the village. Besides providing cool shade to the residents and domestic animals of the villages, the community forest also serves as shelter for the community. The community forest contains many large trees, but no one from the village would ever tamper with them. Using this forest for private purposes is strictly prohibited, and this rule is always followed by all members of a Karen

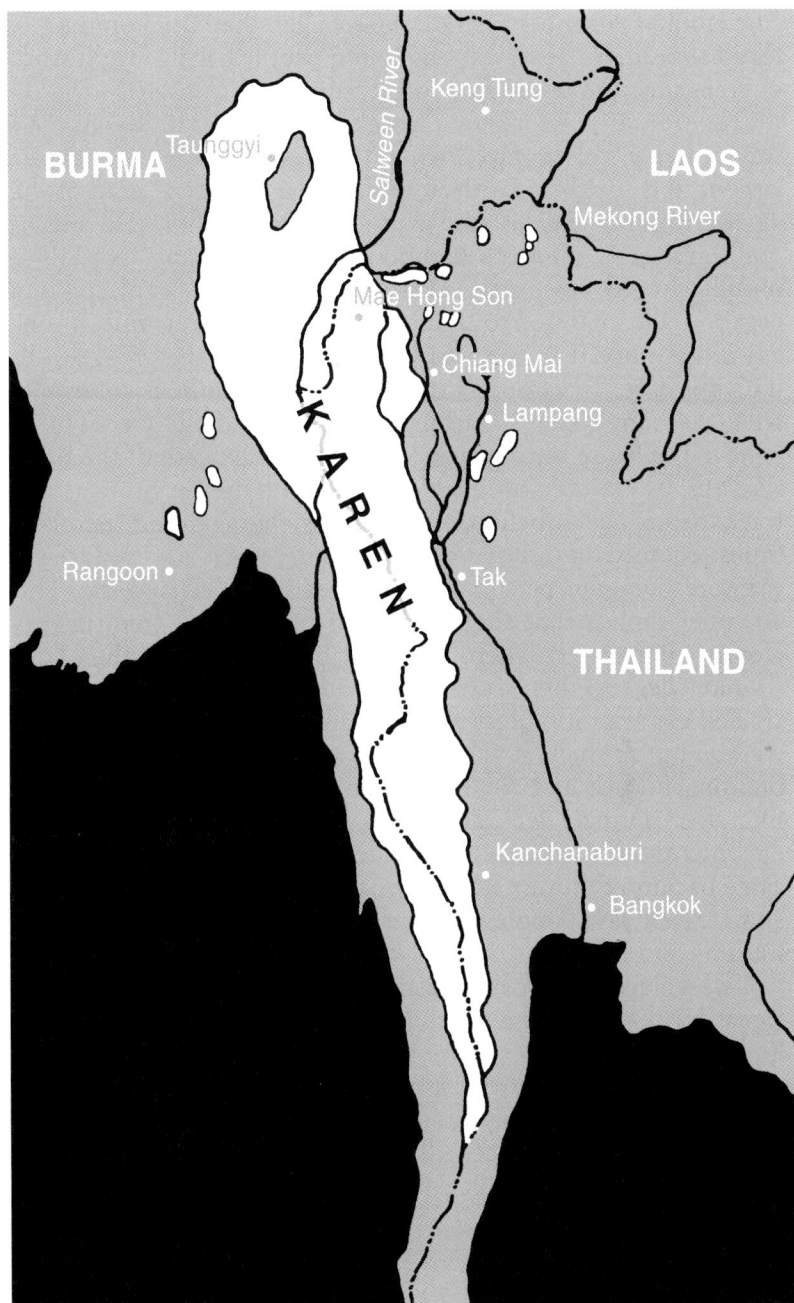

BURMA
Taunggyi
Keng Tung
LAOS
Salween River
Mekong River
Mae Hong Son
Chiang Mai
Lampang
K A R E N
Rangoon
Tak
THAILAND
Kanchanaburi
Bangkok

community. Also, because of their belief that the community forest should be conserved, the Karen people hardly ever disturb or go against the traditional forest rules.

The trees in the forest are closely associated with the Karen's way of living. For example, when there is a birth in the village a large tree is sought as a place to drop the umbilical cord of the newborn. This special tree is called *De-Poh-Tuh* (De means 'umbilical cord', *Poh* is a bamboo tube, *Tuh* means 'tree'). The umbilical cord, once severed from the newborn, is placed in a bamboo tube and tied to the selected tree. The tree must not be cut down since it is believed that the spirit of the child dwells with the tree. To tamper with the tree, therefore, is to tamper with the baby's spirit, causing it to flee from the tree. This is believed to cause serious sickness or even the death of the baby.

Thus, by creating an intimate relation between humans and trees through such beliefs, the Karen encourage their members to protect trees and the forests. A person's spirit is with a tree. If the tree dies, the person might get seriously ill and die. This attitude implies that the survival of people and trees is very closely interrelated. There shall not be one or the other, both should exist together: a crucial attitude toward natural balance.

The community forest is a place for its members to dwell, as well as for animals. It is the source of firewood, materials for building houses and for making fences for domestic animals. Domestic animals, including chickens, pigs, cattle and even elephants, are in turn able to provide people with food or labour. The community forest also provides children with a playground and is used as a training place for activities such as climbing, hunting and trapping.

The villagers can easily distinguish trees in the community forest by their usefulness, such as trees for firewood, building houses, mending fences or for barns to store rice. They are good at carefully selecting trees from the forest. For instance, if the bamboo in one place is found to carry disease, the remaining bamboo in the same place will no longer be used. Such selection thus implies the Karen villager's traditional knowledge of various trees in the forest. Their rationale is to preserve the variety of tree species and ensure a proper balance. This species selection stresses the underlying meaning and importance of the close relationship between people and nature. They must support each other always, so that both can survive forever.

*3) Animal husbandry*
The Karen consider the area outside their living quarters as the place for raising animals, especially large domestic animals such as cattle and elephants, which are considered community property. An arrangement is made in order to separate the community animals from privately owned domestic animals. Especially if something happens to the elephants, the villagers will bring the matter up for discussion. Smaller animals are allowed to roam around the community forest to obtain their own daily food requirements.

**Ownership Shared by the Village Community and Individual Villagers**
*Village land*
The land where the village itself is located is owned by the community. There is no fence or boundary mark. Each family is allowed to build a house and to plant vegetables on a small piece of land around the house. There is a strict rule prohibiting sale and purchase of this land to other villagers and to outsiders. Sale and purchase are thus considered a bad omen for all. Establishing residence in or moving out of the village by any individual is decided by the village headmen according to historical community rules. There is, for instance, a tradition called *taga* or 'consulting the oracles', meaning to ask for assistance in making decisions.

In choosing land, villagers use several important criteria. The ideal is to have long lasting happiness and peace in the community. The criteria include appropriate administrative location of the area, appropriate living area and, most importantly, fertility of the land. Before building houses in the selected community, certain regulations according to their beliefs must be applied. All are aimed at peace and harmony and the sustainable interrelationship among community members. In addition, this includes the balance between humans and nature.

Each Karen house in the village has a small plot of land for cultivating vegetables and fruits for domestic consumption, e.g. mangoes, jackfruit, pomelo, guava, etc. The fruit-bearing trees not only give fruits but also shade and greenery. In all Karen community villages one will find many large and small fruit-bearing trees around the villages as well as around all houses, many of which have been planted there since the time of their ancestors.

As a Karen folk song says:

> Where we are now our mother used to live,
> Where we are now our father used to live,
> Pomelo which our mother planted,
> Orange which our father planted,
> If we help each other care for them,
> They will give us fruits forever.

As metioned before, originally, according to village law, to sell and buy village land was strictly prohibited. However, it could be divided among the villagers by following the tradition of obtaining consent by consulting oracles. It is not allowed to make reserve land because it brings bad fortune which can mean death to the person concerned.

> If our ancestors are incapable of
> setting up a village,
> no matter how large the village,
> it could end up being a small one.

This songs means that if the forefathers did not organise the village well, following the ancient customs and traditions, a large village could end up being a small village.

Catastrophes affecting the village are considered bad omens which necessitate relocation. Such catastrophes may be in the form of diseases related to the forest that bring many deaths or wild animal attacks on the village. When the Karen move to a new location, they usually consult the traditional oracles. However, the new location for villagers must be somewhere near the original site and definitely must not interfere with nature and the ecological balance. It is also held that such catastrophes are by and large related to the former location.

Consider the song which is sung during the wrist-tying 'New Year Ceremony' and the 'August Ceremony':

> We make a living following our forefathers' system and heritage,
> We make a living according to our forefathers' regulation,
> Rice stalks, heavily laden with golden rice bow down,

Sweet scent of wine coming from the central pavillon and all throughout the village.

This means that if we make a living by strictly following our forefathers' system and regulations, the result will be a plentiful rice harvest. For that, we celebrate with wine made from rice in the central pavillon and throughout the village.

The most important step in shifting cultivation is the selection of new land. If wild fowl, a wild buffalo or birds suddenly appear, if a deer makes sounds, snakes cross someone's path or there are dreams of a forest fire, the Karen consider these as bad omens. It means that the forest will not permit them to farm in the area. In all such instances, the land has to be abandoned.

Selection of new swiddens must always strictly follow the old practices. Interference with the natural norms of the forest, thereby disturbing the balance of nature, must be avoided. Shifting cultivation among the Karen is always practised in a large area of land and not on a single small plot. The reason for this is to prevent uncontrollable forest fires. Fire might occur if the preparatory burning of several areas is undertaken by a small number of villagers at one time.

Shifting cultivation is not practised on both sides of the village because it would lead to a 'sandwiched village'. The more practical idea underlying this is to protect the village from fire. In cutting the forest for farming, only the small trees, or at most medium-size trees are cut down. The Karen always preserve the larger ones. But if necessary, a few branches of large trees can be cut. In addition, the Karen do not cut down trees which grow on the long and continuous foothill nor in the valley. The reason is that such places should be preserved for the path of the forest deity. The practical idea is to leave them as a fire-stopper or barrier when burning preparations begin. The method of burning farm lands starts from the top of the plot because the wind at this point is strong. If done the reverse way, the wind from below will be blown upwards, and it will be difficult to prevent the spread of fire to the forest. If the burning starts from the upper part of the farmland, the fire gradually moves down the slope to the middle area. Then they start burning from the lower part of the land and the fire goes upwards. But this will not allow the wind to blow the fire to the top, since that area was already burnt. In case the fire gets out of hand and spreads to the village, the villagers can help each other to quickly put out the fire.

After the planting season is over and the rice has grown to approximately twice the length of a hand (traditional system of measurement), the Karen perform a ceremony called 'fire worship'. It is a kind of ritual dedicated to the earth, forest and trees that were burned. During the ceremony, they ask forgiveness for such deeds as are essential for their livelihood. They also ask that any sufferings disappear with all that was burned and that the cool shade of nature come back as usual. The offering consists of two chickens and a bottle of whisky.

As for the bees which make their hives among trees felled in the rice field, the farmowners do not touch the raised tree stumps. It is believed that if the bee areas are disturbed, production of rice will decline. It would also cause the owners to suffer from all sorts of illnesses.

**Private Ownership: Irrigated Paddies**

Irrigated rice paddies are of vital importance for the Karen people's livelihood. There is an expression that 'swiddens are like standing on bamboo', implying the uncertainty of dry rice production. The productivity depends entirely on the weather and rainfall. Karen villagers who own rice paddies are considered as people of high status in their society.

The Karen seek farmland in the valley where irrigation water from a nearby stream is available. It is these expert foothill farmers who construct rice terraces, utilising an up-hill irrigation method. Since most of the land in the plains has been taken by lowland Thais, the Karen have to use uplands for rice cultivation. However, upland rice terraces are insufficient for their subsistence needs and thus they at the same time have to practise swidden rice agriculture.

A considerable amount of water is needed for rice cultivation. Therefore, the Karen must learn how to use water economically because most of their farm plots are supplied with water from small streams. This is one of the reasons why the Karen always take considerable precautions in protecting the watersheds and water sources in the forest. Water worship is firmly upheld and practised by all Karen. Water sources such as springs are feared as well as highly respected. Swimming in such water sources is strictly forbidden. All of such beliefs are practical means of water and forest conservation. They realise how water is essential to life. As they say: 'Starvation will permit one to last for some time, but without water one will not last even one day.'

## Conservation Forests
There are several types of forest required to be conserved by the Karen. They include watersheds, forests around water sources and forests used as a cemetary or for protection from various natural calamities. Karen forest preservation can be categorised as follows:

*Watersheds*
Pools of water that are derived from various sources of water from the mountains. They are:

*1) 'New forests'*
These are flat and completely surrounded by mountains, protruding slightly in the shape called *Kiat-Laew*, i.e. they appear like 'sitting on eggs'. The surrounding area is wet or moist most of the year. There are tiny springs with pools of water.

*2) Spring forests*
The watershed forest of this type is shady and cool all year round. It is also believed to be haunted by ghosts feared by the villagers. This type of forest is found further from the head of farmlands, but sometimes it is located close to the village.

*3) Farm head forests*
These are forests that also need to be conserved and are an important source of livelihood. They are supposed to be occupied by spirits. When disturbed, the spirits might flee from the place causing the pools and streams to dry up. The owners of farms nearby have to please the spirits by regularly perfoming rituals in order to keep them on the farmland.

## Village Burial Forests
The Karen believe that the souls of ancestors of the villagers are always in this forest. The souls will be disturbed if the villagers cut down trees, hunt or burn the forest. Once disturbed, life will

become more difficult, for instance in the form of various illnesses or natural calamities. Such beliefs and traditions are also aimed at protecting the forest.

## Protected Natural Forests
### 1) Hill ridge forests
Along the hill ridges, according to Karen beliefs, is the pathway for spirits and demons, especially along the ridges of the mountains. These places are not used for settlement or hunting.

### 2) Wind-channel forests
These forests contain a natural channel for the wind, which is also considered the path of demons and ghosts. The Karen will not destroy this type of forest but conserve it. In the final analysis, the Karen preserve such forests for their own protection from forest fire and storms that may naturally occur anytime.

## Use of Trees
There are community laws prohibiting the cutting and use of certain trees, especially those used for building houses. They are:

1) Banyan trees, Pipal and Golden Keruing, all of which are said to be dwelling places of the spirits of their ancestors who determine the birth and longevity of human beings.
2) Se-Koh-Du is a tree species that the Karen specifically use to carry the corpse. It is absolutely prohibited for other uses.
3) Trees that are entwined with vines.
4) Trees with branching trunks.
5) Trees that make certain noises when felled.
6) Trees that remain blocked by other trees.
7) Trees that ants or other animals live on/in.
8) Trees where the umbilical cord is kept.

The laws listed above are strictly upheld by the Karen. Misfortune will befall those who violate them. As the ancestors said: 'Do not resist the law, son, because I did it once and I was indeed punished'.

As can be seen from the aforementioned list of trees, the Karen have plenty of practices aimed at protecting the forest. A blocked tree, if felled, requires the felling of another tree. A tree that houses ants or other animals is a refuge for many lives.

*Traditional Karen resource management: Swidden field with ripening rice and conservation forest in Mu Wae Khi village, Chiang Mai Province, Thailand. Photo: Christian Erni*

## Hunting and Collecting Forest Products

The principal livelihood of the Karen is rice farming. Hunting and collecting of forest products is second. It is said that 'The river smells of fish; the forest has the scent of wild animals.' This implies abundance of both water and earth-bound animals in the old days. The Karen's way of farming is, thus, similar to an old Thai expression: 'In the water there are fish, in the field there is rice.' Both sayings express the belief that survival depends on conservation.

## Hunting

There is a Karen phrase that goes: 'One gibbon dies, seven forests cry in grief; One hornbill is lost, seven banyan trees are in solitude.'

This is why there are so many laws and rules pertaining to hunting. A hunter is allowed to hunt only one bear, one gaur (large wild cattle) or one rhinoceros per year (the latter two are now virtually extinct). Before hunting, the hunter must always ask permission from the forest deities for the number of animals to be killed (usually not more than three).

Animals which are protected from hunting include species such as gibbons, giant hornbills, koels, vultures, woodpeckers, minnervets, crows, owls, hawks, swallows and pythons. The sounds of these birds and animals are loud and characteristically sweet for the forest. Some animals are closely associated with human beings in the myths.

It is prohibited to use poison to kill fish. Some kinds of fish are not allowed to be caught during certain seasons. There is even a rule among certain clans or villagers that earth-dam blocking is not permitted for catching fish.

Birds that are sometimes domesticated and which are considered to bring peace to the household such as cuckoos, doves and pigeons are not allowed to be hunted. Wild animals that happen to stray into the village must not be harmed or killed for food. To oppose these rules is to bring calamity to the village.

If beehives and pythons are found on a field, that field has to be abandoned. It is believed that such incidence represents the transformation of forest deities in order to forbid farming in that location.

## Collecting Forest Products

These are some regulations to be followed:

1) Rattan shoots must be eaten in the woods. However, they can be brought back to the village once a year, sometime in January.

2) Only two bamboo shoots are allowed to be taken home from any single clump. It is considered a sin to take more.

3) Only two bamboo trees are allowed to be cut down from any one clump.

4) Kuy-chai must be eaten only in the forest. If brought home, that person will get lost in the forest.

5) Herbal plants can only be collected during certain seasons and only in specified quantities. Otherwise, the herbs will turn out to be ordinary plants without medicinal value.

6) Certain vegetables are not allowed to be taken home during certain seasons, for instance, cha-om in the rainy season and banana ear during the summer.

7) A certain type of rattan (pluck-ta vine) is not allowed to be taken home and can only be used in the forest. If it is brought home, a tiger will follow.

8) Certain kinds of fruits and mushrooms are allowed to be eaten only in the forest, otherwise they become inedible and useless.

9) Certain kinds of wild animal meats are not permitted to be eaten with outsiders. These include linsang, wild fowl, gibbon, animals with shells and hornbill. Otherwise, they will never see each other again – the reason why hunting such animals is prohibited.

## Conclusion

It is obvious that the Karen lifestyle and the heart of their traditional laws are profoundly focused on conservation of the environment and maintenance of the ecological balance. Consider their management of farm lands, separate from their own forest preserves. Consider the variety of their forest preserves, each firmly directed at continuing processes to conserve the environment. The Karen have a rigid system of rules governing hunting and the gathering of forest products and specifying exactly which animals and plants must be protected. These are traditional rules guaranteeing the life of the forest and a sustainable environment, as well as guaranteeing the maintenance and mutual benefit of people and the forest, living together.

*Problems and obstacles*
A number of problems confront this generation-to-generation handing down of conservation practices:

1. The ignorance of outsiders (whether public or private, individuals or organisations). The failure to recognise traditional conservation practices and the consequent importing of theoretical and technical solutions can lead to disastrous results. Not only does this result in mismanagement, but it severely undermines the local potential to deal with their own problems and natural resources.

2. Religious organisations (whether Buddhist, Christian, etc.) change conventional beliefs and ritual practices, destroying age-old systems of thought and self-confidence. The villagers lose their own indigenous knowledge, without realising it, and adopt external values, often destructive ones.

3. The revision of production methods, requiring change from subsistence to cash cropping erodes local management systems.

4. The introduction of new and official systems of land ownership and structures of community administration upsets the capacity of the village for continuing self-government and self-reliance.

*Suggestions for a way out*
1. Development should begin with the study of indigenous knowledge and local management systems. Programmes should be based on a clear understanding of these and reinforce rather than replace them.

2. Efforts should be undertaken to ensure the continuous transfer of traditional knowledge and practices to new generations and their explanation on the basis of modern science.

3. Integrated subsistence agriculture should be encouraged and supported, with the ecological balance between nature and people maintained.

4. Development activities should provide for a variety of approaches, based on the differing backgrounds and production methods of the different tribes. Efforts to improve should always be founded on existing knowledge and practices.

Jeffrey A. McNeely

# INTERACTION BETWEEN BIOLOGICAL DIVERSITY AND CULTURAL DIVERSITY

'Variety is the spice of life' takes on new meaning at a time when consumers in Bangkok, Bogota, Bangui, Boston, Brisbane and Belfast are eating the same Big Macs, drinking the same Pepsi, watching the same Bill Cosby programme, smoking the same Marlboros, sending faxes over the same Toshiba modem and wearing the same Levis jeans. Does the global consumer culture mean the death of the world's rich diversity of peoples and cultural traditions? If so, what are we losing? What does the loss of biodiversity mean to indigenous peoples? And what does the loss of cultural diversity mean to biodiversity?

## Introduction
Throughout history local societies have ebbed and flowed as their wisdom was challenged by the need to live within the limits of their resources. Those societies that were able to develop the wisdom, technology and knowledge to manage their resources sustainably were able to survive, provided they were also strong enough to stand up to outside pressures. Others over-exploited their resources so they flourished only briefly, giving up sustainability and adaptability for a flash-in-the-pan enjoyment of immediate wealth.

Over the past several generations, the highly diverse and often localised adaptations to local environmental conditions have been profoundly disrupted in most places by a world culture increasingly characterised by very high levels of material consumption, at least for a privileged minority. Economic growth based on the use of fossil fuels as an energy source, greatly expanded international trade, technological advances and improved public health measures have spurred such a rapid expansion of human numbers and consumption of resources that new approaches to resource exploitation have been required to meet the demands. These approaches, often involving powerful machinery, sophisticated technology and arcane economic instruments, have overwhelmed the resource management measures that local communities had developed from their long experience of surviving in an uncertain world.

Perhaps the fundamental problem is that the world has become a single global trading system, bringing new technologies, new approaches and new pressures for exploiting resources. This means that products from local ecosystems are being harvested to feed the demands of distant, unpredictable markets rather than responding to local conditions of supply and demand. Often using heavy subsidies in the form of agricultural chemicals, fossil fuel, pesticides, inappropriate technologies and so forth, governments have replaced traditional systems of resource management with new systems imposed from other parts of the world. These new systems are able to yield considerable income, but the highest profits are earned when the fewest social and economic costs of resource depletion are paid (in economic terms, these costs are 'externalised'). For example, logging is far more profitable when the loggers do not need to compensate traditional owners for their loss of goods and services from the forest. Instead of being included in the prices paid for the timber, these environmental costs are transferred to society as a whole, to be paid either now or in the future.

Throughout the world, resources historically have been managed by diverse human societies who gave social and symbolic value to land and resources beyond their immediate extractive value. These symbolic relationships were based on ecological principles that supported a system of social and economic rules that were highly adaptive in the ongoing struggle to maintain a viable equilibrium between natural resources, individual desires and the demands of society. The traditional symbolic values have helped enable societies to avoid over-exploitation and to live within the limits imposed by the availability of resources and technology. In the past several decades, modern forms of development have often removed the responsibility for managing biological resources from the people who live closest to them and, instead, have transferred this responsibility to central government agencies located in distant capitals. This has not only undermined the local culture, but led frequently to mismanagement of resources as well. The government agencies – depart-ments of forestry, fisheries, protected areas and the like – have seldom developed a capacity to control over-exploitation which is of a sufficient scale to balance the new-found technological capacity to exploit.

Worse, the costs of conservation measures such as national parks which have been designed to control the worst excesses of the new systems of resource exploitation have still fallen on the indigenous people who otherwise would have benefitted from exploiting these resources (in economic terms, they have been forced to pay the opportunity costs involved). And the indigenous and traditional people who live closest to the areas with greatest biological diversity are often among the most economically disadvantaged – the poorest of the poor, who are at the farthest end of a global cash economy and are profoundly affected by every minor fluctuation in the world's ivory, fur, peanut or coffee market or by efforts to establish strict protected areas on their land.

This analysis suggests that we should not be surprised that forests, grasslands, coral reefs, and the species they support have been grossly over-exploited, forcing government officials into pitched battles with 'poachers', conflicts with indigenous peoples, and draconian policy measures such as exclusion of people from resources upon which their lives depend. And since the cultural survival of many rural people depends directly on how they manage natural resources, the 'nationalisation' of resources has had a profound impact on their cultures.

As a result of the global market, both biological diversity and cultural diversity are being depleted. While the loss of biodiversity is now well-recognised (WRI, IUCN, UNEP 1992), cultural diversity is perhaps under even more serious threat. Brazil alone has lost 87 tribes in the first half of this century, and one-third of North American languages and two-thirds of Australian languages have disappeared since 1800 (Durning 1992). In sum, over half of the world's 6,000 languages are now moribund, spoken only by people who are middle-aged or older (Harmon 1992). This depletion of diverse survival strategies and knowledge systems poses a significant threat to humanity, which can exist in the long-term only through a sustainable and interwoven relationship between nature and culture.

Many powerful influences in the world take the opposite view, seeing cultural homogeneity and ecological interdependence among nations as basically desirable. Indeed, the World Commission on Environment and Development has called for greatly expanded interdependence through enhanced flows of energy, trade and finance (WCED 1987). On the other hand, some have suggested that such interdependence – making the world a single global system – is the ultimate source of the global depletion of resources. As the distinguished ecologist Ray Dasmann pointed out two decades ago, when we are all part of one system connected by powerful economic forces, it becomes very easy to over-exploit any part of the global system because it is thought that other parts will soon compensate for such over-exploitation (Dasmann 1975). The damage may not even be noticed until it is too late to do anything to avoid permanent degradation. Perhaps worse, global interdependence enhances the domination of the economically powerful, yet requires a support structure which in itself can be very fragile – the impacts of changes in oil prices, the Mexican bond market and interest rates demonstrate the point.

The system of trade which has enabled the entire globe to be exploited, primarily for the benefit of urban populations, has led to great prosperity for those who have been able to benefit from the expanded productivity, but it has often led to devastation of local ecosystems. And what happens to the local people who remain dependent on the now-depleted living resources, and indeed had developed ways of using these resources sustainably, without depleting them?

The World Commission on Environment and Development provided an answer: growing interaction with the larger world is increasing the vulnerability of these isolated groups since they are often left out of the processes of economic development. Social discrimination, cultural barriers and the exclusion of indigenous people from national political processes makes them vulnerable and subject to exploitation. Many groups become dispossessed and marginalised, and their traditional practices disappear. They become the victims of what could with justice be described as cultural extinction.

This is not a trivial problem. 'It is a terrible irony that as formal development reaches more deeply into rainforests, deserts and other isolated environments,' says the WCED (1987), 'it tends to destroy the only cultures that have proved able to thrive in these environments.'

Unfortunately, the urban centres which characterise modern industrial civilisation have long viewed nature and culture as distinctly different, even opposing, concepts. Today's dominant symbol is money – a very distant and abstract way to characterise resources – and it is replacing natural symbols of proven worth to so-called 'primitive' peoples. Maybury-Lewis (1992) pointed out that as the end of the century draws near, the modern world is marked by unprecedented degrees of confusion, insecurity and yearning for change. Industrial society – today characterised by high unemployment, growing budget deficits, aging workforces and social strife – is losing self-confidence in the face of the future, and indeed the future itself has been brought into question. Under such conditions, the value of tribal wisdom can be fully appreciated, bringing an opportunity to consider new models for living in balance with resources. A return to tribal or primitive' lifestyles is not a realistic answer for the industrialised world or a feasible option for most of the world's 5.5 billion people, or for the projected doubling of the world population in the next century. Rather, new and sustainable systems of resource use can incorporate the traditional knowledge and wisdom of indigenous peoples to develop new and more sustainable relationships between people and resources. Cultural diversity also serves as a form of insurance, helping to expand the capacity of our species to adapt to change. As Maybury-Lewis concludes, the modern world needs traditional wisdom more than tribal peoples need the modern world.

## Forces Driving the Loss of Cultural Diversity: Loss of Control over Biological Resources

The loss of cultural diversity means that people are less well-adapted to specific local conditions, though they may be able to contribute better to the global economy. But the future is uncertain, and the global consumer culture has not stood the test of time. Oren Lyons, a spokesman for the Traditional Elders Circle of the Onondaga Nation in North America, has questioned the values that modern consumer societies are teaching their children. 'Where we come from', he says, 'the natural law is simple in this case: we will suffer in exact ratio to our transgressions and the damage done may be permanent to life as we know it today' (Lyons 1990).

A major effect of economic development has been to tie as many of the world's peoples as possible into the global economy. People in even the most remote areas are expected to produce more for distant markets and to open up their territories for resource exploitation and tourism. Many of them welcome the material goods which result, but the cost is often loss of control of their own resources and a loss of their own culture. Once they become integrated into larger systems, the social and economic centre of gravity shifts away from the community, and rural institutions become increasingly marginalised politically (Murphree 1993).

A major element in traditional relationships between indigenous cultures and the natural world is responsibility over resources. Tenure systems upon which responsibility is built are based on legitimacy drawn from the community in which they operate rather than from the nation-state in which they are located (Lynche and Alcorn 1993). Indigenous systems of resource tenure are extremely variable; complex mixtures of individual and community rights, enforced by the local culture. These systems are flexible and constantly evolving, often in response to changing environmental conditions. Such systems are invariably being disrupted by nation-states claiming ownership of the most environmentally and economically important areas, whether as national parks or national forests which are logged to achieve national objectives.

Where governments have claimed responsibility for resources, this implies that the state has the capacity to perform its assumed managerial role better than the indigenous peoples could. By nationalising forests which are then left unmanaged, or establishing national parks that have no management, the authority of governments tends to be spurious. While many governments have claimed power over resources, they have lacked the capacity to implement their responsibilities, thereby creating among indigenous peoples a lack of confidence in the capacity of either state or local institutions to regulate access to resources. This creates controversy about legal rights to resources, resulting in the conversion of common property systems which have well-defined rules and regulations into open access systems which often lead to widespread over-exploitation and loss of resources upon which local cultures are built.

Cultural diversity is threatened by the new global consumer culture which is spreading through television, trade and other means. A few examples will indicate the range of factors driving this process.

Land use management throughout much of Sub-Saharan Africa has been evolving from a pre-colonial communal land system to more formal and individualistic land title systems. Most traditional communities do not have effective title or control of their land systems, or any effective way to make their views felt at the national policy level. The colonial period was marked by a taking of many of the most desirable lands from long-term resident communities. The post-colonial period of nationhood has further served to provide legal means for the taking of land and resources from local communities under the guise of 'national interest'. Added to this are population pressures on the land, contributing to a breakdown of traditional methods of control. For the Shona of Zimbabwe, this scenario of divestiture of land has been all too evident. Traditionally, the Shona managed their lands communally based on ancestral relationships. Sacred sites and sites of historical importance traditionally were preserved throughout the Shona domain, though outsiders were generally unaware of these areas or of the values attached to them. Consequently, the breakup of Shona lands into small parcels under individualistic ownership schemes has failed to maintain traditional land use protection and management systems, and has resulted in a loss of cultural heritage and associated sustainable farming practices (IUCN 1993).

The Tuareg of West Africa are nomadic pastoralists. During the brief West African rainy season, the Tuareg move their herds of camels and other livestock such as sheep and goats into the desert to take advantage of the ephemeral seasonal grasses. As the dry season returns, the Tuareg withdraw their herds back to more permanent grazing areas close to water sources. This continuous cycle of movement allows the vegetation to regenerate and replenish itself. Tenuous water sources are also allowed to replenish themselves. The Tuareg rely on their livestock for transport, milk and blood, clothing and, occasionally, cash. Like many pastoralists, the Tuareg also rely on their livestock's manure for cooking and heating fuel (Burger 1990). The French colonisation of the region in the early 20th century profoundly changed the Tuareg economy. Raiding, a traditional component of Tuareg culture, was suppressed, and the trans-Saharan caravan trade declined in the face of modern transport methods. The imposition of political boundaries, customs duties and other governmental restrictions caused many Tuareg to abandon their nomadic lifestyle and settle permanently, despite their deeply-rooted dislike of agriculture. In their new agricultural lifestyle, the Tuareg have become more susceptible to drought such as the major drought of the early 1970s that drove thousands of Tuareg into Niger and Nigeria (Gaisford 1981).

The Sámi of northern Scandinavia are a distinct ethnic group who migrated to the region from Russia perhaps 10,000 years ago (Gaisford 1981). The majority, around 20,000, live in Norway, with 10,000 in Finland, 3,000 in Sweden, and perhaps 2,000 in Russia. Sámi live in permanent settlements in the northern tundra, although some live to the south in the coniferous forests, and many live along the coast. Sámi culture was traditionally decentralised, with families organised into loose associations. This has created tensions with central Scandinavian governments who have sought to establish political control over the Sámi. Today, only about 10 per cent of Sámi are still engaged in the traditional occupation of reindeer herding. For most Sámi, reindeer husbandry is no longer economically viable (Rogers 1993), and many also continue to practise traditional fishing, trapping and farming. Most Sámi have become thoroughly assimilated within the national Nordic cultures, but the Sámi continue to possess a strong ethnic identity and determination to preserve their culture (Rogers 1993). Since much of their language and culture is closely linked with their nomadic past, this has proved difficult. Sámi today face the dilemma of trying to find a means of economic survival that will enable them to

*Struggling to maintain their cultural identity without the roots in traditional economy: Only ten per cent of the Sámi are still engaged in reindeer herding. Photo: IWGIA Archives*

preserve their culture without forcing them to live on reservations or become tourist attractions.

Baines (1991) has written about the efforts of indigenous peoples in the South Pacific to nurture economic development while maintaining control over resource management. In the Solomon Islands of the South Pacific, the last 20 years have witnessed growing conflict between development interests and traditional land/sea tenure systems. Governmental agencies have grown increasingly frustrated with legislative provisions that safeguard the rights of indigenous peoples to maintain control over their lands and coastal areas. Pressure is mounting to introduce legislation to override customary tenure and associated rights. This would give the government access to large areas that could be opened for mining, logging, tourist development and other forms of development. To a large extent, this movement has been promoted by some Pacific islanders who perceive their ancestral systems as impediments to a 'progress' they believe only 'western' forms of development can provide.

The conflict between indigenous uses of wildlife and contemporary societal values attached to certain species by urban people is vividly illustrated by the current situation facing indigenous Greenlanders. In Greenland, the indigenous peoples have gained self-governance over their land and resources. Hence, the perennial issue of title and control of land is not the problem. Rather, some indigenous Greenlander communities have experienced economic hardships because of the decline in demand in North America and Europe (with the exception of Denmark) for sealskins, one of Greenland's traditional export products. The indigenous Greenlanders argue in favour of increased sealing based on assurances that seals would be harvested sustainably; sealing is locally regulated, certain protected areas are off limits for sealing, and sealing by non-residents is prohibited. However, while some indigenous hunting communities may still be dependent on wild harvests, over 90 per cent of Greenland's GNP now comes from the commercial fishery sector. Resolution of this issue thus depends largely on the willingness of foreign markets to sanction increased sustainable harvests of seals or on finding alternative economic solutions (such as within the commercial fishery sector) for indigenous Greenlanders that will nevertheless preserve their cultural heritage (IUCN 1993).

Robinson (1993) describes how colonists have been moving into the territory of the Yuqui indigenous people in Peru, primarily for the purpose of producing coca. These colonists tend to remain on their farms only during the planting and harvesting of the coca, and return to their highland settlements at other times of the year. Their activities appear to have had a major impact on the fish and game available to the Yuqui, using technology (such as dynamite fishing) that leads to considerable over-exploitation of resources. This is just one of many examples that could be provided of how new colonists have moved into traditional lands and disrupted traditional systems which had worked over a period of many generations. Crosby (1987) describes the impacts Europeans have had on both cultures and ecosystems during the thousand years of their 'ecological imperialism'.

On the island of Sumbawa, in the eastern part of the Indonesian archipelago, hunting has long been an important part of the economy. Because most of the villagers are Muslims, pigs are not a particularly desirable game animal, but feral buffalo and cattle, as well as the local species of deer *Cervus timorensis* are popular game animals. As grazers, they do far better in grasslands than in the forest that would normally cover the island. Today, grassland covers 17 per cent of Sumbawa's land area. These grasslands are at least several hundred years old and have been used for grazing and hunting for at least that long. The grasslands are maintained by annual fires which replace older and less edible grasses with younger and more edible ones, as well as eliminating dead plant material and thereby actually increasing overall herbaceous productivity as well as preventing reforestation. The creation of grasslands by people is a sensible reaction in habitat management, creating conditions which favour the grazing animals at the expense of pigs (which prefer the forest). Furthermore, the replacement of forest by grassland has been of net benefit to the wild herbivores that are hunted, with populations kept at such a high level that they could be harvested virtually at will. The hunters accepted communal control on hunting methods, prohibiting hunting during the period from November to May when the deer bear and rear their young. Government conservation programmes prohibited both burning of the savannas and hunting of the main game animals (ironically excluding pigs, the only species the Islamic islanders avoided), thus breaking down a genuine symbiosis which had proved sustainable over long periods of time. Because of its insensitivity to the local reality, this programme has both failed to win acceptance among peasant hunters and undermined their traditional conservation measures, thus achieving the worst of results (Dove 1984).

In conclusion, over-exploitation is to be expected in times of very rapid cultural change as traditional controls break down and humans learn to exploit resources in new ways. The movement of Europeans into the Americas is only the most dramatic example of this process (Crosby 1987), but similar factors appear to affect the entire globe (Roychowdhury 1992). Technological innovations such as plantation agriculture or industrial logging tend to favour exploitation of biological resources and the weakening of traditional approaches to conservation, especially when a group with 'modern technologies' moves into a region occupied by groups that use traditional technologies. The dominant society has the option of moving on to fresh resources when an area is exhausted and would derive no particular advantage from adopting the traditions of sustainable, conservative use that characterised the groups it has overwhelmed. It is able to earn virtually all the cash benefits of the forest but pay almost none of the long-term environmental costs. These costs remain with the indigenous peoples, who must live with the consequences of the resource management decisions made by external groups (Gadgil 1987).

At the same time, the indigenous groups lose any advantage from traditions of conservative use that were effective when they could exclude other groups from their territory. These traditions evolved when costs and benefits were internalised in the decisions made by communities, but since the local people are now paying far higher environmental costs of resource degradation, their only rational response is to join the exploiters to try to seek greater benefits as well and thereby contribute to the undermining of their culture.

Finally, the dominant economic forces in the world have relied on a vast government machinery to facilitate foreign exchange earnings through international trade. This economic expansion has the implicit (and sometimes explicit) goal of promoting more complete exploitation of biological resources. As an inevitable result, cultural diversity is also reduced, for two main reasons (Gadgil 1987). First, a significant component of cultural diversity which enables people to earn a living from the local biological environment is no longer functional; and second, subordinated groups begin to imitate the culture of the dominant group, thereby losing a major portion of their cultural diversity.

This is the *real* tragedy of the commons: traditional management systems that were effective for thousands of years become obsolete in a few decades, replaced by systems of exploitation which bring short-term profits for a few and long-term costs for many. This leads to the loss of both biological diversity and cultural diversity.

## Conserving Cultural and Biological Diversity: Approaches for Adapting to Change

Are all traditional systems doomed to failure, falling victim to state and private ownership? Or do traditional community-based resource management systems still have something to contribute? This section examines a few of the major issues involved in answering these questions.

Development – action that alters the environment so that it caters more effectively for human needs – is essential if the world is to be free from poverty and squalor, but such development must be based on resources that regenerate naturally and can meet our needs indefinitely. Destruction of tomorrow's biological and cultural foundations in order to satisfy today's needs is self-evident folly.

Within the process of development, room must be found for nature, which is both a spiritual enrichment and in a very practical sense the foundation of cultures. The processes of wild nature renew the oxygen in the air, maintain the cycles of essential elements, sustain the fertility of the land and regulate the flow of rivers. Humans turn to wild nature for new crops and new drugs, as well as for the beauty that enriches life. In many parts of the world, wildlife has played a dominant role in developing the culture of indigenous peoples. In tropical Asia, for example, tigers, elephants, crocodiles and large birds of prey help define the relations between people and their environment and even the relations among people (McNeely and Wachtel 1991). In short, conservation and development are not opponents, but are inseparably one (IUCN 1980, WCED 1987).

Similarly, cultural diversity and biological diversity need to be conserved together if either is to prosper; the local knowledge that people have about their resources and how they should be managed provides a critical resource for all of humanity. Perhaps 'biocultural diversity' is a useful phrase to describe conserving both biological and cultural elements to support the way people relate to their environments, and can provide a useful concept for bridging the current gap between biological and cultural approaches to conservation.

## The Convention on Biological Diversity: International Support for Cultural Diversity

The tropical developing world holds the lion's share of the world's genetic diversity as well as a vast body of indigenous knowledge of flora and fauna. The developed world, however, holds the technological capability in biochemistry, genetic engineering and biotechnology needed to develop genetic resources into commercial products. This disparity continues to generate controversy over whether genetic resources and traditional knowledge are part of the 'global commons' or whether such resources are the exclusive heritage of their native regions.

Under the Convention on Biological Diversity, which entered into force at the end of 1993, most countries now recognise the 'sovereign right' of countries to control the utilisation of their genetic resources and traditional knowledge. Pharmaceutical, biotechnology and agricultural companies in signatory nations must now reach cooperative agreements with countries from which genetic resources are to be obtained. Under this system, the potential exists for indigenous peoples to have their traditional knowledge recognised (through Intellectual Property Rights) and to benefit from it.

The Convention also specifically recognises the important contributions that indigenous peoples can make to the conservation of biological diversity. In its preambular section, the Convention recognises the

> close and traditional dependence of many indigenous and local communities embodying traditional lifestyles on biological resources, and the desirability of sharing equitably benefits arising from the use of traditional knowledge, innovations and practices relevant to the conservation of biological diversity and the sustainable use of its components.

Article 8 of the Convention establishes the obligation of each Contracting Party to

> respect, preserve and maintain knowledge, innovations and practices of indigenous and local communities embodying traditional lifestyles relevant for the conservation and sustainable use of biological diversity and promote their wider application with the approval and involvement of the holders of such knowledge, innovations and practices and encourage the equitable sharing of the

benefits arising from the utilisation of such knowledge, innovations, and practices.

Finally, Article 10 obliges each Contracting Party to

protect and encourage customary use of biological resources in accordance with traditional cultural practices that are compatible with conservation or sustainable use requirements; and to support local populations to develop and implement remedial action in degraded areas where biological diversity has been reduced.

It is to be hoped that this will provide an incentive both for cultural preservation and sustainable utilisation of natural resources that will allow biodiversity on tribal lands to be preserved. But the danger of further exploitation of both resources and people is never far from the surface.

**Protected Areas and Cultural Diversity**

Some innovative ways to link culture and conservation in protected areas are being tested in various parts of the world (Kemf 1993). Wasur National Park, in Indonesia's Irian Jaya province near the border with Papua New Guinea, for example, protects a savanna habitat which has been managed by people for generations. All areas of the park have strong mythological, spiritual and food links to the people. One area in the sanctuary zone is considered the centre of origin of the Marind tribe. Other areas, called *dusun*, are traditional gardening, hunting or sacred sites, usually owned by the clans or families to whom they were originally assigned in tribal mythology. A number of *dusun* are sprinkled throughout the park. As part of the management of the national park, people who traditionally own *dusun* may have continued access and carry out traditional management practices. The people residing in the 13 villages within the national park may remain there. Traditional hunting (especially of deer) is allowed only for park residents (Craven 1992).

Siberut is the northern-most island in the Mentawai chain, located off the west coast of Sumatra in the Indonesian Archipelago. The Mentawais are home to a rich biological diversity of which 65 per cent of the mammals are endemic, including four species of endemic primates. Only on Siberut, however, do expansive stands of tropical rainforest remain, although these too have been heavily logged by foreign timber concessionaires during the last decade. Sharing the forests are indigenous people who live in reasonable ecological harmony with their forests.

Only on Siberut does this indigenous Metawaian culture remain largely intact (Schefold 1972, 1974). The indigenous Metawaians are heavily dependent on harvesting primates for food, yet the harvest is conducted sustainably and primates remain abundant. As increasing development (e.g. timber concessions and oil palm plantations) pressures began to affect Siberut in the 1970s, the WWF and the IUCN launched a programme to conserve Siberut's biological diversity and indigenous people (see McNeely et al. 1980). This programme has been successful in designing protected areas that incorporate traditional, sustainable uses by indigenous peoples and providing a system for conserving biodiversity in those areas not officially declared as protected areas. Continuing work to implement the conservation programme is being carried out with financial support from the Asian Development Bank. The island has also been declared a Biosphere Reserve under UNESCO's Man and the Biosphere Programme. Sadly, implementation of the conservation measures has not yet lived up to the design.

Aboriginal land claims are now recognised under Australian law in several states, particularly in the Northern Territory. As a result of this recognition, traditional uses are frequently incorporated into national park management. Several national parks (Uluru, Kakadu, Nitmiluk) were returned to traditional owners and in turn leased back for continued use as protected areas for conservation and recreation. The Anangu Aborigines of Australia have gained title to Uluru National Park, but with the leasing arrangement, in practical terms, title only ensured joint management of Uluru by the Anangu and the Australian National Park and Wildlife Service. However, sacred sites were granted full protection and access to the park for ceremonial purposes and aboriginal hunting was guaranteed. The joint management approach was designed to achieve two objectives: the mediation of conflicts over traditional uses of the park and the regulation of tourism. In addition, Anangu knowledge of local ecosystems and animal behaviour has played a central role in coordinating surveys of animal populations and in resource management decisions. However, the joint management plan has been criticised for employing a framework that is completely non-Aboriginal in form. While the framework has enabled Anangu to achieve significant gains in controlling their lands, it has not yet eliminated conflict over Aboriginal and non-Aboriginal uses of Uluru National Park (IUCN 1993).

### Enabling Local People to Maintain Responsibility for Managing their Resources

Governments are now recognising the capacity of local people in managing their own resources. Villages in the coastal zone of the Philippines have long been dependent on the productivity of coral reefs, but as traditional management systems break down, over-exploitation has increased. A new project is enhancing fisheries' resources by building new systems of responsibility for resource management in three island villages, each having a coral reef small enough to patrol.

Accepting that the only effective resource management would come at the community level, project staff encouraged individuals interested in the problem of marine conservation to form Marine Management Committees (MMCs). The MMCs matured into working groups which received community respect, a process involving give-and-take among project staff, local officials and residents. As the marine reserve began to function and illegal fishermen were repelled, the community gave more support. Building an education centre with local participation and supervision provided a source of community pride. MMCs became more effective as they were given new responsibilities for projects such as placing *Tridacna* clams in the fish sanctuary areas for the community to manage and harvest; refining the marine reserve guidelines into a legal document adopted by the municipal town councils; training MMC members in the management of tourists to the coral reefs; developing education programmes for all parts of the community; and initiating alternative income schemes such as mat weaving and sea cucumber mariculture.

Three marine reserves with municipal legal support are now demarcated by buoys and signs, and managed by MMCs which actively patrol for rule infractions by local residents or outsiders.

Copies of the municipal ordinances are posted on the islands in the local language and published in a brochure. Each site now has a fishery breeding sanctuary and a surrounding buffer area for ecologically-sound fishing. Destructive fishing methods – such as using dynamite, cyanide or other strong poisons and very small mesh gill nets – which were formally widespread have now been effectively banned. Increasing numbers of tourists are visiting the sanctuaries and bringing economic benefits to the villages.

Species diversity and abundance have significantly increased for certain families of fish, especially the favourite targets of fishermen; mean percentage increases in species diversity ranged from 25 to 40 per cent, while increases in the numbers of all food fishes ranged from 42 per cent to 293 per cent over the three sites. In addition, and of crucial importance for the sustainability of the new reserves, the total fish yield for the fishermen has also increased; protection of part of the sea from fishing pressure has thus led to a total net increase in productivity and economic benefits for fishermen (Savina and White 1986, White and Law 1986).

In the Pacific, many islanders are growing increasingly resistant to development, and more concerned about traditional values. Debate over a barrage of development proposals (including agriculture, fishing, mineral prospecting, logging and tourism) for the Marovo Lagoon in the Western Solomons led to an alliance between the Marovo village council and the Western Province. Working together, the Marovo Lagoon Resource Management Project was established to provide villagers with greater input into development planning for the area (Baines 1991). Other Solomon Islands communities are taking similar action. Some communities have resisted logging by developing their own conservation organisations, which have been active in managing local, small-scale, silviculturally-sound commercialisation of forest timber. Villagers on the island of Vella Lavella, concerned about improving the management of their customary natural resources as their population is rapidly growing, have chosen the year 2000 as their deadline for becoming fully involved in resource management decisions (Baines 1991).

## Organising for Political Power

Faced with rapidly diminishing living space as a result of deforestation and occupation of tribal lands by new settlers, some Amerindian groups have organised themselves to defend their interests. Two international congresses of indigenous peoples have been held, in 1989 and 1991, to develop strategies for blocking colonisation and unsustainable development, and to explore the connections between land rights and natural resource management. In El Salvador, some indigenous people have been campaigning, with partial success, for communal lands at the community level, working through the National Agrarian Reform Act (Chapin 1992). In Honduras, several federations have joined forces to work with MOPAW, a development organisation, to secure titles to tribal lands and forestall colonisation of these areas. As part of this programme, the Tawahka Sumu have been granted the Tawahka Biosphere Reserve. The Miskito in Nicaragua have formed an organisation called Miskito Kupia (or 'heart of the Miskito') to advocate an Indian-managed reserve encompassing the entire Miskito Cays area. Similarly, the Kekchi and Mopann Maya of Belize are campaigning for a homeland of some 200,000 hectares. In Panama, the Kuna, Embera and Wounnaan have sought to establish tribal homelands as well. However, similar efforts in Panama by other, less politically organised tribes, such as the Guaymi and the Veraguas, have had little success because of conflicts with private and governmental economic interests in these tribal lands (Chapin 1992). But organisation is not only needed to recover or have access to land. Indigenous peoples need to have the possibility to choose their destiny for themselves. Nobody can decide in their name to keep them marginalised or unexposed to the national and global economic systems. Having the possibility to choose often requires having access to the information, techniques and legal and political systems of dominant societies. Indeed, what will happen in the coming decades can not be, as it has been for so long, the result of policies and decisions coming from outside.

## Conclusions

Examples of ecologically and culturally sensible interactions between people and their environment can be found in all parts of the world. Such traditional communities often have profound and detailed knowledge of the ecosystems and species with which they are in contact and effective ways of ensuring they are used sustainably (IUCN 1980). Cultural diversity, which is provided above all by the great variety of indigenous cultures in all parts of the world, provides the human intellectual 'gene pool', the basic raw material for adapting to the local environment. The challenge is in applying this knowledge and, where appropriate, transferring associated techniques and thinking to conservation management systems appropriate to today's circumstances.

The key element of linking cultural diversity with biodiversity is that indigenous peoples need the right to self-determination and to set their own development agenda. This certainly is no guarantee of success, but it does put responsibility firmly in the hands of those who will earn the benefits and pay the costs. We might reasonably expect that communities will behave in their enlightened self-interest, if empowered to do so.

Security of tenure offers opportunities for communities to gain benefits from their resources, but at least some market forces typically exist exclusively outside local communities; therefore, resources are perceived differently at national and community levels, and the benefits are derived differently. Therefore, governments should consider returning at least some nationalised resource systems such as forests and wildlife to community-based tenure systems, which can often be more cost effective. Putting resource management back in the hands of local communities also helps governments divest themselves of responsibilities for functions they have proven incapable of providing adequately. The legitimacy of community-based tenure systems can be recognised through cadastral surveys, assessments of wildlife populations, demarcation, registration and community infrastructure which can defend against outside pressure.

For example, in November 1991, Brazil's President Fernando Color de Melo issued a decree to give the Yanomani, the largest indigenous group in the Amazon rainforest, partial control of their traditional lands (Michaels 1991). The decree came after apparent last-ditch efforts by the Brazilian military to prevent it because the Yanomani lands, in the north of the Amazon Basin, include the border with Venezuela – a militarily sensitive area. The Yanomani will gain control of their land after the government has formally surveyed the forest and established the boundaries, at a cost of some US$ 2 million. Mineral rights will rest with the government.

The decree comes as part of a zoning process which will involve dividing the forest into zones for protected areas, traditional indigenous farming and hunting or for rubber tappers and others who use the forest without destroying it, and those areas where logging, roads, mines, dams and other ecologically destructive development can take place.

The full implications of such an 'indigenous privatisation scheme' need to be considered. Transferring the control of access rights from a national to a local authority puts power into those making the local decisions. As Murphree (1993) points out, the way that natural resources are used in any particular place and time is the result of conflicting interests between groups of people having different objectives. Seldom does any one group dominate, and resources can be used in a number of different ways at the same time and place. So the variation in resource management is part of an ongoing process in which the different interests and struggles of the various actors are located; some local actors are likely to benefit more than others, thereby creating new tensions in the community.

Providing power of control of access rights to a local community also implies powers of exclusion, often calling for the use of negative sanctions (i.e. violence, public ridicule).

Cultures tend to be comprehensive, containing within them everything that is required to enable people to function within that culture. Modern government, on the other hand, tends to be much more fragmented and organised into 'sectors' which lead to more effective harvesting of resources but less effective conservation action. Many of the structures of modern society are maladaptive, impeding the capacity of social systems to respond to change. Indigenous peoples have tremendous disadvantages relative to the political and economic elites which control modern countries. These elites, however, cannot ensure sustainable management of local resources without the full cooperation of indigenous peoples.

All who follow will share the loss of traditional knowledge about the local environment. The consumer culture will not last forever, but the earth abides. The numerous local cultures which are adapted to sustainable use of locally-available resources may well provide the resilience which will enable our species to adapt to whatever changes the future may bring.

### References

Baines, G.B.K. 1991. 'Asserting traditional rights: community conservation in Solomon Islands'. Cultural Survival 15: 49-52.

Burger, Julian 1990. *The Gaia Atlas of First Peoples: A Future for the Indigenous World*. New York: Doubleday.

Chapin, M. 1992. 'The view from the shore: Central America's Indians encounter the quincentenary'. Grassroots Development 16: 2-10.

Craven, Ian 1992. 'Conflicts between Integrating Traditional Peoples into Protected Area Management Systems and Park Zoning: Case examples from Irian Jaya, Indonesia'. Paper from workshop on People and Protected Areas, IVth World Congress on National Parks and Protected Areas, Caracas.

Crosby, Alfred W. 1987. *Ecological Imperialism: The Biological Expansion of Europe 900-1900*. Cambridge: Cambridge University Press.

Dasmann, Raymond 1975. 'National parks, nature conservation, and "future primitive"'. Ecologist 65(5): 164-167.

Dove, Michael R. 1984. 'Man, land and games in Sumbawa: Some observations on agrarian ecology and development policy in Eastern Indonesia'. Singapore J. Tropical Geography 5(2):12-24.

Durning, Alan T. 1992. 'Guardians of the Land: Indigenous Peoples and the Health of the Earth'. Worldwatch Paper 112: 1-62.

Gadgil, Madhav 1987. 'Diversity: Cultural and biological'. TREE 2(12): 369-373.

Gaisford, J. (ed.) 1981. *Atlas of Man*. London: Marshall Cavendish Books, Ltd.

Harmon, D. 1992. 'Indicators of the world's cultural diversity'. IVth World Congress on National Parks and Protected Areas, Caracas. IUCN.

IUCN 1980. World Conservation Strategy: Living Resource Conservation for Sustainable Development. Gland: IUCN-UNEP-WWF.

IUCN 1993. Indigenous Peoples and Strategies for Sustainability. Summary of a Workshop on Strategies for Sustainability: 31 March – 2 April 1993. Gland: IUCN.

Kemf, Elizabeth 1993. *The Law of the Mother: Protecting Indigenous Peoples in Protected Areas*. San Francisco: Sierra Club Books.

Lynch, Owen J. and Janice B. Alcorn 1993. 'Tenurial Rights and Community-based Conservation'. Paper prepared for the Liz Claiborne-Art Ortenburg Foundation Workshop on Community-Based Conservation, Airlie, VA.

Lyons, Oren R. 1990. 'Traditional native perspectives'. Orion Summer: 31-34.

Maybury-Lewis, David 1992. *Millennium: Tribal Wisdom and the Modern World*. New York: Viking Press.

McNeely, J.A. et al. 1980. Saving Siberut: A Conservation Master Plan. WWF-IUCN Indonesia Programme, Bogor.

McNeely, J.A. and Paul S. Wachtel. 1991. *Soul of the Tiger: Searching for Nature's Answers in Southeast Asia*. Singapore: Oxford University Press.

Michaels, J. 1991. 'Brazil creates homeland for Yanomamis'. The Christian Science Monitor, 19 November 1991.

Murphree, Marshall W. 1993. 'The Role of Institutions'. Paper prepared for the Liz Claiborne-Art Ortenburg Foundation Workshop on Community-Based Conservation, Airlie, VA.

Robinson, John G. 1993. 'Community-Based Approaches to Wildlife Conservation in Neotropical Forests'. Paper prepared for the Liz Claiborne-Art Ortenburg Foundation Workshop on Community-Based Conservation, Airlie, VA.

Rogers, A. (ed.) 1993. *The Guinness Guide to Peoples and Cultures*. London: Guinness Publishing.

Roychowdhury, Anumita 1992. 'Environment history: Past lessons, future strategies'. Down to Earth. 31 July: 33-36.

Savina, Gail C. and Alan T. White 1986. 'A Tale of Two Islands: Some Lessons for Marine Resource Management'. Environmental Conservation 13(2): 107-13.

Schefold, Reimar 1972. 'Religious Conceptions on Siberut, Mentawai'. Sumatran Research Bulletin: 12-24.

Schefold, Reimar 1974. 'Schlitztrommeln und Trommelnsprache in Mentawai'. Z. Ethnol. 98: 66-73.

WCED (World Commission on Environment and Development) 1987. *Our Common Future*. Oxford: Oxford University Press.

WRI, IUCN, UNEP 1992. *Global Biodiversity Strategy: Guidelines for action to save, study, and use Earth's biotic wealth sustainably and equitably*. Washington D.C.: WRI, IUCN, UNEP.

ELIZABETH KEMF

# INDIGENOUS PEOPLES AND CARING FOR THE EARTH

'Life trees' are revered, whether in North or South America, in Asia or the Pacific, Europe or in Africa. They are often part of what are universally recognised as 'sacred groves'. The Kuna indigenous people of Panama call these forests *kalu*, while the Mijikenda, the tribal peoples of Kenya's coast, refer to their sacred groves as *kayas*. In northern California – where remnants of some of the Americas' last old growth forests remain – the Hupa Native Americans still live, dance, fish, raise their young and bury their dead with great ceremony on the land where their ancestors have lived for thousands of years. They also maintain sacred groves where outsiders cannot enter without special permission.

Many of these sacred forests now overlap with officially-declared protected areas and are encompassed inside the boundaries of national parks or nature reserves. For centuries, indigenous peoples have been the traditional keepers of such woodlands and other sacred habitats. Compared with protected area managers, who control over five per cent of the world's land mass, indigenous peoples are the stewards of a much greater proportion of the remaining wild lands. These ethnic, native or tribal peoples occupy some 19% of the earth's surface in habitats where their ancestors lived for up to thousands of years. Anthropologists and demographers estimate that they number between 200 and 600 million, comprise 4% of the world's population and live in over 70 countries from the Arctic to the Amazon (Kemf 1993, 1994). But their cultures are dying. Over the past 150 years between 30 to 50 million indigenous people have died, including 87 entire groups in the Amazon alone. Today, 6,000 languages are spoken. It is feared that by the end of the next century 50% of these will be lost (Durning 1992, Kemf 1993). Already half of the world's languages are moribund, spoken mainly by grandparents – and unknown to their grandchildren. Since language is considered the single best indicator of a culture, the future of the world's indigenous peoples is precarious.

197

In an attempt to reverse this tragic trend of the loss of cultural diversity and to draw attention to the plight, the needs, the dreams and the hopes of the world's indigenous peoples, the United Nations declared 1993 the International Year for the World's Indigenous People. During that year there was a lot of fanfare and grandstanding, but the Secretary of the UN Working Group on Indigenous Populations, Julian Burger, said his group was still operating on a shoestring budget. The financial backing for projects for indigenous peoples fell far short of expectations. Presently, it appears easier to raise funds for flagship species such as pandas, tigers and whales or marine habitats, symbols of biological diversity, than it is to raise money for cultural diversity, alone. The irony is that the world's last remaining areas of biological diversity have been maintained in the regions of the richest cultural diversity. It has taken over a century for most conservationists to realise that the two are inextricably linked, and often interdependent.

Initially, it was believed that officially-declared protected areas should be free of all human interference. In so-called wilderness areas, selected for the creation of national parks and reserves, the local inhabitants, whether seasonal migrants or permanent residents, were often moved off their land – and their sacred groves or traditional methods of land or marine resource management were never acknowledged or ignored entirely.

Consequently, protected areas were usually modelled after the world's first national park, Yellowstone, established on Crow, Blackfeet and Shoshone-Bannock territory in 1872. A sub-tribe of the Shoshone lived year round in the present park boundary while the other tribes used the area for hunting and fishing on a seasonal basis. Burial grounds accidentally uncovered in 1941 revealed that Native Americans were resident – at least 800 years earlier – on Fishing Bridge, one of Yellowstone's most popular campgrounds. When the park was created in the 1870s the Native Americans did not leave willingly as many historical accounts imply. In the summer of 1877, 300 people were killed in a series of pitched battles between tribal groups and civilian superintendents. In 1886 administration of the park was turned over to the US Army who managed it until 1916.

In conformity with the 'Yellowstone model', many national parks around the globe were developed as wilderness preserves – for public recreation – without permanent human habitation or extractive use. Yellowstone's outstanding beauty and natural features – the largest mountain lake in North America, its geysers, breathtaking waterfalls, snow-covered peaks and abundance of wildlife – spawned the birth of thousands of parks around the world. To date, some 25,000 protected areas of varying size have been created. Of these, over 9,000 meet the criteria for inclusion in the United Nation's list, and 1,470 of these are based on the Yellowstone model (IUCN 1994).

Recognising the limitations of a global application of the Yellowstone model, which was adopted in good faith with the best intentions at the time, park managers today are developing new approaches, methods and guidelines for establishing protected areas with the assistance of the World Conservation Union's (IUCN) Commission on National Parks and Protected Areas (CNPPA). These guidelines, which have been under serious review by the CNPPA since 1984, were revised by IUCN in 1994. They reflect the evolution of conservation thinking and management, taking into account that protected areas must 'meet people's needs', and 'that they should not be islands in a sea of development, and that they must be part of every country's strategy for sustainable management and the wise use of natural resources must be set in a regional planning context' (Lucas 1994).

The new guidelines acknowledge (under a sub-category of the strictest Category I, Strict Nature Reserve/Wilderness Area) objectives which should 'enable indigenous communities living at low density and in a balance with the available resources to maintain their lifestyle'. This category also recognises the need 'to provide for public access ...which will serve best the physical and spiritual well-being of visitors and maintain the wilderness qualities of the area for present and future generations'. The National Park (Category II) guidelines define that this category should 'provide a foundation for spiritual, scientific, educational, recreational and visitor opportunities, all of which must be environmentally and culturally compatible'. This category also notes that organisational responsibility including ownership and management may also be vested in a 'council of indigenous people, foundation or other legally established body which has dedicated the area to long-term conservation'. Categories IV to VI lend themselves to a harmonious interaction between people and protected areas. Some of their objectives include

> delivering benefits to people living with the designated area as consistent with the other objectives of management; maintaining harmonious interaction of nature and culture through the protection of landscape and/or seascape and the continuation of traditional land uses, building practices and social and cultural manifestations; to bring benefits to and to contribute to the welfare of the local community through the provision of natural products (such as forest and fisheries products) and services (such as clean water or income derived from sustainable forms of tourism)(IUCN 1994).

Since these guidelines have just been revised, it is inevitable that it will take time for protected area managers to familiarise themselves with them and to accept them. One of WWF's own immediate tasks is to ensure that these guidelines are known, accepted and put into place across its entire conservation programme.

## WWF Nature Conservation with Indigenous Peoples

Regrettably, over the years many protected areas were created without consultation with the communities which lived in or near them, whether they were by definition indigenous or other long-term residents. Ironically, it was indigenous peoples who were for millennia the custodians of the earth. Often, but not always, they cared for their habitat so well that it maintained its natural ecosystems in a relatively unspoiled state. Frequently, when protected areas were established, indigenous and local residents were moved out, often to the detriment of the land itself.

In the past, it was generally believed that protected areas were places where boundaries of protection were established and people were either kept out or removed. Today, as population pressure increases and the rights of indigenous peoples and local communities gain recognition and respect, an expanded approach to protected areas is emerging. Wilderness areas are shrinking and human activity is spreading. For example, in Latin America 86 per cent of the national parks and protected areas are inhabited or affected by people (Amend and Amend 1992) Gerhard Heiss, a consultant to the Council of Europe and to the EEC, estimates that in western and northern Europe, 80 to 90 per cent of the national parks and protected areas are used seasonally, mainly by pastoral people grazing their flocks. According to Heiss, 30 per cent are probably permanently inhabited. In some cases, this is having devastating effects (Kemf 1993).

Yet, in many areas, the presence of local people upholding long held traditions has had a positive effect on the environment. The underlying message which is being made by indigenous and rural peoples today is that unless property rights (land tenure) of long-term residential people are respected and economic benefits from the creation of protected areas accrue in part directly to the communities living in and near them, it is unlikely that the nature reserves will endure. Local communities must be involved in the planning and boundary marking of reserves. Most importantly, their traditions must be respected. That means staying away from their sacred sites, no matter how fascinating or attractive they might be. Uninvited visitors are not welcome in these very special places, such as in the 'Land of the Dead', the Sacred Groves or *Kayas* of Kenya, the *dusuns* or Gardens of the Forest in Irian Jaya, or other holy places of ancient ritual and human burial.

It must also be recognised that aboriginal, rural, tribal, native or remote dwelling people may want to exploit their land whether it be through hunting, timber harvesting, plant collection, farming, oil refining, fishing, etc. And WWF is – at their request – helping them develop management plans for the areas which they own and want to conserve.

Among the growing number of rural communities who have approached WWF for help in setting up or helping them increase involvement in and management of protected areas are the Hupa Native Americans of northern California in the USA, the Inuit of Isabella Bay in Canada, the Zoque indigenous peoples of Mexico, the Karen of Thailand, the Shona people in Zimbabwe, the Kuna of Panama, the Shimshali of Pakistan, the Phoka people of northern Malawi, the Imagruen of Mauritania, the Ewenk of Siberia and many others scattered all over the globe. Groups such as these are, with increasing frequency, asking WWF and other NGOs to assist them in developing management and land use plans for buffer zones of national parks or multi-use zones of protected areas.

Two notable regions where WWF has been asked for assistance are in Mexico, where Zoque communities want to establish the country's first Campesino Ecological Reserve, and in Irian Jaya where Indonesia's Directorate General of Forest Protection and Nature Conservation (PHPA) sought WWF's expertise in developing a management system in Wasur National Park. The park is comprised entirely of traditional sacred sites or *dusuns*, which are owned mainly by four indigenous tribes. These two models illustrate two different approaches to biodiversity conservation. Mexico's example shows how a group, which already owned land, decided to create its own protected area, while the model in Irian Jaya shows how a government decided to declare a protected area and discovered it was comprised entirely of land revered and claimed by four indigenous groups.

**Mexico's Campesino Ecological Reserve**
In Mexico, WWF, together with a Mexican NGO (Maderas del Pueblo del Sureste, A.C.) based in the region of Chimalapas in the southern state of Oaxaca, is working with indigenous and rural peoples in the hope of creating the first peasant farmer's or Campesino Ecological Reserve *(Reserva Ecologica Campesina)*. This reserve would be controlled and managed mainly by indigenous peoples. Located inland on the Isthums of Tehuantepec, the Chimalapas is comprised of some 600,000 ha of woodland including tropical moist and dry forest, cloud forest, elfin and pine-oak forest. Around 300,000 ha of the mountainous terrain is uninhabited primary forest, owned by the Zoque indigenous communities of Santa Maria Chimalapa and San Miguel Chimalapa.

WWF began supporting ethnobotanical research in Oaxaca with help from the MacArthur Foundation in 1985. Collaboration began mainly with the Chinantec, Mixtec and Mixe people. In one village alone six local women interviewed members of some 150 households to help document the classification of 1,000 species of plants. Local support and technical assistance has been sponsored by the Sociedad para el Estudio de los Recursos Bioticos de Oaxaca, A.C (Serbo, A.C), a Mexican non-

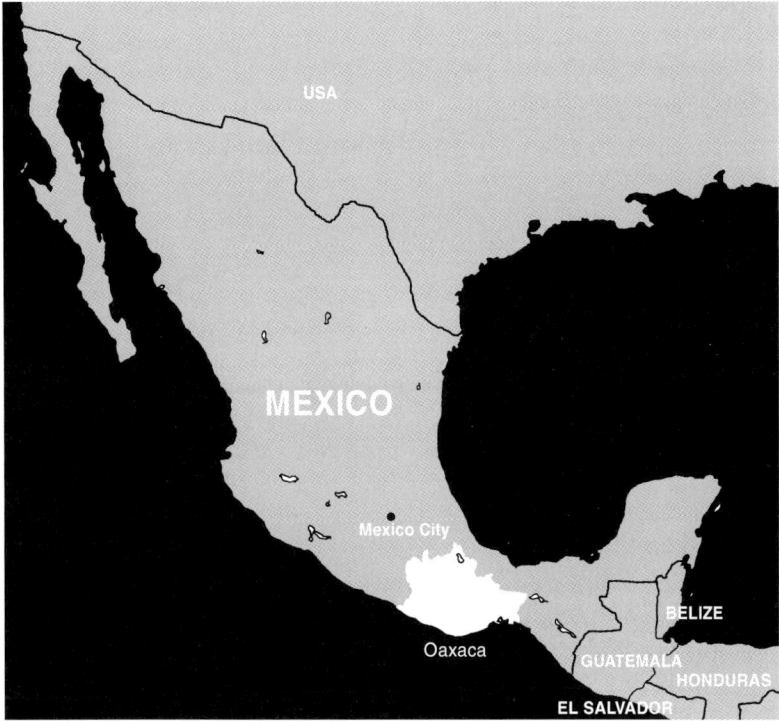

governmental organisation that combines participatory studies of ecology and ethnobotany with communal management of forest resources.

The primary goal of the ethnobotanical research is to discover and to describe biologically important areas as a first step towards conservation and sustainable use of Oaxaca's remaining forests, according to Dr. Gary Martin, WWF project executant in WWF/Unesco/Kew Gardens/Darwin Initiative's People and Plants Programme. The SERBO team, together with ethnobotanists like Dr. Martin, who has been working on the WWF project since 1987, have collected more than 3,000 botanical specimens. Under the leadership of a local agronomist, Juan Areli Bernai Alacantra, a preparatory school (the Instituto Comunitario Mixe or 'Kong Oy') has been established. The Institute, which averages an enrolment of about 30 students, offers course in Mixe literacy, music, agriculture, traditional medicines and sustainable use of

*Harvesting grains in the village of Chuparrosa, Santiago Comalte-pec municipality, Oaxaca, Mexico. Photo: WWF/Tony Rath*

forest resources. A course in the Mixe language on local ecologi-cal knowledge is ongoing and the institute hopes to create a community herbarium. Methods of marketing plants are also being examined, with recognition of intellectual property rights. GIS (Geographical Information System) maps have been com-pleted to aid the area's residents to determine the highest priori-ties for plant conservation. A workshop to review the past 10 years of ethnobotanical research, involving Chinantec, Mazatec, Mixe, Zapotec and other indigenous communities, is planned for early 1996. (Martin, personal communication 1995) The ethno-botanical work is expected to contribute significantly to the creation and management of the Campesino Ecological Reserve.

In the early 1990s, WWF's former field representative, Alejan-dro de Avila, reported that title to part of the communal lands had been encroached by loggers and cattle ranchers, a situation precipitated and aggravated by a state boundary conflict be-tween Oaxaca and Chiapas. In order to control illegal logging, grazing and drug cultivation, the local communities began to seek a way in which to protect their natural resources by creating a community-managed reserve (Kemf 1994).

Resolution of land-tenure and access disputes is one of the first and most pressing activities of this people-centred project. The work in Chimalapas, carried out mainly by local residents with partial support and guidance of WWF, achieved noteworthy success in late 1994: about 40,000 ha of land in the Chimalapas was granted special protected status. Cattle ranchers who had illegally occupied the area, called 'La Gringa', left the area at the request of Mexico's Federal authorities and returned the land to the local community. It is hoped that this area will become part of the planned Campesino Ecological Reserve.

A variety of conservation activities have been spawned as a part of the *people-centred* conservation and development project that has been funded by WWF in Chimalapas since 1989. Project workers have established improved methods of maize production and propagation of valuable timber and fruit species including mahogany, cedar and orange trees in six settlements within the Zoque communal lands. These communities, known locally as *congregaciones*, are populated by impoverished people who have migrated from outside the area and include Chinantec indigenous families displaced by the construction of the Cerro de Oro dam in northern Oaxaca; Tzotzil people from highland Chiapas; and Mixe, Mixtec, and other indigenous and non-indigenous groups who have sought refuge in the biologically rich mountains.

The present WWF project, part of a long-term community development programme proposed by the NGO Maderas, has been collaborating with the Chimalapas communities since 1989 to lay the foundations for this project and has been the channel for the provision of existing financial support. With initial support from USAID and WWF-US, Maderas has provided technical assistance to the communities and stimulated the social cohesion necessary for launching this venture. Maderas is the only NGO to have continued, with great tenacity, to work in the difficult physical and demanding socio-cultural conditions of the area, and in spite of attacks and threats from outside political groups with economic interests in the region, according to Peter Newborne, WWF-UK's project manager.

Funded as part of the Eco-development programme supported by the European Commission and the Overseas Development Agency (ODA) in the UK with a matching grant from WWF-UK, the project focuses on three forest areas of outstanding significance in Oaxaca: the Selva Zoque (site of the Campesino Ecological Reserve), the Sierra Norte and the Coastal Zone.

The budget for eight components in the Oaxaca programme, comprising a total of 40 activities, amounts to around US$ 1.8 million over a two-year period, plus additional funding from US and Mexican sources. Originally, it was supported by USAID through the Biodiversity Support Programme, a consortium between WWF, The Nature Conservancy and the World Resources Institute.

WWF and other NGOs working on the people-centred conservation project hope that the ecological reserve will be demarcated and declared officially by 1998. Indigenous communities are still negotiating with 400 settlers who moved off the land known as 'La Gringa'. WWF is part of a committee which is negotiating with the settlers, who are ranchers, and helping the communities develop a management plan. The highest priority for the project in 1995 is resolving land tenure questions and bringing about a peaceful settlement to land claims. WWF hopes that this bottom-up approach, originating at the grassroots, can be replicated throughout Mexico.

During the project, full-time legal advice and assistance to communities and the Campesino General Assembly is being provided to Maderas. Before the Campesino Ecological Reserve can be established, a just and lasting solution to the land tenure conflicts must be found. For example, two full-time people will work with the Maderas team to concentrate on agrarian, human rights and conservation law. This is just one of the 40 activities, but it is seen as the highest priority.

Nearby, in Santiago Comaltepec in the Sierra Juarez of Oaxaca, the Chinantec indigenous municipal and communal authorities approached WWF and requested advice and support to develop their municipal legislation, including a land use plan.

This is very rare in Mexico, according to Martin Goebel, a Mexican forester and former director of WWF's Mexico office. In 1990 WWF offered technical and financial assistance to help draft legislation for land use, not yet approved by the communal assembly or state government. The second phase of the project involves a study of the natural resources of the community and mapping vegetation types and land use patterns. WWF hopes it will lead to a communal definition of the activities allowed in different ecological zones. Despite internal conflicts regarding the management of the communal forestry enterprise, WWF is trying to work with the different factions in the area, which is considered to be one of the most biologically diverse municipalities in Mexico.

The situation in Oaxaca is extremely complex as nearly one quarter, or 570 of Mexico's municipalities are resident in this state which is about the size of Portugal. It also has the greatest mix of cultural diversity in Mexico with 15 distinct ethnic and linguistic groups. Apart from Spanish, over 50 native languages are spoken throughout Mexico. It must be recognised in this and in all conservation projects that external factors including long-standing rivalries between local groups, drug-traffickers and conflicting and usually competing economic interests, can delay or disrupt progress or halt activities entirely. The conservation community is slowly recognising that there are no overnight success stories, and that laying just the groundwork by the communities themselves in such a complex and biologically rich region as Oaxaca has taken over a decade. It will be at least another three years probably until the Campesino Ecological Reserve is realised.

### Irian Jaya's Gardens in the Forest
In Irian Jaya in Indonesia, WWF has worked with local NGOs and government officials in helping create two protected areas, Wasur National Park and Arfak Mountains Strict Nature Reserve. At first there were differences of opinion over whether or not indigenous peoples or long term residents should be allowed to stay in Wasur National Park or have access to its resources and to their sacred sites, or *dusuns*. One tribal elder spoke for many: 'To restrict our access to these sites would be the same as barring the door of your church, mosque or shop.'

One of the prerequisites for WWF involvement in helping develop the national park's management plan was recognition of

INDONESIA

Arfak Mts
Native Reserve

PAPUA NEW GUINEA

Wasur National Park

the *dusuns* and the rights of the four tribal groups to continue to use them as they had for centuries. The priority aim of the WWF project was to find ways to utilise sustainably the natural resources of the park, while at the same time generate direct economic benefit to the park's residents. Economic poverty remains, as it has always been, the biggest threat to Wasur National Park and its residents. In order to obtain cash people hunt deer and pig and sell the meat in the nearest town of Merauke, log, harvest leaves for oil distillation and collect plants for medicinal uses.

Over 2,500 Kanum, Marind, Marori and Yei tribal peoples inhabit 13 villages inside the Wasur National Park. 'Most of them live in a delicate balance with nature and manage its resources well,' according to the late Ian Craven, a former WWF project executant, who worked for WWF in Irian Jaya since 1985. Craven, who was a dedicated and hard-working conservationist, died in a plane crash in 1993 while surveying the introduced deer population in Wasur National Park. Craven realised from the beginning of his work in Irian Jaya the need to work closely with local people and forged strong partnerships with government officials, including Wahyudi Wardoyo, with whom he co-authored a chapter on Irian Jaya for the WWF/IUCN book, *The Law of the Mother: protecting indigenous peoples in protected areas* (Kemf 1993). Wardoyo is Director General of Forest Protection and Nature Conservation with the Department of Forestry in Indonesia.

According to Wardoyo and Craven, 'In Irian Jaya, each clan and family has traditional sacred sites called *dusuns*, predefined by past generations for hunting, gardening and spiritual events.' When WWF, together with a local NGO, YAPSEL, and local landowners mapped and catalogued hundreds of *dusun* sites, they discovered that they spread over the entire 413,810 ha of the park. There was no unclaimed land at all. This was the same situation that Craven had found earlier when he worked with the Hatam people to delineate the Arfak Mountains Strict Nature Reserve. The tribal people own the land.

The ideas of the tribal elders are contained in the management plans for the park, which was drawn up with help from WWF at the request of the PHPA (Indonesia's Directorate General of Forest Protection and Nature Conservation). Until 1991 the PHPA's understanding of the tribal peoples of Wasur was limited, but the situation is continuing to improve. Mr. Sutisno, who is the highest authority over protected areas in Indonesia, states: 'The cultural aspects of Wasur National Park must be considered and supported during planning and management, the people must continue to use their *dusuns* in a traditional manner.'

The Wasur National Park Management Plan states that the park is 'vitally important as an area for conserving a significant part of Indonesia's cultural variety, and this significance is considered of equal importance to the park's biological value...'.

Although the lifestyles of the four tribal groups have changed because of contact with settlers and visitors to the Wasur area, they are still hunter-gatherers with long established ancestral ties to their land, especially the *dusuns*. The somewhat unusual style of management and some of the objectives of the park allow for this. Traditional use zones and village zones are being demarcated inside the park boundaries. Before the park was established in 1990, on the border with Papua New Guinea's Tonda Wildlife Reserve, these types of zones were usually excluded from protected areas in Indonesia. In mid-1991, when the government authorities agreed that the residents could remain inside the park, Mr Sutisno said: 'We acknowledge the importance of bottom-up planning and wish the local communities to be involved in designing the zoning systems for Wasur National Park'

*Traditional Hatam house in the village of Kwok. Arfak Mountains Natural Reserve, Irian Jaya, Indonesia. Photo: WWF/Ian Craven*

(Craven and Wardoyo). By the end of 1994 survey work on the establishment of boundaries for utilisation in four villages was completed.

Another difference between Wasur National Park and most other established protected areas in Indonesia is that economic development of the park's resources is encouraged and the products marketed with returns to villagers. Deer marketing schemes, small business establishment, community based tourism and creation of an essential oils enterprise are all underway. In 1994, the deer marketing scheme and community shop were streamlined into one cooperative venture involving four villages. Additional revenue is returned to the communities living inside the park as all of the park's rangers are indigenous.

Training in business planning, marketing and management is currently being given to indigenous people through the Wasur non-governmental organisation, which WWF has helped to set up with the assistance of the Ford Foundation. There were delays in setting up the NGO and in establishing its charter because the Department of Forestry was concerned that the NGO could become too independent in its activities within the national park, which it considers its responsibility. In October of 1994, following a number of discussions between WWF, forestry officials and communities, WWF held a large planning workshop on buffer and village zones and community integration. The workshop brought together a wide range of interests groups and increased understanding and agreement was reached regarding the role of the NGO vis-à-vis the national park. Presently, there are nine NGO staff and a director is being sought. After further training in management and administration, WWF hopes to reduce its involvement to a minimum except for scientific input regarding utilisation of natural resources. WWF's position will then be mainly that of a facilitator in bringing the Wasur NGO, the Forestry Department (the Conservation of Natural Resources Section-KSDA) and the park communities together regularly.

Two objectives which have to be met before the NGO can run itself independently and with an initial degree of success are to strengthen the role of women and community representation and to establish a firmer self-supporting business structure.

However slow progress may seem in Wasur, it has been steady and events are promising. 'In March 1991, when the Wasur National Park Project opened its office doors for the first time, infringements on the Park's resources were numerous: sand quarrying, road building, settling, logging, small plantation development and motorised hunting with rifles and machetes on an unprecedented scale ... the Provincial Department of Forestry considered Wasur National Park the most threatened of any protected area in the province,' according to Craven.

Communities questioned why their land had to be included in protected area. Today, in 1995, some communities – whose land is being eaten away by uncontrolled excavation for sand – are asking if their villages can be gazetted inside the national park boundary.

Now that the guidelines for protected area establishments have been adapted and revised, many of these enacted even before the new IUCN Guidelines were published, indigenous and rural communities are welcoming a concept that once was and is still often abhorred. In cases such as in Oaxaca in Mexico and Wasur in Irian Jaya, indigenous peoples and rural communities were involved in developing new models which would benefit them directly – economically, culturally and biologically. It is these models and approaches that we can learn from and can apply elsewhere.

**Park Management at the Crossroads**

Although a modicum of recognition has been given to the rights of indigenous peoples over their homelands, much more needs to be done. However, conservationists are divided into several schools of thought: those who think resident people should be able to fish, hunt and forage in national parks, those who do not, and those who think there should be a compromise between the camps. But it is also becoming increasingly apparent that the human factor in creating and managing national parks and protected areas had long been overlooked and misunderstood. In 1992, IUCN's IV World Park Congress embraced this issue, most notably in a six-day long workshop chaired by WWF's Director-General Claude Martin. IUCN's new Categories of Protected Areas also reflect this (see Appendix 1).

Classical and modern park management methods are at a crossroads. If they can meet together on the same road, they have great potential for creating protected areas that conserve and enrich cultural and biological diversity. It is evident from the growing number of news reports over the first couple of years – including the international outcry over the deaths of the 70 Yanomami indigenes in Brazil and Venezuela, the Senate decision to recognise native title in Australia and the battle between the Zapatista Army of National Liberation (comprised mainly of indigenous peoples) and Mexican authorities – that the voices of indigenous peoples are being heard and heeded.

Some progress is being made by indigenous peoples in reclaiming ancestral land. For example, in 1989, the government of Colombia returned nearly 25 per cent of the country to its indigenous peoples and in neighbouring Venezuela and Brazil, the Yanomami and other Amerindians have regained – after 500 years – partial rights over 109.000 km² of the Amazon. In 1991 Venezuela created the Alto Orinoco Biosphere Reserve in order to protect a vast tract of virgin rainforest and to safeguard the survival of the Yanomami and Yekuana people who have lived there for millennia. Land rights for the indigenous peoples on the Venezuelan side of the border are more advantageous for the Yanomami than on the Brazilian side, where the government retains control over mineral exploitation. Thousands of gold miners still invade the Yanomami reserve despite a presidential decree announced in November of 1992. In August of 1993, Brazilian gold miners massacred scores of Yanomami Indians including 16 in Venezuela.

In Canada's far north various native organisations have been negotiating with the federal government for over twenty years over land claims. In 1984 a settlement was reached with the Inuit of the western Arctic, or Inuvialuit. The terms of this agreement included the establishment of an Inuvialuit Game Council (IGC) and an Inuvialuit Regional Corporation (IRC). In July, 1992, the IGC, the IRC, the Northwest Territories government and Canada reached an agreement to establish a National Park on Banks Island. Under the terms of this agreement, the Inuvialuit obtain exclusive rights to harvest wildlife in the park, their fishing is given priority over sports angling, and they will have the power to screen archaeological research.

In November, 1992, the Inuit of the eastern Arctic and sub-arctic ratified the largest land claim agreement in Canadian history, covering one-fifth of the country. The landmark agreement will resolve land claims and lead to the establishment of a Nunavut Territory encompassing a huge chunk of the Arctic. The Territory of Nunavut (which means 'our land' in the Inuit language, Inukitut) gives the Inuit direct control over 560,000 km² of land, including 57,600 of subsurface mineral rights. The agreement also provides for the creation of three national parks, at Auyuittuq, North Baffin and Ellsmere. The Inuit themselves pushed for the creation of these protected areas. WWF-Canada has worked with the Inuit community of Clyde River, Baffin Island, to devise a conservation plan to protect critical habitat for endangered bowhead whales at Isabella Bay. Igalirtuuq, the community's proposal for a Marine National Wildlife Area and

Biosphere Reserve, is moving forward through the approvals process for the new territory of Nunavut.

One of the most controversial land claims in history is ongoing in Australia today. For ten years the members of the Meriam community of Murray island waged a legal battle to regain their rights to 9 km$^2$ of islands in the Torres Strait, a narrow body of water separating Papua New Guinea and Australia. In June of 1992 Australia's High Court ruled in the islanders' favour. The Court said that their 'native title' to the land was recognisable under Australian common law. The concept of *terra nullius* (land belonging to no one), 'cryptic legalese for the fiction that pre-European Australia had been an empty, unoccupied continent, was thrown out of Australia's High Court'. Today, the High Court case, dubbed 'Mabo', for one of the original Torre Strait Islander plaintiffs, is raising land rights questions across Australia.

Commenting on the evolution of Australia's national park system, David Foster of the Phillip Institute of Technology, and an IUCN consultant, says:

> Park managers have had to come to terms with a whole new set of issues, concepts and ideas as well as to learn to communicate with a group of people with a different language, culture and world view. Of particular concern to many has been the challenge to their fundamental beliefs about the very nature of national parks themselves.

The parks, co-owned and managed by Aboriginal people and Australian government park officials, serve as models for what creative communities could do – or should not do – to satisfy the cultural, environmental and economic requirements of indigenous and non-indigenous peoples.

At a glance, the chain of events affecting a tiny, distant island between Australia and Papua New Guinea and the struggle over land rights in southern Mexico might seem to have little relevance to the international community concerning people and protected areas. Yet the aftermath of Mabo and the hope of Oaxaca's campesinos and Wasur's indigenous residents foreshadow the shape of things to come in the changing relationship between indigenous peoples and protected areas.

**Appendix 1:**

*The 1994 IUCN system of Protected Areas Categories*

I. Strict Nature Reserve/Wilderness Area.

Areas of land and/or sea possessing some outstanding or representative ecosystems, geological or physiological features and/or species, available primarily for scientific research and/or environmental monitoring; or large areas of unmodified or slightly modified land, and/or sea, retaining their natural character and influence without permanent or significant habitation, which are protected and managed so as to preserve their natural condition.

II. National Park: Protected Areas Managed Mainly for Ecosystem Conservation and Recreation.

Natural areas of land and/or sea designated to (a) protect the ecological integrity of one or more ecosystems for this and future generations, (b) exclude exploitation or occupation inimical to the purposes of designation of the area and (c) provide a foundation for spiritual, scientific, educational, recreational and visitor opportunities, all of which must be environmentally and culturally compatible.

III. Natural Monument: Protected Areas Managed Mainly for Conservation of Specific Features.

Areas containing one, or more, specific natural or natural/cultural feature which is of outstanding or unique value because of its inherent rarity, representative or aesthetic qualities or cultural significance.

IV. Habitat/Species Management Area: Protected Areas Managed Mainly for Conservation Through Management Intervention.

Areas of land and/or sea subject to active intervention for management purposes so as to ensure the maintenance of habitats and/or to meet the requirements of specific species.

V. Protected Landscape/Seascape: Protected Areas Managed Mainly for Landscape/Seascape Conservation and Recreation.

Areas of land, with coast and sea as appropriate, where the interaction of people and nature over time has produced an area of distinct character with significant aesthetic, cultural and/or ecological value, and often with high biological diversity. Safeguarding the integrity of this traditional interaction is vital to the protection, maintenance and evolution of such an area.

VI. Managed Resource Protected Area: Protected Areas Managed Mainly for the Sustainable Use of Natural Ecosystems.

Areas containing predominantly unmodified natural systems, managed to ensure long-term protection and maintenance of biological diversity, while providing at the same time a sustainable flow of natural products and services to meet community needs.

## Bibliography

Amend, Stephen and Thora 1992. 'Human occupation in the National Parks of South America: a fundamental problem'. *Parks Magazine.* Gland: IUCN, January.

De Alejandro, Avila B. 1992. WWF's Conservation programme in Oaxaca, Mexico. September, unpublished.

Bowe, Michele and Linke Rawawarin 1994. Interim Report to the Ford Foundation (and to WWF Int.): Development of Wasur National Park NGO and Community Development. December, unpublished.

Burger, Julian 1990. *The Gaia Atlas of First People: a Future for the Indigenous World.* London: Gaia Books.

Craven, Ian and Wahyudi Wardoyo 1993. Gardens in the Forest, in *The Law of the Mother: protecting indigenous peoples in protected areas*, Elizabeth Kemf (ed.). San Francisco: Sierra Club Books.

Craven, Ian et al. 1992. Wasur National Park Management Plan. Department of Forestry, Directorate General of Forest Protection and Nature Conservation/WWF Int., unpublished.

Durning, Thein Alan 1992. Guardians of the Land: Indigenous Peoples and the Health of the Earth, *Worldwatch paper* No. 112, December.

Foster, David 1992. Applying the Yellowstone Model in America's Backyard: Alaska, in *Aboriginal involvement in Parks and Protected Areas*, Jim Birckhead, Terry de Lacey, and Laura Jane Smith (eds.). Canberra: Panther publishing and printing.

Haines, Aubrey L. 1974. Yellowstone National Park: its exploration and establishment. Washington, US Department of the Interior: National Park Service.

Harmon, David 1992. Indicators of the World's Cultural Diversity. Paper presented at the Fourth World Congress on National Parks and Protected Areas, Caracas, Venezuela, 10-21 February.

Hulse, David L. and Seri Thongmak 1993. The Winds of Change, in *The Law of the Mother: protecting indigenous peoples in protected areas*, Elizabeth Kemf (ed.). San Francisco: Sierra Club Books.

IUCN 1994. *Guidelines for Protected Area Management Categories*. IUCN Commission on National Parks and Protected Areas with the assistance of the World Conservation Monitoring Centre. Gland and Cambridge: IUCN.

Kemf, Elizabeth 1993. *The Law of the Mother: protecting indigenous peoples in protected areas*. San Francisco: Sierra Club Books. London: Earthscan. Switzerland: Birkhauser Verlag.

Kemf, Elizabeth 1994. Indigenous People and Protected Areas: WWF and IUCN, a new approach, in *Indigenous peoples and International Organisations*. Lydia van de Fliert (ed.). UK: Bertrand Russel House.

Lucas, Bing 1994. *Introduction to IUCN Guidelines for Protected Area Management Categories*. Switzerland and UK: IUCN.

McNeely, J.A. and J. Harrison and P. Dingwall 1994. Protecting Nature: Regional Reviews of Protected Areas (based on contributions to the IV World Congress on National Parks and Protected Areas, Caracas, Venezuela in 1992). Switzerland and Cambridge: IUCN.

Morrisson, Jim 1993. Protected Areas and Aboriginal Interests in Canada. A WWF-Canada Discussion Paper. Canada.

Nelson, Byron Jr. 1988. *Our Home Forever, The Hupa Indians of Northern California*. Salt Lake City: Howe Brothers.

Scharff, Robert 1966. *Yellowstone and Grand Teton National Parks*. New York: David Mckay Co.

DARRELL A. POSEY

# BIODIVERSITY CONSERVATION, TRADITIONAL RESOURCE RIGHTS & INDIGENOUS PEOPLES

## I. The Convention on Biological Diversity and Enhancement of Community-based Conservation

The Convention on Biological Diversity (CBD) contains several provisions which if implemented could provide ways to secure a greater degree of community empowerment (see Posey 1994, IUCN Report).

*Article 6* calls for strategies, plans, and programmes for conservation and sustainable use of biological diversity. Indigenous peoples should be actively involved in these *National Studies*, not only as participants and executants, but intellectually through the development of their own criteria and value systems. Likewise, *Article 7* calls for identification and monitoring of biodiversity, which should include indigenous criteria and full participation.

*Article 8* deals with *in-situ* conservation, which in effects calls for support of indigenous and local communities, since they are intricately a part of the overall ecosystem. *Article 8(j)* specifically deals with indigenous peoples, according to which Signatories to the Convention have pledged to:

> respect, preserve and maintain knowledge, innovations and practices of indigenous and local communities embodying traditional lifestyles relevant for the conservation and sustainable use of biological diversity and promote their wider application with the approval and involvement of the holders of such knowledge, innovations and practices and encourage the equitable sharing of the benefits arising from the utilisation of such knowledge, innovations and practices.

To ensure implementation, activities should include the following:
* indigenous land demarcation and guarantees of security;
* support for indigenous-based and designed conservation and sustainable development efforts;
* research centres to develop strategies and models to apply traditional technologies in a larger context;

219

- support for and strengthening of indigenous organisations, including local, regional, national and international indigenous alliances, councils, federations, unions, etc.;
- development of enforceable international legal structures to develop mechanisms for protection of and equitable sharing of benefits from indigenous and traditional knowledge, innovations and practices.

*Article 10(d)* states that Contracting Parties shall: 'support local populations to develop and implement remedial action in degraded areas where biological diversity has been reduced.'

In the absence of a clear idea of what is meant by 'support', indigenous peoples should formulate their own guidelines. Both the CBD and Agenda 21 stress restoration and remedial action in degraded areas. It is predictable that funding priorities will reflect this emphasis and that restoration and revitalisation projects will proliferate. Indigenous peoples should be prepared to offer their own projects for their own lands and territories, utilising their own conservation technologies and management models as the basis for such projects.

*Articles 11, 12* and *13* call for 'Incentive Measures' to finance research, training, public education and awareness in order to effect conservation and sustainable use of components of biological diversity. These sections should be interpreted by indigenous peoples in order to strengthen their own research agendas. Emphasis should be given to Collaborative Research and Community Controlled Research (CCR), in which indigenous communities themselves set, guide and control the research priorities, standards and guidelines for non-indigenous research partners or contractees. Indigenous peoples should seek support, financial and otherwise, to establish their own programmes for scientific and technical education and training in 'measures for the identification, conservation, and sustainable use of biological diversity' (cf. Article 12(a)). Likewise, they should seek support in their own media projects as provided for in Article 13(a).

*Article 14* deals with impact assessment and minimising adverse impacts'. Section 1(a) calls for the Parties to:

> introduce appropriate procedures requiring environmental impact assessment of its proposed project that are likely to have significant

adverse effects on biological diversity with a view to avoiding or minimising such effects, and where appropriate, allow for public participation in such procedures.

Effective implementation of this Article depends upon local participation in projects that affect indigenous, traditional or local communities. Environmental Impact Assessment (EIA) studies themselves should include local guidance and full participation, as indigenous criteria and mechanisms for assessment are fundamental. A critical part of the EIA procedures must include Prior Informed Consent (see Principle 10, Article 8), meaning that local communities must be afforded full disclosure of all relevant information regarding the project, including its background, technical surveys and feasibility studies, as well as already existing assessments of the projects in question. Furthermore, EIA results must be made available to indigenous communities as provided for under the access to information provisions (Principle 10 of the Preamble).

---

ENVIRONMENTAL IMPACT ASSESSMENT (EIA)

Indigenous, traditional and local communities require the following to make effective provisions for Environmental Impact Assessment studies:

- *full participation in all phases of conceptualisation, implementation, and analyses;*

- *inclusion of their own guidelines, criteria, and mechanisms for EIA studies;*

- *full disclosure of all information relevant to the project, including technical and feasibility studies and assessments;*

- *access to information on the results of the EIA;*

- prior informed consent is obligatory to undertake or implement studies;

- *national and international mechanisms with legal jurisdiction to handle matters of redress, liability, restoration and compensation.*

---

*Article 16* deals with 'Access to and Transfer of Technology'. Indigenous and traditional technologies have rarely been considered as 'technologies' *per se* in international parlance. This pattern is part of the larger trend to downgrade, overlook and minimise the knowledge, innovations and practices of indigenous and traditional peoples. The CBD, however, specifically elevates these elements to a central concern (see Articles 8(j) and 18.4) as technologies relevant to the conservation and sustainable use of biological diversity. Thus, it is clear that 'indigenous and traditional technologies' are covered under the technologies section of Article 16.

• *Article 16.2* provides that access and transfer of technologies subject to patents and other intellectual property rights must occur on mutually agreed terms which 'recognise and are consistent with the adequate and effective protection of intellectual property rights'.

• *Article 16.3* calls for Contracting Parties to take legislative, administrative or policy measures to provide access to and transfer of technology, including technology protected by patents and other intellectual property rights. It is important that this is to be carried out 'in accordance with international law'.

• *Article 16.4* calls on Contracting Parties to take legislative, administrative or policy measures to facilitate the private sector's 'joint development and transfer of technology'.

• *Article 16* recognises that 'patents and other intellectual property rights may have influence on the implementation' of the CBD, but States are called upon to cooperate to ensure that such rights are supportive of and do not run counter to the Convention's objectives.

In some ways, Article 16, when seen together with Articles 8(j) and 18.4, is one of the most important sections for indigenous and traditional peoples. The article specifically provides for 'national and international legislative, administrative and policy measures to protect the intellectual property rights of technologies, which must be interpreted to include indigenous and traditional technologies'. Specific mention of the private sector in 'joint development and transfer of technology' is subject to mutually agreed terms that require legal recognition and protection of patents and other intellectual property rights. There could be no clearer call for intellectual property rights protection for indigenous knowledge, innovations and practices. Furthermore, international measures are specifically called for necessitating an international system to regulate IPR, including intellectual property rights for indigenous and traditional technologies[1].

*Article 18* refers to technical and scientific cooperation. *Article 18.2*, calls for the promotion of cooperation to develop and strengthen not 'national capabilities, but means of human resources development and institutional building'. Section 18.3 specifically calls for the establishment of a CLEARING HOUSE MECHANISM to promote and facilitate technical and scientific cooperation. This mechanism would be established by the Conference of the Parties and could include a central base with many satellites, including community-controlled research and training centres developed in partnership with indigenous and traditional peoples. In addition to a central Clearing House, additional Clearing House Mechanisms can include such things as indigenous designed and maintained databases, monitoring and conservation centres which should be afforded funding priorities under the financial mechanisms established by the CBD *(Articles 20 & 21)*. Whatever the solution or combinations of solutions, the concept of a 'Clearing House' implies the establishment of ethical and legal guidelines governing access to and use of information secured through Intellectual Property Rights agreements.

---

*CLEARING HOUSE MECHANISMS*

*Article 18 provides for a Clearing House Mechanism to be established by the Convention of the Parties. This should include:*

*- indigenous participation in all phases of conceptualisation, implementation and maintenance;*

*- establishment of priorities and guidelines developed by communities embodying traditional lifestyles;*

*- creation of community-controlled regional Clearing Houses;*

*- securing Intellectual Property Rights agreements to insure protection and compensation for information transfer.*

---

*Article 23* establishes the Conference of the Parties, which has full authority to establish, review, consider and adopt measures, acts, subsidiary bodies, protocols and implementing mechanisms. There are two especially interesting possibilities written into this section:

(1) possibility for the establishment of a Special Subsidiary Body on *Indigenous and Traditional* Scientific, Technical and Technological Advice. This Body would be especially constituted to advise the Conference of the Parties on all aspects of *in situ* conservation and sustainable development as it relates to indigenous and traditional technologies, as well as knowledge, innovations and practices of local communities embodying traditional lifestyles.

(2) develop a SPECIAL PROTOCOL on Indigenous and Traditional Technologies Based on Knowledge, Innovations and Practices of Local Communities Embodying Traditional Lifestyles. This could be utilised to develop mechanisms for strengthening indigenous, traditional and local communities. It would have an international legal basis, since it would be subsidiary to the CBD which is a legally-binding international agreement (see Article 25).

*Article 24* establishes the CBD Secretariat to implement the functions of the Secretariat, as defined in sections 1 (a-e): *indigenous and traditional peoples need to be permanent members and staff of the Secretariat.*

*Article 25* gives details about the 'subsidiary body on scientific, technical and technological advice', which is open to participation by all parties and *shall be* [notice the mandatory language] multidisciplinary. The Conference of the Parties is to provide guidelines and establish the authority of the advisory group. The CBD outlines its functions as providing:

(a) scientific and technical assessments of the status of biodiversity' (24.2.a);
(b) assessments of measures taken in the implementation of the CBD (24.2.b);
(c) identification of innovative, efficient and state-of-the-art technologies and knowhow, while promoting 'development and/or transferring such technologies' (24.2.c);
(d) advice on international cooperation in research and development (24.2.d);

(e) responses to technical, technological and methodological questions that arise.

This provision for the establishment of a *Subsidiary Body on Scientific, Technical and Technological Advice* should be well represented by indigenous and traditional peoples. Since knowledge, innovations and practices of local communities embodying traditional lifestyles is highlighted elsewhere (e.g., Articles 8(j) & 18.4) as being relevant to conservation and sustainable use of biological diversity, then the Subsidiary Body should give research into and application of traditional technologies a central focus of highest priority. The Body should also give priority to the establishment of indigenous criteria for evaluation, assessment, monitoring and advising. It should be instrumental in identifying traditional technologies, knowledge, innovations and practices in state-of-the-art applications to wider contexts. It should also seek Collaborative Research efforts with indigenous peoples and foster Community Controlled Research (CCR) controlled by local communities. To facilitate international co-operation, it should develop guidelines and propose model legislation to develop adequate Intellectual Property Rights (IPR) and Traditional Resource Rights (TRR) at national and international levels. Finally, it should propose guidelines for the establishment of monitoring and enforcement institutions and mechanisms to insure the respect, preservation and maintenance of knowledge, innovations and practices of indigenous and local communities embodying traditional lifestyles relevant for the conservation and sustainable use of biological diversity.

Alternatively, a Special Subsidiary Body on *Indigenous and Traditional* Scientific, Technical and Technological Advice could be established to exclusively deal with these matters (see section on Article 23).

SUBSIDIARY BODY ON SCIENTIFIC, TECHNICAL AND TECHNOLOGICAL ADVICE.

*Indigenous and Traditional Peoples should seek a Special Subsidiary Body on Indigenous and Traditional Scientific, Technical and Technological Advice. Alternatively, the already established Subsidiary Body on Scientific, Technical and Technological Advice' would have to:*

- include a fair representation of scientific and technical specialists from indigenous, traditional and local communities;

- identify relevant traditional technologies, innovations and practices;

- apply and seek wider application of indigenous and traditional knowledge, innovations and practices;

- develop methodologies, techniques, and strategies for use of indigenous criteria for evaluation, assessment and monitoring;

- give priority to and develop guidelines for Collaborative Research and Community Controlled Research (CCR) with indigenous, traditional and local communities;

- develop guidelines and proposals for model legislation on Intellectual Property Rights (IPR) and Traditional Resource Rights (TRR) for indigenous, traditional and local communities;

- develop guidelines and proposals for model legislation to establish monitoring and enforcement institutions to insure that the CBD is fairly and properly implemented and that indigenous, traditional and local communities benefit from the Convention on Biological Diversity.

*Article 28* deals with the process of Adoption of Protocols. Protocols establish a subset of agreements within the framework of a Convention. Thus, a Protocol to the CBD would define specific aspects of items provided for in the Convention on Biological Diversity. Two interesting possibilities exist:

(1) as previously suggested, a special protocol on Indigenous and Traditional Technologies Based on Knowledge, Innovations and Practices of Local Communities Embodying Traditional Life-styles could be negotiated. The disadvantage to this strategy is that few States would support the negotiation of such a protocol because it would be controversial and of little interest to most contracting parties.

(2) include the well-being of indigenous and traditional communities as a major aspect in a protocol on biosafety. Indigenous and local communities embodying traditional lifestyles are recognised as having knowledge, innovations and practices relevant to the conservation of biological diversity and the sustainable use of its components (Preamble). Furthermore, these local communi-

ties are seen as fundamental to *in situ* conservation and, indeed, as integral parts of the ecosystems they inhabit (Article 8).

Article 8(g) calls for 'the establishment and maintenance of means to regulate, manage or control the risks associated with the use and release of living modified organisms resulting from biotechnology which are likely to have adverse environmental impacts that could affect the conservation and sustainable use of biological diversity, taking also into account the risks to human health'. Indigenous, traditional and local communities would clearly be some of the most affected by these modified organisms.

There is already a strong international movement to implement a biosafety protocol for the CBD. This proposed Protocol *should also deal with the impacts of biotechnology and its risks on local communities.* This should include guidelines for equitable sharing and intellectual property rights protection, since these are the mechanisms that guarantee benefits for local communities and insure their continued conservation of biological diversity.

---

*POSSIBILITIES FOR SPECIAL PROTOCOLS TO THE CBD ON INDIGENOUS AND TRADITIONAL TECHNOLOGIES BASED ON KNOWLEDGE, INNOVATIONS AND PRACTICES OF LO-CAL COMMUNITIES EMBODYING TRADITIONAL LIFE-STYLES to:*

*- define and develop mechanisms for the implementation of 'sharing equitably of benefits arising from the use of traditional knowledge, innovations and practices relevant to the conservation of biological diversity and the sustainable use of its components' (Preamble);*

*- define, document and investigate 'knowledge, innovations, and practices of indigenous and local communities embodying traditional life-styles relevant for the conservation and sustainable use of biological diversity' (Article 8(j));*

*- define and develop effective mechanisms to promote the 'wider application' of traditional knowledge, innovations and practices (Article 8(j));*

*- establish guidelines and mechanisms for training and surveying programmes in indigenous and traditional knowledge (Article 17);*

*- develop a 'Clearing-House Mechanism' for technical and scientific cooperation (Article 18);*

*- develop financial mechanisms to strengthen local communities to preserve and maintain their knowledge, innovations and practices (Article 20).*

*POSSIBILITIES FOR A SPECIAL PROTOCOL ON BIOSAFETY & TRADITIONAL TECHNOLOGIES to:*

*- develop criteria and mechanisms to identify and develop baseline inventories of existing components of biological diversity utilising local communities and their own criteria;*

*- develop criteria and mechanisms to identify and develop baseline inventories of knowledge, innovations and practices of traditional communities that currently maintain and conserve biological diversity;*

*- develop criteria and mechanisms to assess the impact of intended new technologies and genetically modified organisms on traditional lifestyles and conservation and sustainable use of biological diversity by local communities;*

*- develop criteria and mechanisms to monitor change, including adverse effects of external technologies and genetically modified organisms on traditional lifestyles and conservation and sustainable use of biological diversity;*

*- develop equitable sharing mechanisms for biotechnology developed based upon or derived from traditional technologies.*

## An Important Warning

Despite what are generous words, indigenous and traditional peoples are faced with a difficult conundrum. On the one hand, their contributions, central role in sustainable development and conservation, and rights as decision-makers and beneficiaries are recognised far beyond any previous international binding legal conventions. On the other hand, by accepting the terms of these agreements, indigenous peoples must accept that ultimate control over resources lies with nation-states. Many indigenous groups are unwilling to allow this *a priori* usurpation of their fundamental rights no matter what promises and favourable interpretations may arise.

Unless decisive and significant actions are taken at national and international levels to empower (financially, socially, culturally and politically) local communities, there is no reason to expect that the Rio Declaration, Convention on Biological Diversity, Agenda 21 or Forest Principles will significantly contribute to the resolution of basic issues raised in the Draft Declaration of Rights for Indigenous Peoples, namely their staunch and unified call for self-determination. The UNCED agreements may, however, pave the way for the creation of useful instruments which work toward true partnerships with indigenous, traditional and local communities.

## II. Traditional Resource Rights

Until international agreements are in place specifically to protect traditional knowledge and biogenetic resources from unwanted exploitation, local communities are vulnerable to scientific and business interests. Intellectual Property Rights (IPR) for indigenous and local communities has become a very critical topic in international discussions. The classic instruments for IPR protection are patent, copyright, trade secret, know-how and appellation of origin, augmented by mechanisms of royalties, franchises and licensing agreements. But the issues of protection, recognition and compensation for indigenous peoples' knowledge and resources are not just legal matters; they are profoundly ethical questions based on concepts of universal fairness and justice. In fact, avoiding legal instruments may be the best policy in the long run, since the legal system has always been stacked against indigenous peoples (access to legal instruments, legal fees, fairness in courts, etc.).

Contracts are not technically IPR instruments but can be used to define and guarantee rights and conditions. Contracts are probably the most accessible and easily instituted legal instruments because they are internationally recognised and require little legal assistance. Downes et al. (1993, 255-289) and King (1994, 69-83) have discussed elements of model contracts which are now being effected in various parts of the world.

One such model contractual arrangement has been developed by The Global Coalition for Biological and Cultural Diversity. To reflect the long-term and serious nature of market links with indigenous peoples, the model has been called a Covenant on Intellectual, Cultural and Scientific Resource Rights' (Posey

1994) to guide contracting parties with essential principles. It is intended to guide negotiating partners into ethical and equitable associations of mutual benefit. The 'Covenant' is meant to be more than just a contract. It establishes a basic set of principles to be followed by all partners, while emphasising that, in order to strengthen local communities and biodiversity conservation, a long-term commitment is necessary.

*Essential elements of the Covenant include:*
1. The establishment of a legal fund for the local community as part of 'upfront payment'. In principle, this helps to offset the financial handicap of indigenous and traditional peoples in access to legal assistance and litigation.

2. An independent monitor to evaluate the state of the agreement. This element is essential to the development of any TRR arrangements and is perhaps the weakest link in the chain, since few institutions or individuals are sufficiently knowledgeable about traditional and indigenous cultures, as well as TRR, to serve in this capacity.

3. Informed consent and joint planning are other critical elements in the Covenant.

4. Concern for the environment. There is no point in discussing equitable agreements, just compensation and IPR if biological diversity is not conserved and ecological concerns do not have priority by all partners. This is explicitly stated in Principle VIII, 'Insuring ecological and cultural sensitivity in all phases of any project, including collecting, screening, sourcing, production and manufacture'.

Contracts and IPR tools are inadequate to encompass indigenous and traditional knowledge and biogenetic resources. The term TRR (Traditional Resource Rights) has been coined to reflect the necessity of reconceptualising the limited and limiting concept of IPR, while emphasising that a wide range of relevant international agreements exist to form the basis for a *sui generis* system of protection for traditional and indigenous peoples and their resources. A number of overlapping areas of international law and practice (BOX 6) can be identified to provide the synthesis for an ideological basis for a newly designed (i.e. *sui generis)* TRR system (see Posey 1994).

# WHAT ARE TRADITIONAL RESOURCE RIGHTS?

TRR are based on the following 'bundles' of rights and legal concepts:

1. *Human Rights:* Universal Declaration of Human Rights (UDHR), International Covenant on Economic, Social and Cultural Rights (ICESCR), Draft Declaration on the Rights of Indigenous Peoples.

2. *Collective Rights:* ICESCR, International Covenant on Civil and Political Rights (ICCPR), International Labour Organisation Convention 169 (ILO 169), Draft Declaration on the Rights of Indigenous Peoples.

3. *Self-determination:* ICESCR, ICCPR, ILO 169, Draft Declaration on the Rights of Indigenous Peoples.

4. *Land and Territorial Rights:* ILO 169, UDHR, CBD, Draft Declaration on the Rights of Indigenous Peoples.

5. *Religious Rights and Religious Freedom:* UDHR, ICCPR, national laws.

6. *Development Rights:* ICESCR, ICCPR, ILO 169, Draft Declaration on the Rights of Indigenous Peoples.

7. *Rights to Privacy:* UDHR, ICCPR.

8. *Environmental Integrity:* CBD, Declaration of Rio.

9. *Intellectual Property Rights:* World Intellectual Property Organisation (WIPO), Paris and Berne Conventions, GATT-TRIPS, establishing: Patent, Copyright, Trademark, Appellation of Origin, Trade Secret, Know-how; National Laws.

10. *Neighbouring Rights:* Rome Convention.

11. *Prior Informed Consent and Full Disclosure:* CBD, Contracts, Draft Declaration on the Rights of Indigenous Peoples; National Laws.

12. *Contracts and Covenants:* National Laws.

13. *Farmers' Rights:* FAO.

14. *Cultural Property:* National Laws, UNESCO Convention on Cultural Property, UNESCO World Heritage Convention.

15. *Cultural Heritage:* UNESCO World Heritage Convention.

16. *Customary Law and Practice:* Soft Law, ILO 169, Draft Declaration on the Rights of Indigenous Peoples.

17. *Folklore:* UNESCO, especially UNESCO/WIPO Model Provisions.

18. *Cultural Landscapes:* UNESCO World Heritage Convention.

Traditional resources include plants, animals and other material objects including cultural property, which may have intangible (e.g., sacred, ceremonial, heritage or aesthetic) qualities. Traditional resources may also be totally intangible, metaphysical or non-quantifiable with no physical manifestations (Posey & Dutfield, in press). The term 'property' is inappropriate, since property for traditional peoples frequently has intangible, spiritual manifestations and, although worthy of protection, can belong to no human being. It is suggested that the TRR concept can be implemented nationally and internationally in the following ways:

- by guiding the development of national laws, the *sui generis* system for the protection of plant varieties as permitted in accordance with the GATT-TRIPS Agreement, and codes of ethics;

- by its inclusion in implementation mechanisms of the CBD;

- by its inclusion in funding guidelines for projects involving traditional communities.

### III. Other Mechanisms and Options
As interest in traditional knowledge has grown – and along with it the awareness of indigenous, traditional and local communities as to their intellectual, cultural and scientific property rights – a number of ideas, mechanisms and strategies have emerged. A Handbook (*Beyond Intellectual Property Rights*. Posey & Dutfield 1994) has been developed to familiarise local communities with these options. A few of the principal possibilities are outlined here.

*1. Material Transfer Agreements (MTAs)*
MTAs are common forms of contract governing the details of access and use of biogenetic materials in *ex-situ* collections.

Lesser (1994) has suggested that MTAs are already effective tools for indigenous peoples to utilise to impose their cultural stipulations for use of traditional resources and that they are even more powerful with the CBD in vigour.

## 2. FAO and Farmers' Rights

Farmers' Rights were defined as a way of compensating traditional farmers for the knowledge vested in them and their forebears upon which modern plant breeding is founded. They were introduced at the 1987 meeting of FAO's Commission on Plant Genetic Resources and defined as:

> ... rights arising from the past, present and future contributions of farmers in conserving, improving and making available plant genetic resources particularly those in the centres of origin/diversity. Those rights are vested in the international community as trustees for present and future generations of farmers, and supporting the continuation of their contributions as well as the attainment of overall purposes of the International Undertaking (FAO Conference, Resolution 5/89).

By 1992 the International Undertaking on Plant Genetic Resources had been signed by 107 countries (Ayad 1994). Plant Breeders' Rights are vested in individuals and companies, whereas Farmers' Rights are a collective right, vested in the International Community as trustee for present and future generations of farmers (FAO 1991)

At the Intergovernmental Conference on the Convention on Biological Diversity (ICCBD) which met in Nairobi (June – July 1994), the difference between Plant Breeders' Rights and Farmers' Rights were emphasised:

> the issue of Farmers' Rights and *ex situ* collections is the issue of IPR. The particularities of farmer and local community innovation, conservation, use and ownership of biological resources are quite different from corporate IPR needs.

Farmers' Rights need to be kept separated from IPR systems because they are grounded in the concept of shared knowledge.

## 3. Community Intellectual Property Rights (CIPR)

Indigenous farmers have begun to assert their right to save seed through Community Intellectual Property Rights. CIPR suggest that the government of India should simultaneously adopt PBR and Farmers' Rights as a form of community protection. The Farmers' Movement in India are using CIPR to assert their rights to seed claiming that any corporation using their local knowledge or local resources without the permission of local communities is engaging in intellectual piracy (e.g. the neem controversy). By asserting this right an opportunity is created to define a *sui generis* system centred on farmers' rights arising from their role in protecting and improving PGR. The Farmers' Movement claim that the CBD recognises the role of local communities of farmers and indigenous peoples in the conservation of knowledge about PGR and their rights to protection of that knowledge, and gives states sovereign rights on biodiversity (CBD: Preamble, Article 10c, and 18.4) which override the GATT requirements (Shiva 1994).

Within the Crucible Group (The Crucible Group 1994) the view was expressed that to be effective, CIPRs would need both appropriate national legislation and reciprocal recognition in other countries. In addition, the creation of an international database for tracing germplasm may be needed and a 'Public Defender': an internationally recognised mediator or ombudsman.

*4. UNESCO/WIPO Model Provisions*
In 1985 UNESCO and WIPO produced their Model Provisions for National Laws on Protection of Expressions of Folklore Against Illicit Exploitation and Other Prejudicial Actions. The intention was to go beyond conventional copyright by protecting intangible expressions as well as works. The document avoids a definition of folklore but does explain what the term 'expressions of folklore' should encompass (Section 2). The rights provided are similar to neighbouring rights as described above, an important difference being that there is no fixed time limit.

According to the Model Provisions, certain uses of expressions of folklore are subject to prior authorisation by a competent authority or the community itself if they are 'made both with gainful intent and outside their traditional or customary context' (Section 3), and would therefore constitute 'illicit exploitation' if used without this authorisation. 'Traditional context' here means remaining 'in its proper artistic framework based on continuous usage by the community' (WIPO 1989: 6).

234

'Customary context' means in accordance with 'the practices of everyday life of the community' (Ibid).

There are four types of 'other prejudicial action' which may be subject to criminal sanctions (Section 6):

- failure to indicate the ethnic and geographical source of an expression of folklore in printed publications and other communications to the public;

- unauthorised utilisation of an expression of folklore where authorisation is required;

- deliberately deceiving the public about the ethnic source of a production;

- any kind of public use which distorts the production in a manner 'prejudicial to cultural interests of the community concerned'.

A 'competent authority', which could be the communities themselves, would be set up to deal with applications for use of expressions of folklore and perhaps to fix and collect authorisation fees for safeguarding national culture or national folklore. Although the Model Provisions were not drawn up with genetic resources in mind, traditional resources could be considered 'expressions of folklore' for the purposes of legislation based on this document.

*5. Model Draft Community Intellectual Rights Act*
The Model Draft Community Intellectual Rights Act is suggested as a means of bringing about the evolution of new criteria for claiming patent rights compatible with cultural values and practices of indigenous peoples. It could be used in the context of the GATT TRIPS call for *sui generis* forms of IPR protection and would accord with the requirements of the CBD, particularly Article 8(j).

The purpose of the Act would be to prevent the 'privatisation and usurpation of community rights and knowledge through existing definitions of innovation'. It would assert the existence of knowledge that is communally owned and shared, given that ownership of property is not a concept accepted by many indigenous peoples. Therefore, a more suitable form of description for knowledge that is of value, not privatised, and cumulative would be 'community intellectual rights' (CIR).

To meet the novelty or innovation requirement of regular patent protection criteria, indigenous peoples are described as 'innovators' because the knowledge they have accumulated has been hitherto unknown to the outside world.

Two legal bases are suggested for 'vesting in local communities custodianship rights of an innovation',

i) Constructive Trustee: local community leaders are nominated or appointed to act for the whole community as trustees for the beneficiaries (the community)[2].

ii) Higher Trust: this builds on the concept that government in possessing sovereign rights, as declared in the CBD and UNCED documents, is in fact holding those rights in trust for the community[3]. It also refers back to FAO Resolution 4/89, on Farmers' Rights being vested in the international community 'as trustees for present and future generations of farmers',

As suggested in the concept of Farmers' Rights, the right is to be held in perpetuity because knowledge and practice will evolve as a community evolves.

Section 5 of the CIR Act suggests the creation of a Registry of Invention (ROI). Here a community may register its innovation by the simple method of declaring the existence of that innovation to the world. The idea is similar to copyright law whereby 'protection generally arises with no need for formal acceptance by a registering authority', and more flexible than filing a patent. Failure to register does not surrender the innovation rights.

Sections 6.1 and 6.2, Proof of Invention states that: 'a declaration by the duly constituted representatives of the community that they have been using the innovation or are the custodians of the innovation will suffice to vest the innovation in the community'. Anyone challenging this declaration will have the responsibility of proving their challenge, rather than requiring the innovators to prove their customary use.

## 6. Proposed Collectors Act
Based on the concept of 'prior informed consent', the Act would set out the obligations required of collectors and grant them a license if they are deemed able to fulfil the requirements made of them. The license would be given for a prescribed period,

subject to conditions. The powers of the Act would be strong enough to enable contravention of the conditions of the Act to be subject to penal sanctions. This would go as far as making directors and employees of companies contravening the Act liable to imprisonment, in addition to withdrawal of the license. The collector would be required to provide:

- plans for prospecting;

- details of types of material to be collected in terms of species and quantities;

- details of the evaluation, storage and use of the collected material, including the uses to which it would be put;

- details of the benefit the host country or community may derive from the collection of the germplasm.

Conditions relating to collection and obligations related to post-collection activities would be enumerated, in order that the community or state receive fair recompense for sharing their resource.

Sums of money to be paid include:
- a sum payable by the collector, representing not less than a fixed percentage of any income arising from the supply of germplasm extracts to commercial organisations;
- a similar sum for any royalties obtained as a result of the creation or invention of a marketable product from the collected materials.

An endorsement would be required from the collector's country (an accredited representative) agreeing to indemnify the source country for any losses it may sustain should the collector breach the agreement, plus surrender of the results of any report made of studies or experimentation made on the collected specimen. The obligation imposed on the collector shall read:

> No patent application shall be filed within or outside the country in respect of the collected specimens or any part thereof, its properties or activity or any derivatives which utilise the knowledge of indigenous groups or communities in the commercialisation of any product as well as to a more sophisticated process for extracting, isolating or synthesising the active chemical in the plant extracts or compositions used by indigenous peoples or if the same represents the intellectual right of the indigenous communities.

By including in the Act the requirement for a contract to be drawn up between government and collector, a country will have greater scope for enforcing penalties associated with any breach of contract. A country's legislation has no extra-territorial power, whereas many countries customarily have reciprocal enforcement arrangements with other countries, which will include breach of contract provisions. A contract is also more flexible in that it can be tailored to a particular circumstance, and the existence of one contract does not preclude others being taken out, if they are not in conflict[4] (Singh Nijar 1994).

## Conclusion
Community Intellectual Property Rights (CIPR), and the even broader concept of Traditional Resource Rights (TRR), need to be implemented in order to enhance the viability of local communities, whose indigenous knowledge systems are critical to biodiversity conservation. The development of *sui generis* systems should be a consultative process between government, non-governmental groups and peoples' organisations. The process itself may become as important as the final national legislation, since it will be through consultation and co-management that the practical issues of access to and control over resources is effectively defined. Mechanisms called for in the Convention on Biological Diversity (CBD) can be utilised to facilitate the process. National Biodiversity Studies, Environmental Impact Assessments, Clearing House Mechanisms and technical advisory bodies can all be implemented in a way that local criteria and priorities lead, and even control, the research, planning and implementation of conservation and development projects. There are many other 'bundles of rights' that can be borrowed from legally- and non-legally-binding international instruments that can form the basis for national laws. The wide range of options points to one problem: the political will to recognise, enhance, protect and equitably compensate local communities for their knowledge and biogenetic resources.

## Bibliography
Ayad, W. G. The CGIAR and the Convention on Biological Diversity, in *Widening Perspectives on Biodiversity*. Krattiger, A.F. et al. (eds.). Gland: IUCN.

Crucible Group 1994. *People, Plants and Patents: The Impact of Intellectual Property on Trade, Plant Biodiversity, and Rural Society.* Ottawa: International Development Research Centre.

Downes, D. & S. A. Laird & C. Klein & K. Carney 1993. *Biodiversity Prospecting: Using Genetic Resources for Sustainable Development.* Reid, W. V. et al. Washington, D.C.: WRI.

FAO 1991. Biotechnology and Plant Genetic Resources, and Elements of a Code of Conduct for Biotechnology. UN FAO Commission on Plant Genetic Resources, 4th Session, Rome, 15-19 April. CPGR191/12.

IUCN/UNEP/WWF 1991. *Caring for the Earth: A Strategy for Sustainable Living.* Gland: IUCN/UNEP/WWF.

King, S. R. 1994. Establishing Reciprocity: Biodiversity, Conservation and New Models for Cooperation between Forest-Dwelling Peoples and the Pharmaceutical Industry. *Intellectual Property Rights for Indigenous Peoples: A Sourcebook.* Greaves, T. (ed.). Oklahoma City: Society for Applied Anthropology.

Lesser, W. 1994. Intellectual Property Rights and Indigenous Peoples. Working Paper. Geneva: International Academy of the Environment.

Posey, D. A. 1994. International Agreements and Intellectual Property Rights for Indigenous Peoples. in *Intellectual Property Rights for Indigenous Peoples: A Sourcebook.* Greaves, T. (ed.). Oklahoma City: Society for Applied Anthropology.

Posey, D. A. and G. Dutfield. (In press). *Beyond Intellectual Property Rights: Protection, Compensation and Community Empowerment.* Gland & Ottawa: Worldwide Fund for Nature & International Development Research Centre.

Posey, D. A. (In press). *Indigenous Peoples, Traditional Technologies and Equitable Sharing: International Instruments for the Protection of Community Intellectual Property and Traditional Resource Rights.* Gland: IUCN.

Shiva, V. 1994. The Need for Sui Generis Rights. *Seedling,* Vol. 12, No. 1.

Singh Nivar, G. "Towards a Legal Framework for Protecting Biological Diversity and Community Intellectual Rights – a Third World Perspective". The Third World Network Discussion Paper, 2nd Session ICCBD. Nairobi, 20 June-1 July 1994.

## Notes

1. For a discussion of relevant Intellectual Property Rights (IPR) instruments, see Glowka et al. 1994. A Guide to the Convention on Biological Diversity. Environmental Policy and Law Paper No. X. Gland: IUCN.

2. For further reading on constructive trusts see Snell's Principles of Equity, 28th edition (1982), p. 192. Beatty v. Gugenheim Exploration Co. (1919). 225 N.Y. 380 at 386 (Cardozo, J.).

3. See Megarr., v, V.C. in Tito v. Waddell (No.2) 1977. 3 all E.R. 129 at 222 – a decision of the English Chancery Division Court.

4. Source (v) and (vi): G. Singh Nijar 1994. Towards a Legal Framework for Protecting Biological Diversity and Community Intellectual Rights – a Third World Perspective. Third Word Network Discussion Paper, 2nd Session ICCBD. Nairobi, 20 June - 1 July 1994.

JEREMY NARBY

# DNA AND THE ORIGINS OF SHAMANIC KNOWLEDGE: TOWARDS A NEW PARADIGM?

In the early 1980s I began studying anthropology. My main interest was 'Third World development'. A professor suggested that I look into the rights of indigenous people, who tended to live in out-of-the-way places like the Amazon, surrounded by vast natural resources like tropical forests, that they did not use in ways Western experts considered 'rational'.

These were the days when the rainforest was called 'jungle', and taking it away from the Indians and cutting it down was called 'development'. I decided to do the fieldwork my training in anthropology required in a place where this was occurring.

From this rather theoretical perspective I strolled into the Peruvian Amazon in 1984, fresh from the suburbs and the library. I wanted to study how the Ashaninka indigenous people use their resources to demonstrate that they used them rationally and therefore deserved the right to own their lands.

My methodology consisted of accompanying people in their activities. This often involved walking through the forest. During these walks I would ask people about plants. I soon saw they had an encyclopaedic understanding of plant properties. They knew plants that accelerate the healing of wounds, cure diarrhoea or heal chronic backache. I would try these remedies on myself, only to find that they worked. So I started asking my Ashaninka consultants how they knew what they knew.

Their answer was enigmatic: they said that their botanical knowledge came from the plants themselves; and that shamans drink a hallucinogenic brew called *ayahuasca* and talk in their visions with animate essences, or spirits, that are present in all living beings and are sources of knowledge.

They said that nature is intelligent and speaks a visual language. It not only communicates in hallucinations and dreams, it also gives everyday signs. The plant that cures the bite of the snake has two white hooks next to the stem of its leaves, similar in shape to the snake's fangs. 'Look at the form,' they said, 'this is the sign that nature gives us.'

I did not take these ideas literally. These Indians could say what they wanted, they were not going to convince me that they had learned their botanical knowledge from hallucinations or from hidden signs in nature. Besides, hallucinations *could not* be the source of true knowledge because to consider them as such is the definition of psychosis.

Also, I wanted to demonstrate that the Ashaninka used their resources rationally. To emphasise the hallucinatory origin of Ashaninka ecological knowledge would have been counter-productive to the central argument underlying my research.

Nevertheless, one evening after four months of fieldwork, I was chatting with some men and came to ask them once again how they had learned all they knew about plants.

One man answered: 'Brother Jeremy, to understand what interests you, you must drink ayahuasca. And if you like I can show you some time.'

I accepted. Several nights later, I sat with this *ayahuasquero* on the platform of a quiet house and drank ayahuasca. The ensuing experience shattered my understanding of reality.

With the shaman singing beautiful melodies, I sank into deep hallucinations. Suddenly I found myself surrounded by enormous fluorescent snakes, 15 yards long, one yard high, looking more real than real; and these snakes began explaining things to me about myself that were painfully true. They said: 'You are just a human being.' It was true that I was just a human being, and that my rational perception of reality had limits starting with its capacity to grasp what my eyes were seeing. My world-view collapsed in front of me. Then I vomited colours, saw in the dark, and flew out of my body. I also saw extra-ordinarily fast sequences of images, like the veins of a human hand flashing back and forth with the veins of a green leaf: they looked the same. Relentless images; impossible to remember everything.

In the following days, I tried to come to terms with this experience. Overall, it was disturbing because it confirmed what the Ashaninka said: one could learn things in the hallucinatory world of *ayahuasqueros*. And there was a further mystery: just who were those snakes, anyway?

However, I was young, and was also stalking a doctorate in anthropology. I was afraid my colleagues would not take me seriously. I chose not to look into the matter much further and not to include it in my official research. I completed my field-work on Ashaninka resource use and went home to write my dissertation. Two years later I became a doctor in anthropology.

In 1989 I started working as an activist for the rights of indigenous people, gathering funds in Europe for land titling projects in the Amazon. To do this I would give talks explaining that the best way to save the rainforest is to entrust it to its indigenous inhabitants, who are the only ones who know how to use it rationally, that is, without destroying it. But the more I talked the more I realized there was something I was *not* saying: namely, that these Amazonian Indians say their botanical knowl-edge comes from plant-induced hallucinations.

After four years of successful fund-raising, I decided the time had come to look into this mystery. My employer granted me a paid sabbatical to do this. So eight years after my encounter with the fluorescent serpents, I decided to investigate the enigma of hallucinatory knowledge.

I read the literature on shamanism for months, with an emphasis on the hallucinatory shamanism of western Amazonia. I categorised and cross-referenced it, Cartesian style. This re-vealed a rather strange picture. Across western Amazonia, doz-ens of indigenous cultures take ayahuasca and say that it is the source of their botanical knowledge. Anthropologists have docu-mented this extensively, but most seem to consider that the Indians are talking in metaphors and that their botanical knowl-edge is actually due to experimentation and chance. But it suffices to look at their botanical recipes to see that this explana-tion is improbable.

Curare is a case in point. This Amazonian hunting poison revolutionised modern medicine in the 1940s. It makes possible surgery of the vital organs because it paralyses all muscles, including breathing muscles. Curare is a combination of plants that must be boiled together for 72 hours. The final product is a paste that is inactive unless you inject it under the skin. If you swallow it, it has no effect. It is difficult to see how anybody could have stumbled onto this recipe by chance experimentation particularly considering there are 80,000 plant species to choose from in the Amazon.

Having examined the ethnographic, botanical and neurological data in some detail, I came to consider the possibility that Amazonian shamans were truly gaining access to information in their hallucinations. I followed this hunch to discover with stupefaction that what these people say about the spirits or animate essences common to all life forms corresponds on many levels to what scientists say about DNA, the informational molecule at the centre of each cell of each living being.

For instance, scientists say DNA is shaped like a ladder, a twisted rope ladder, two vines wrapped around each other or two entwined snakes. And shamans from around the world talk of an *axis mundi*, an axis of the world, that is shaped like a ladder, a twisted rope ladder, two vines wrapped around each other or two entwined snakes. They say the axis is so long it connects heaven and earth and that they get their knowledge from spirits going up and down the axis. As Mircea Eliade pointed out, the axis mundi and the serpent are often linked to the creation of life and to *twins*. Quetzalcoatl, the feathered serpent of the Aztecs, is the twin child of Coatlicue, the cosmic serpent, and symbolises the sacred energy of life; in Aztec the word *coatl* means both 'serpent' and 'twin'.

Meanwhile, DNA is a *single* molecule that is a *double* helix. The two strands that wrap around each other are complementary versions of the same text. When a double helix unzips, it becomes two separate and complementary strands; duplication enzymes then reconstruct these into double helixes that are exactly identical, in other words *twins*. This twinning is at the centre of life and has been since the beginning. Without it, one cell could not become two, and life would not exist. The very essence of DNA is to be both single and double, in other words duplicable.

A good number of the world's cosmic serpents are shown to be both single and double. Taoists represent the vital principle of cosmic origin, yin-yang, as two snakes wrapped around each other in complementary fashion. Like DNA, the yin-yang is androgynous.

Molecular biologist Christopher Wills writes: 'The two chains of DNA resemble two snakes coiled around each other in some elaborate courtship ritual.'

Many mythical serpents are extremely long. The monster-serpent of Greek mythology, Typhon, touches the stars with its head. Chuang Tsu's fish-bird is 'who knows how many thousand miles long'. African representations of the Ouroboric serpent show it wrapping itself around the world. Meanwhile, the DNA in a human cell is a two-metre thread that is a billion times longer than its own width. Relatively speaking, it is as if your little finger stretched from Paris to Los Angeles. If you lined up all the DNA threads in your body, they would stretch 200 billion kilometres. This distance is equivalent to seventy return trips between Saturn and the sun.

I discovered one could focus simultaneously on shamanism and molecular biology, and gain an enhanced perspective on both.

For instance, the shamans of western Amazonia say that certain psychoactive plants (containing molecules that are active in the human brain) influence the spirits in precise ways. They say that spirits have an almost unquenchable hunger for tobacco because it gives them energy. I went looking for an analogous connection between nicotine and the DNA contained in the nerve cells of a human brain. I found that science has recently discovered that when a molecule of nicotine fits into the nico-tinic receptor on the outside of a brain cell, it causes a channel to open, through which positively-charged atoms rush; these atoms activate the DNA contained in the nucleus of the cell, in such a way that it starts coding for the construction of more nicotinic receptors. Give nicotine to the DNA in your brain, it asks for more. Like the spirits, it has an almost unquenchable hunger for tobacco.

I spent a year exploring molecular biology. It would be diffi-cult here to discuss all the common points it has with shaman-ism. These two domains of knowledge, which seemed separate until now, complement each other on many levels. I wrote a book about this common ground called *The cosmic serpent: DNA and the origins of knowledge.*

The analogous connections between what shamans say about spirits and what molecular biologists say about DNA prove nothing. However, the hypothesis that these two domains are truly complementary can be tested; and if it is exact, it means that indigenous people hold, in their shamanism, an unsuspected source of bio-molecular knowledge which is financially inestimable and mainly concerns tomorrow's science.

However, there are obstacles. The idea that shamans communicate with a DNA-based consciousness is not receivable by current biology, which is founded on the notion that there is no intelligence in nature. As Jacques Monod wrote, one cannot admit that nature has a goal, 'even provisionally or in a limited area, without departing from the domain of science itself'. Currently, scientists consider DNA to be an inert chemical, 'desoxyribonucleic acid'.

Who can say what the future has in store?

# IV
# Indigenous Culture and Development: The Question of Identity, Equity and Cooperation

NEVER TUESTA CERRON

# BEYOND LAND RIGHTS:
# INDIGENOUS INTERCULTURAL EDUCATION

It is a well-established fact for proponents of indigenous issues
that we conceive of our land as a unity. It is our life. We educate
ourselves in the land and learn how to live together in harmony
with each other and with the natural resources that satisfy our
needs.

Land is the source of such sacred places as waterfalls, lagoons,
hills, etc. These places aid the indigenous youth, who through the
taking of *toé*, *ayahuasco* and tobacco attempt to make contact
with the ancestral spirits who pass on the 'vision' and the power
which should guide all future activities.

The land is also the home of the spirits which the shaman
must appeal to in order to gain sufficient strength and ability to
cure sicknesses. Likewise, it is from the land that women find the
resources for the manufacture of utensils which allows them to
attend to their family and guests of all kinds with pride.

It is for these reasons that in our societies the first question
you are asked is whether or not you have undergone the process
of obtaining the 'vision', and if you have, what did you learn. It
was not more than fifteen years ago that an indigenous youth
who had not had a vision was considered to be a coward, dirtying
his family name, without hope of having a secure home, full of
social problems and destined to die at an early age.

For all indigenous people, our territory is our life. It provides
all of the resources necessary to satisfy our food, transport,
communication, healing, clothing and other needs. Our notion
is: 'Indigenous people and the land are an undividable oneness'.
A major concern of the organised indigenous people is that we
can not discuss the environment or development issues without
an educational component. That is why the topic 'Beyond land
rights: indigenous intercultural education' is discussed in this
article.

## Indigenous Education

Indigenous education was a constant, transmitted orally from generation to generation, without a fixed school or an established timetable. The father, grandfather and older brothers were in charge of educating the males and the mother, grandmother and sisters, the girls.

It was a practical education, the theoretical part was based on the stories and history of our villages. This knowledge was passed on in the early morning or twilight hours each day. It is through the stories and history that an understanding of indigenous philosophy would be obtained. In the first years, the education was orientated towards activities that are connected to the home, recreational areas, washing areas, the people that one encounters as well as including tales appropriate for young children.

Later, both men and women demonstrate the appropriate activities for the different sexes: for men this was the construction of houses, canoes, blow pipes, bows and arrows, chairs and darts; for women, the production of ceramic objects, *masato* (a drink made from fermented maize or rice) and meals.

Subsequently, after approximately the tenth birthday, young men and women began to be further educated in these activities by undertaking them together with their parents, grandparents or siblings.

*The young man's education was focused on:*
-Refraining from the consumption of sweet foodstuffs (certain species of banana, pineapple, sugar cane, *caimito*, etc.) because too much sugar causes the muscles to become slack and fragile. Gluttony, as concerns the consumption of meat, should also be avoided.

-Learning to fast so that the body remains in good condition when food is unavailable, for example in times of war or all day hunting excursions.

-Young women encountered along the paths should not be approached, otherwise the spirit who brings the vision will not be able to draw near.

-Prepare and keep clean the road and lodgings that will be travelled and used after having taken *ayahuasca*, otherwise the spirit imparting the vision will withdraw.

252

*Asháninka women and children at a community meeting in Ucayali, Peru: Ensuring the passage of traditional knowledge and culture to the younger generation requires the development of specific educational programmes in schools. Photo: Alejandro Parellada*

-Practice and fulfilment of this behaviour will aid the young indigenous person to obtain the vision after drinking *ayahuasca*. For the indigenous boy it is important to have the vision because it will give him the strength and security to plan his activities throughout his lifetime with respect to an already determined objective, be it warrior, farmer, hunter, fisherman or gatherer. In addition, he should learn in which parts of the year and points of the day and where he should realise these activities. In this way he learns to respect certain prohibitions and learns the *icaros* that will facilitate his ability to make use of the surrounding resources.

-Knowledge to choose the proper trees to construct houses, canoes, *manguare*, oars and fuel (firewood). To do this he should understand when the proper time of the year or day is to carry out this activity, as well as the restrictions both before and after the activity and the *icaros* to be able to use the resource.

-Knowledge of the types of vegetation, animals and insects as indicators of the land's suitability for agriculture.

-Knowledge of the different plants and lianas which can be consumed directly or in another form in order to maintain a body free of impurities. To select them, the shape, taste, and colour of the leaves as well as the stalk should be considered.

*The young woman's educated was directed towards:*
-Obtaining all of the necessary knowledge to be able to distinguish between the different species of domestic plants (yucca, banana, sacha potato, pineapple and *cocona*) to be sown at the small farm. Furthermore, she should know the specific sites and with which species the individual species will best thrive. She should also be aware of the subsistence allowance for each of the sown seeds, the treatment the seeds must undergo before they are sowed and the *icaros* which will help to obtain a successful harvest. A woman who knows all of these rules and yields a large harvest will gain prestige in her society.

-Knowledge to be able to select clay and high quality accompanying components in order to make utensils for the home (pots, large earthen jars, *mocahua*). The quality and number of utensils that the indigenous woman has gives her prestige.

This is a concise summary of a portion of the knowledge that an indigenous education imparts. At present, many families from several villages still practise these traditions.

## Development in the Indigenous Villages
For indigenous peoples, both the notion of development as well as that of civilisation have represented nothing less than a show of superiority and imposition on their way of life on the part of the church, governmental representatives, researchers, lumbermen and small-time dealers from the mestizo society.

Formal education was almost entirely in the charge of the Summer Institute of Linguistics whose headquarters are at Yarinacocha, near Pucallpa, and internees from the Jesuits. At present, other religious orders continue to intervene in education.

This formal education was orientated towards evangelisation, with the goal of training the indigenous students to be good practitioners of the national culture in order for them to be able to integrate into it without any major difficulties. To fulfill these aims, the school curricula for indigenous children are the same as those used at the national level, with a few adaptations of the tasks.

Government representatives assigned to the mestizo settlements, but living in indigenous regions are, in general, placed in these villages as a form of punishment and have as their sole goal the making of their fortune by any means available.

It is not uncommon to see military leaders and their personnel panning gold or felling trees for commercial sale, or the authorities in charge of education receiving bribes for the allocation of a place or a transfer.

Until recently, the presence of the government in indigenous villages was carried out through the Special Projects and Colonisation Programmes, with the goal of overcoming the entire Amazon region. None of these colonisation programmes ('New Nazareth' in the Bagua province) and special projects (Pichis-Palcazu in the Junin department – 'Alto Mayo' in the San Martín department) have benefitted indigenous people in the least, rather they have served to enrich those carrying them out. We can see the result now; all of the settlers who have called the Amazon the 'bread basket of Peru' were involved in the extraction of timber, and when the trees were felled, they began to sow coca which, to make matters worse, resulted in the appearance of the Shining Path Guerrilla Movement and the Túpac Amaru Revolutionary Movement.

The lumbermen and small-time dealers, who ought to be referred to as the 'plunderers of the Amazon', are those who are pillaging, with the help of certain industry, the flora and fauna from our Amazon in complicity with government representatives alluded to above. They act as the agents who help convince the indigenous population that those concerned with the protection of resources and the environment are the developed countries, because they do not want indigenous peoples to have access to the services that they have. A second argument is that the sale of wood and meat from the mountains will generate income that will benefit the nation's development. Persuaded, the indigenous peoples yield to these arguments and accepting a payment of some basic goods, they end up selling the valuable timber in their community for a pittance. In some cases, they have even been paid to help fell the trees or hunt the animals.

As regards researchers, it is worth mentioning that they have played an extremely important role in the encounter between indigenous villages and Western society, and many of them have participated in educational programmes for indigenous villages. Nevertheless, we believe that in general they have treated us as research objects for the benefit of other scholars of indigenous peoples and languages. Whatever they learn is used to further their professional interests or to get closer to the state bureaucracy. The fruits of the studies have not benefitted indigenous peoples by way of concrete programmes in which our participation is a part of the process as a whole (research, planning, execution and evaluation). Other researchers have focused on insects, birds, animals and plants but without considering the indigenous peoples as an integral component of nature.

In sum, it is clear that none of these representatives of civilisation and development have ever taken into consideration that indigenous peoples of the Amazon have a different language, culture, territory and form of social organisation than the national society. It is regrettable and worrisome for us that there is still talk of creating 'living frontiers' in the Amazon, when these territories are actually inhabited by indigenous peoples.

We ask ourselves what we need to do to be considered as 'alive' by the government. Perhaps we ought to pillage all our resources, pollute the environment, grow coca and, finally, take up arms.

### Approaches of the Organised Peoples: AIDESEP

In the face of the effects created by this encounter, thirty years ago indigenous peoples began to organise themselves into federations. The first federations were formed in total geographic isolation from one another but with the same aim: protection of the territory in the face of expansionist advances and destruction of forests. The first organisations formed were: the Amuesha Council, the Centre of the Native Communities of the Central Rainforest (CECONSEC) and the Aguaruna-Huambisa Council. The work that these federations carried out as regards the government necessitated a national organisation, which was created in 1989, the Asociación Interétnica de Desarollo de la Selva Peruana (Interethnic Association for the Development of the Peruvian Rainforest) (AIDESEP). At present, AIDESEP consists of 36 regional federations. AIDESEP's programme of action is the following:

1. Integral protection of the territory

2. Reassessment of the language and culture, through the Development of Bilingual Teachers in the Peruvian Amazon Programme.

3. Indigenous health

4. Defence of political and human rights

5. Reassessment of indigenous ecology

6. Development of indigenous organisation and autonomy

In order to strengthen the implementation of these actions, the organised indigenous peoples propose:

- That all projects and programmes to be implemented in areas belonging to indigenous peoples include the participation of their representatives throughout the entire process: background studies, planning, execution and evaluation.

-That the governmental agencies or NGOs responsible for the execution of development or social programmes take into consideration that indigenous peoples have a language, culture and knowledge about their means and customs that are totally foreign to the national society and that it is not possible to implement models which do not correspond to these differences.

- That all types of programmes for indigenous peoples correspond to the needs and approaches of our society and that their execution contain a follow-up process which studies the events in order to identify the results and that these findings be passed on to the representatives of each people.

In order to ensure the continued existence of indigenous peoples, we are aware of the urgent need to reappropriate our knowledge as concerns the treatment of forests, our culture, language and social organisation. To achieve this, we want to develop 'Educational Programmes' in the schools which include these subjects so that they be passed on to future generations, in combination with Western society's scientific developments. If this is not understood and made into reality, we will continue to write manifestos and declarations about indigenous knowledge and its value, but in reality we will not affect the process of imposition and alienation that have resulted in the marginalisation of our cultural heritage.

SONA JHARIA MINZ

# FEMALE VOICES: INDIGENOUS WOMEN
# AND DEVELOPMENT STRATEGIES

Ninety per cent of the world's people have no control over their
lives, in spite of recent changes around the world favouring
market economies, multi-party democracies and grassroots activities declares the *Human Development Report* 1993, released in
New Delhi on 25 May 1993. 'Many of today's struggle are more
than struggles for access to political power, they are struggles for
access to the ordinary opportunities of life: land, water, living
space and basic social services,' states William H. Draper III,
UNDP Administrator, in a foreword to the report. The report,
prepared by an independent team of economists for the UNDP
and published by Oxford University Press, USA, shows that
ethnic minorities – the poor, rural dwellers, women and the
disabled – often have little power to change their lives. Dr.
Mahbub ul Haq, former Finance and Planning Minister of Pakistan and the chief architect of the report, says that the basic
message of human development has not changed: economic
growth is imperative for a nation's development, but this growth
must be translated into the lives of people. Dr. Haq says 'income
is essential but it is only a means, not the sum total of human
life'. People make many choices, besides making money, which
affect their lives in areas ranging from health and education to
employment and the way they are governed.

To promote societies built around people's genuine needs,
what the report calls '*five new pillars* of the people-centred world
order' is of paramount importance. The first two, which interest
me personally in congruence with my presentation, are the
following:

1. New concepts of human security that stress security of the
people, not just of the nation and the territory. This means
accelerated disarmament, using defence cuts to boost human
development. The means is the UN's increasing intervention to
provide more human security in countries where people are
fighting within the countries rather than between countries.

259

2. New strategies of sustainable human development that weave development around people, not people around development.

The Human Development Report 1993 focuses on participation as a key to human development (a new shift from the conventional line of thinking). Quoting again Principle 20 of the declaration on environment and development from Earth Summit 1992, at Rio: 'Women have a vital role in environmental management and development. Their full participation is therefore essential to achieve sustainable development.'

### Ideological and Political Subordination of Women

The issue of gender has yet to gain adequate attention in development planning for India's large population of Tribals, the Adivasis. Not withstanding Article 15 (3) which empowers the state to make special provisions for women and children in order to help them achieve the fundamental rights of 'equality before law' as laid down in Article 14 of the Constitution, Adivasi women remained the most deprived and neglected section of the population. While the reasons for this neglect vary across region and tribes, part of the plight stemmed from the general perception that Adivasi women are a distinct category whose conditions are distinct from those in the mainstream society. The seemingly egalitarian ethos of the Adivasi social organisation and relative autonomy of the women in personal and economic matters in many Adivasi societies created an impression that Adivasi women do not suffer from gender discrimination.

That this egalitarianism is a compulsion of subsistence level production, is apparent from the widening gender gap which occurs with economic differentiation and modernisation. This implies that gender inequality is not an alien phenomenon among Adivasis but is obscured by their poor economic condition which forces men and women to cooperate and share in common productive activities. Sociological research on the family and kinship in India also shows that as the interaction of the Adivasis with the caste groups increases women's autonomy in the family, the workplace gradually erodes as they adapt the ideas and values of caste societies.

In many Adivasi societies women suffer from serious ideological and political subordination. Some of the examples I would like to cite may be already well-known. The Toda women are debarred from having anything to do with the buffaloes which are considered sacred animals. Among the Kota and the Santhals, women are forbidden to participate in communal and other rituals. Also, in the maintenance of community and public morality women have no role as these are functions of *Panchayats* from which women are traditionally excluded. Even the regional councils set up after Independence in some of the tribal areas have resisted the efforts of a few women to obtain any position on these bodies. A glaring instance of this kind of male hegemony can be found among some of the Adivasis of North-East India where, while women shoulder heavy reproductive and productive responsibilities (sometimes more than men) they are traditionally debarred from political participation as politics is defined as an arena for mature and physically fit (read: men) persons only. The exclusion of women from politics has not only affected their integration into the development process, it has also resulted in their isolation from the area of decision-making and policy formulation which in turn has contributed to the persistence of blatant gender bias in development policies.

Interestingly, the policy of protective discrimination which singles out the Adivasis, scheduled castes and other socially underprivileged sections of the population for constitutional safeguards has not only increased the polarisation between the Adivasis and the non-Adivasis, but in some ways it is detrimental to the interest of Adivasi women. While it is true that this policy has brought the issue of tribal development to the centre of the stage, it has also resulted in marginalising women's development from the planning process. To cite a recent example, the Seventy Third Constitutional Amendment, which places special emphasis on the empowerment of women and reserves one-third of the seats in the local *panchayats* for them, has been exempted from application in the majority of Adivasi areas on the grounds that these areas have their own local self-government and are adequately covered in the Fifth and Sixth Schedules of the Constitution. The fact that among many Adivasi societies women are excluded from participation in *panchayats*, and the fact that the Fifth and the Sixth Schedules are completely silent on the question of development or empowerment of women does not seem to worry the policymakers.

There appears to be a dual standard in the state's approach to tribal development, and this is amply demonstrated by its land and forest policies which show little respect to the special safeguards enshrined in the Fifth and Sixth Schedules on the rights of tribal people, the Adivasis. In the name of public purpose and economic development the state reserved the right to take away certain categories of land and forest from the people. For instance, the forest, consisting primarily of trees once saved by the women of the Chipko movement, are no longer accessible to them.

Based on a survey taken amongst Adivasis in Madhya Pradesh and Orissa in India, close to 47 per cent of Adivasis depend on 'minor forest produce' as their primary or secondary source of essentials and means of livelihood, yet are debarred from any access to the forest. The major 'minor forest produce', timber and some other items, go to urban Indians – its collection and smuggling often destroying the tribal area at an alarming rate. Paharia Adivasis, one of India's most backward and impoverished, have resorted to extensive tree-felling and deforestation to raise the few rupees they need to survive. Development programmes come and go, leaving no major impact. These are the consequences because development programmes rarely take into account the features and sentiments of the differing cultural uniqueness (source: Integrated Rural Development Programme for Paharias Distribution of cows).

Birhor, a nearly extinct tribe which was originally comprised of hunters, have much to offer us about rational utilisation of resources (environmental resources) as they have lived in complete harmony with the great jungles around them for ages. Their settlements did not normally exceed more than ten families in a certain area, all of them well-spread throughout the forest. This allows the different clusters of families fair access to the forest (home) and equal and just share of the game. According to the 1991 census, there are only 2,000 Birhors (whereas indigenous peoples number over 60 million); not even one Birhor child (not to mention a girl) goes to school.

Adivasis in India continue to be the weakest and usually the first targets of land grab, displacement or 'development'. A prime example is the Military Field Firing Range displacing inhabitants of 245 villages in and around Neterhat and the zoological parks in the Southern India.

It must also be emphasised that the major brunt of the state's land and forest policies fall on women. There is the case of Adivasis of Orissa who have been displaced three times due to the Hirakud dam project which has snatched away the means of traditional livelihood. The women have now no option but to sell firewood; (the following information was obtained first hand by a surveyor) in order to go through this daily chore, a 16 year old girl from a certain village had to walk 16 km to the forest and back to the village market carrying 25-40 kg of firewood on her head, only to fetch 5 or 7 rupees.

It is clearly evident that while the reservation of forests directly cuts into the resource base of women who largely depend on minor forest produce for their fuel, fodder, food and income, the acquisition of land by the state also triggers land alienation and impoverisation. This spells dangerous portents for the future of Adivasi women. The opening up of national boundaries and liberalisation of the economy would further accentuate their problem, for instance the provisions laid down for deep-sea fishing versus small indigenous traders.

## Gender Sensitivity

There is a dire need for the adoption of a gender sensitive approach in tribal development. Reflecting back on the Gandhian philosophy of production and development, 'not mass production but production by the masses' was his message. (However, this is neither the time nor the platform to advocate an ideological stand of one individual or the other). Partly as a result of the Earth Summit at Rio, the term *sustainable development* has become fashionable all over the world. It is apparent that decades of industrialisation and mass production have failed to produce sustainable development. Rather, they have led to environmental disaster and large-scale human misery.

The plight of material production as well as human development at Heavy Electrical Corporation (HEC), Ranchi, is only a drop in the ocean which robbed the Adivasis off their fertile paddy fields which have now reached a production level of nearly nil. There may be numerous examples of such cases.

Human Development Report 1991 included the following extract 'Development has to be woven around people not people around development. It has to be development of the people, by the people, for the people.'

A gender sensitive approach in tribal development is crucial because Adivasi women do not only suffer from the adverse impact of development, like their counterparts in non-Adivasi societies, but the majority of them also experience acute disability in gaining access to material and social resources such as nutrition, income, health and education.

Take education for instance: in Medak, a constituency in Andhra Pradesh from where the Prime Minister was elected, not even two out of every 100 Adivasi women are literate. Even seen in the light of the national scenario, where about 70 out of every 100 Indian women are illiterate, the plight of Adivasis is desperate. Using the land to population ratio, even though the rural areas account for three-fourths of the population, they receive (officially) fewer resources for education than the well-to-do, who have access to the privately managed 'quality' institutions located in urban areas and take away a large share of unreserved seats (*reserved seats* are meant to be exclusively for the Adivasis and other minority committees) in the professional institutions. Children from rural areas face great disadvantages due to the relative poor quality of the rural schools, the family background of poverty and social stigma that they are labled with. Adivasi girls and children have made considerable progress since the late 1970s and early '80s, although most of them are still on the bottom rung of the ladder of educational attainment. While the girls suffer social prejudice, as mentioned above, and are committed to the care of siblings and household chores, they also suffer from disabilities of which reservation policy in education and job opportunities is not the final solution. Currently, a majority of them suffer from the limitations of the first generation learners; those hailing from the rural setups also suffer from the after-effects of childhood malnutrition, a sense of social isolation, unsuitable work habits and lack of self confidence in realising their academic potential. To obviate the resulting psychological strain, special programmes are needed for enhancing their competence and facilitating their adjustment. The need of

*'A gender sensitive development programme ... is like investing in a recurring deposit, it meets a whole family and prepares ground for the whole next generation'. Bhilala woman and daughter, India. Photo: Diana Vinding*

the hour now seems to be not the scrapping or revision of the reservation policy but a greater effort to ensure that the greatest number possible enter the formal schooling stream.

At this point I am not trying to sound insensitive to indigenous knowledge and the handing down of traditional knowledge through the generations. The importance of maintaining and reviving indigenous knowledge and thoroughly embedding it in day to day life remains essential. Nevertheless, the ideology of motherhood, which emphasises women's psycho-physical and reproductive capacities, may clothe in an aura of prestige and status parts of the structure of patriarchy and male domination prevailing in the politico-juridic domain, thus ensuring their continued subordination.

Today, Adivasi women are also increasingly coming under the attack of domestic and public violence. The former is driven by the masochistic appeal to control female sexuality whereas the latter is rooted in caste and class prejudice. Analytically, these two forms of violence are interrelated: a direct fall out of the ideological and political subjugation of women. A situation resulting from absence and lack of education of Adivasi women, recently identified as a crisis, is that of the domestic helpers (unskilled women and young girls move from the rural or village settings to cities to look for means to survive). They are continually subjected to inhuman treatment and sexual harassment. Thus, what is urgently needed is the empowerment of women to counter the ideology of subordination and structure of domination within which they are shunned.

This is not to say that women's development can be delinked from the issue and development which affect the Adivasis, but systematic subordination of women inside and outside the family across cultures and the failure of the development paradigm to curb the increasing impoverisation of women do point to the necessity of a gender specific approach in development planning for the Adivasis.

A gender sensitive development programme does not meet a section of society of a particular generation, but it is instead similar to investing in a recurring deposit, it meets a whole family and prepares ground for the entire next generation. Consider the marginalised and underprivileged sectors, the Adivasis in which men and women are being subjected to oppression. Here women are the doubly oppressed ones. While education may resolve the issue of reviving value systems imbibed in various tribal cultures, it should also address some of the local issues such as witch hunting of Adivasis of Central India.

In India some (maybe only a handful) of the parachurch organisations involved in social work have come to the realisation that social concerns and especially issues related to Adivasis must be addressed. As their style is the holistic approach, they are working as awareness builders amongst other church-based organisations to make them aware and sensitive to social concerns and to put social, rural or tribal development on their respective agenda, besides their own work. Their efforts and experiments are met with encouraging feedback from Adivasi communities for having provided opportunities for women to read and write, giving them a chance to learn new skills and build confidence. By empowering the women in this way, women are provided with an ability to take a more active role in their own development, in resisting exploitation, becoming aware of their rights, building a healthy family and in organising their community for change.

In conclusion, I believe that a gender sensitive approach may prove to be just one step forward towards sustainable development, as it gives hope towards the development of not just one person or people but generations. From my personal experience, the participation of women in the ongoing movements has given an additional dimension to the sustainability of the movements. A case in point is that one of the inevitable factors in the people's movement for the protest against the Field Firing Range in Neterhat was that women and youth had been given some important participatatory and decision-making roles.

PEDRO GARCIA HIERRO

# REFLECTIONS ON INDIGENOUS
# SELF-DEVELOPMENT

I want to express my satisfaction with being part of an encounter that has gathered indigenous representatives from five continents. At the last moment, the speaker who was going to give this presentation announced that he would not be able to attend. Therefore, I have prepared some notes about the relationships between indigenous economy, or self-development, and external cooperation, taking inspiration from the title of the original presentation. The presentation was going to discuss 'The surprises of sovereignty' referring to the disillusionment with certain initiatives carried out by indigenous peoples who upon obtaining their territories initiated mining activities, began to exploit forestry resources or even entered into the profitable activity of speculation.

Surprises and disillusionment are always present in relations between foreign cooperation aid and indigenous peoples when this relationship is concerned with the issue of development. It is the consequence of the distortions of a strange play of images to which, frequently, indigenous peoples' economic initiatives must adjust if they want to gain access to the benefits of foreign cooperation.

## The Urgent Need for Economic Success

The indigenous movement of the Peruvian Amazon has worked arduously for two decades and has achieved considerable success in the opening up of political niches for dialogue with the surrounding society, as well as in the process of defining their principal grievances. In other American countries such as Bolivia, Ecuador, Mexico or Colombia, this indigenous movement has even become the protagonist of the renewal of popular social processes.

But if we ask ourselves about the success we had when we were to create new economic models or were going to strengthen indigenous creativity in order to respond to economic challenges of the day or, more simply, if we raise the question of the organisations' ability to resolve the most basic economic needs of their members, the panorama is different. The fact is that there is a significant difference between the success and diffusion of indigenous grievance platforms and the quality of life of the communities. Speaking of images, for example, the vision of a healthy and proud indigenous person, self-possessed, is more commonly disseminated but less frequently the case than that of the sick indigenous person, humiliated and dependent on *patrones*.

The issue of the economy is, however, of the utmost importance as the political evaluation American governments make of indigenous organisations is based on economic success. Many of the governments' shock policies, principally on the local level, are based on reports of ineffectiveness on the part of indigenous organisations as regards economic issues. On the other hand, any indigenous leader knows that political successes achieved during times of struggle could be reversed should solutions not be found for domestic economies as they face daily community life.

## Images and Development

A major distortion exists between images of the indigenous economy and the real setting in which the communities function. It concerns an aggressive political and economic framework in which national or transnational companies enjoy the freedom to essentially operate as they please. National legislation discharges them from all obligations and grants them the legal, economic and technical tools they need to prosper.

This model is perpetuated by the countries of the North, from where a great part of cooperation funds originate. It is the model that has made them prosperous. And although it does not lead to sweet dreams, it has allowed their bad conscience to rest comfortably.

And what is missing in this model? Solidarity, reciprocity, proper treatment of nature, labour satisfaction, self-development, cultural identity, sustainability, human development, equality and mutual respect. These are the deficiencies of the prosperous societies of the North. And these are the same issues that have become obligatory topics when evaluating support for indigenous peoples. Everything which Western economies have not been able to integrate and, as a consequence, discarded in order for them to develop, have subsequently become the dominant paradigms when evaluating indigenous development, the test of the 'truly indigenous'.

Thus, on the one hand, we have a real framework for the indigenous economies in which capitalism is seen with its most vicious features and absolutely free from constraint. On the other hand, a series of ideal images and paradigms affecting support to indigenous peoples is found. Both models have their origin and theoretical development in the countries of the North.

In the first context, indigenous peoples are an inconvenient obstacle to development; in the second, indigenous peoples are the panacea for the problems. This provokes a schizophrenia which infects indigenous economies and generates singular problems to the point of not knowing which to hold to: reality or desired reality. This is a problem because the economy is the terrain of clear thinking and ideas, not hypothetical constructions.

To illustrate the point does not require more than a simplification of the normal behaviour of the economic agents in contact with indigenous peoples. To start with, they are rated as poor, idlers and ignoramuses. Based on this, a development policy is proposed which excludes them and is aggressively predatory. When the disaster has already become irreversible, and when the 'development' destroys hundreds of hectares of forests, they turn to the indigenous people and treat them as sages and experts in the proper treatment of nature and then ask them to demonstrate these virtues in the management of their economic activities.

Ecology, that wailing wall of development, is accustomed to having, in the Amazon, the melancholy cadence of funeral songs. Industrialised societies become intoxicated with economy and they suffer ecological hangovers which they want to cure with a 'cooperation with the indigenous peoples pill'. Nobody assumes that intoxication is harmful in and of itself, and that an aspirin, in these cases, is nothing more than a placebo. Demanding a result from indigenous peoples in these conditions is, at the very least, abusive. If we compare the possibilities of economic success of an oil company and, just as an example, of an indigenous organisation, the perspective is pathetic at best. The oil companies have real rights that allow them to move about freely on indigenous lands, establish their services, drill, extract and transport their products. They have special taxation laws and accountants. They can mercilessly exploit their workers. They have the possibility to control the destination of their production. And, above all, they have a 'right to piracy' allowing them to pollute with absolute impunity. They are, after all, props of the economy.

The necessary conditions to practise 'their style of economy' have been provided. And in the case of the indigenous community? A surface soil title-deed is not sufficient to be able to maintain their type of economy. It is often not definitively secured; or it has been reduced to a minimum; or it is plagued by regulating norms and subject to servitude such as in cases where indigenous territories contain oil or minerals. The laws are not acquainted with the particularities of the indigenous economy and are usually a major obstacle in its development. Most of the time they are fighting to defend their resources from aggressions. Authorities and armed forces collaborate against them.

But, moreover, in the face of total liberal deregulation of the oil industry, the community is expected to be egalitarian, reciprocal, sustainable, self-sufficient, treat nature properly, maintain cultural identity, respect a human conception of development, etc., if it wants to obtain foreign cooperation aid. This is an additional ethical regulation which contrasts with the tacit consent to freedom of action for large corporations.

## Some Hypotheses for Indigenous Development with Identity

A concept which forms part of the package of paradigms for indigenous economies is self-development. This concept can be defined as the process which involves the indigenous people themselves in attaining an improvement in quality of life in order to guarantee transgenerational self-sufficiency and maintenance of control over territories and resources, without losing or damaging the cultural base which lays the foundation for the people.

We are speaking of control. We are speaking of indigenous people, from their own perspective, beginning to generate new and more effective answers, from a humane point of view, in order to resolve economic problems. This model assumes that the conditions have already been provided, that indigenous peoples have achieved a state of social tranquillity and a level of control of their resources which allows them to demonstrate a new type of economic approach which could serve as an example for us in an intercultural utopian society.

The reality is another story. The Amazonian process is extremely conflictive, very violent and not very propitious to control. The invasion is global, sped up. The number of players involved, together with the indigenous peoples, who determine the fate of the Amazonian forests is increasing in number, the network of interests is daily more complex, and decision-making centres are more distant and indefinite as each day passes. What chances does an indigenous people have of showing us the type of knowledge that we are requesting of them?

During the last five years, the Candoshi, Shapra, Shuar, Quichuaruna and Achual peoples of Alto Amazonas, in the northern rainforest of Peru, have achieved a high degree of organisation, and consequently initiated their entrance into a sustainable economy with identity. Overnight, they were informed that there exists a number of oil concessions, for a period of 30 or 40 years, that give corporations freedom of action in an area consisting of more than 2 million hectares occupied by indigenous people. Opposing the situation is not easy because it militarises the response. How is self-development going to be for the affected peoples in the decades to come?

How can self-development be asked of the Ashaninka people of the central rainforest who were successfully producing varieties of an approved organic export coffee until they suffered the loss of more than five thousand people, plus ten thousand displaced, as a result of the government's war with the Shining Path guerrilla movement over the last ten years? They are further confronted by a colonisation bent on producing coca in conjunction with drug trafficking in their territories.

The Harakmbut of the southern rainforest in Peru are estimated to have numbered 30,000 before the onslaught of rubber exploitation at the turn of the century. Since then they have been subject to the ravages of gold panning on the banks of the Karene and Inambari rivers and today total just over 1,500 persons.

273

Currently, the threat of large-scale oil exploration threatens the Amarakaeri Communal Reserve, one of their last territorial bastions.

The premise that indigenous self-development is possible is in most cases usually just a fictitious notion. It is almost certain that indigenous peoples could have shown us new economic paths, but nobody listened to them at the time they were able to do so. Indigenous peoples could have incorporated important concepts in economic theories. Rejecting the exploitation of man by man (which they condemn in capitalism) and of country by country (the definition of imperialism), indigenous peoples incorporate a healthy rejection of the exploitation of one generation by another (the transgenerational concept of traditional economies). The usual division and confrontation between work, capital and resources have given way to demands for one or another of the two main factors of production. In traditional economies there exists a demand for a third factor, nature, and a unified understanding without the factors being set up against each other. At any rate, what is certain is that many things have changed and would-be future Nobel Prize winners for work on indigenous economy are today devoted to fighting for their land.

I recently took part in a conference at which there was a search for new 'niches' for indigenous economies. For example, there was mention of the Inuit peoples' ice and possibilities of converting it into mineral water. In this context, the word niche was synonymous with opportunity. I then responded to the speaker with the example of the Huitoto invention of practical uses for rubber. This is a product that has provided many millions to many corporations, revolutionising the industry. In the case of the Huitotos, their invention cost the lives of nine out of every ten inhabitants. In this context, the synonym for niche is funeral. The same could be said today of that proverbial invention of the Ashaninka people, the *uña de gato* (cat's claw): its success has only resulted in a violent new wave of invaders.

It is not about searching for opportunities. They clearly exist. The real issue is about creating conditions so that indigenous people maintain control of their economic issues. And this does not occur because across the American Amazon indigenous peoples are colonised by those who are always able to rob them and seemingly are impelled to do so.

Thus a hypothesis for indigenous self-development can be put forth. Self-development will never come about as long as some degree of self-determination for indigenous peoples is not attained. The United Nations has already put into practice a process of decolonisation, but a second process is still lacking. Perhaps it is one with different characteristics, perhaps created under other parameters, but it must permit indigenous peoples to control their entire decision-making process, all their resources, all their culture, their innovations, their territories, who enters and who does not, establish the rules of the game, and define and apply their own law. Only then will we be able to expect the contributions of true indigenous self-development.

This is an essential requirement which means that if cooperation efforts seek to support indigenous self-development, they have to lay down very concrete goals in order to support – not only financially but politically as well – the processes of self-determination of each one of these peoples.

I want to leave this point here in order to return to the topic of images. But it is important to insist on another assumption that is present in all indigenous platforms: territorial security. Why this obsessive indigenous demand? In my view, this demand is realistic and sceptical towards ideas. Indigenous peoples know that discourses pass, economic theories as well, just like 'in' images and governments and their political proposals. But each piece of territory that they succeed in conserving or that they succeed in recovering puts them on top of the world and hope is kept alive.

Lands – as a demand which keeps alive the possibilities of being a people – and self-determination – as the ultimate struggle which will allow these peoples, when the time is right, to specify their possibilities and contributions to the rest of humanity – are the foundations of indigenous demands throughout the world. It seem obvious that they have a clearer vision of them.

## Attributes and Essences

Returning to the question of images, over the last years images have become of great importance for American indigenous peoples, procuring alliances and opening niches for the recognition of their rights. In fact, at the end of the 1970s ethnic and ecological repercussions in the capitalist economy of developed countries produced a sentiment of revulsion. In the search for more humane models, many young people looked back to indigenous peoples and pointed out their attributes. These attributes produced strong feelings and sympathy, helping to open doors to the indigenous movement.

It is necessary to make it clear that the emotions of the countries of the north are of great importance in the countries of the south. With respect to indigenous peoples, there are almost no American governments interested in protecting their rights. American *criollismo* prides itself in direct relation to the *conquistadores* and in inverse relation to their proximity to native people. Politicians conceal their indigenous features and had it not been for exceptions, it is possible that the process of conquering would have been completed once and for all (remember the slogan on the walls of Quito which said: 'the only good Indian is a dead Indian').

The indigenous policies of the governments of the South respond, almost unfailingly, to the pressures of the North. These pressures impart emotions which respond to images generated, in many cases, by intellectuals and solidarity organisations. That is why it is extremely important that images and emotions are carefully selected. Up till the present time, as concerns the indigenous question, images and emotions have developed with regard to attributes and not essence. And that makes support fragile or dangerously conditioned. For example, indigenous peoples have been supported for many years because they take conscientious care of the woodlands, maintaining its natural purity. But when due to circumstances it becomes necessary for indigenous people to fell timber in order to survive, kill animals for food, or do the unmentionable, breed cattle, the image is resented, positive feelings end, and political support is deflected toward natural intangible areas, within whose objectives indigenous people again become an obstacle.

At other times, as well, the images revolve around physical features, external attributes or false conceptions. I believe that one of the greatest deceptions of many people who approach indigenous peoples with this devote attitude is when they verify how much they often resemble the poor who wander around

*'Self-development will never come about as long as some degree of self-determination for indigenous peoples is not attained'. Boca Inambari, Harakmbut community in Madre de Dios, Peru. Photo: Alejandro Parellada*

their cities (in many cases, African Asian or American indigenous people, of course).

Thus, these types of images can work against indigenous peoples' interests. It is important to generate emotions about the essence and more lasting or unconditional support. Indigenous peoples from the African deserts, from the frozen steppes of the Arctic circle and from the Amazonian plains have spoken at this conference. The similarity of their problems is amazing. What these problems have in common is not ecology, traditional dress or spiritual songs. Nor is it marginalisation. Their common problems are related to exclusion: political, cultural and economic exclusion. This exclusion is also present when the alternative is integration conditioned by ethnocidal factors which reject them as a different people, or genocide, which threatens to exterminate them. This is an essential problem. At this point support for indigenous grievances is then framed in contexts like justice or decolonisation, of much more permanence than enthusiasm which hinges on aesthetics or other passing fashions.

These feelings clearly bring about changes in the countries of the North. The mention of decolonisation of the indigenous peoples affects economic interests of the developed countries and that's another story. But we will return to this issue later.

For the moment, I would like to focus on the idea of the importance of images – and the emotions that they provoke – in supporting the political process of indigenous peoples and the importance of selecting them with seriousness and with regard to essence, rather than attributes.

We all agree that the Swiss are the most skilful watchmakers in the world, but nobody would dare to lay the foundation of Swiss national rights by using that quality as a basis. Nobody would justify razing Swiss forests, enslaving their citizens or taking their possessions for the sole reason that they did not wish them to continue making more watches. Swiss national rights have intrinsic roots laid down in the rights of peoples.

The same is true for indigenous peoples. Their rights are intrinsic and, at the moment, they are denied them. We will speak more of this when we discuss the issue of self-determination. Once they have reached the same level as the rest of the world's peoples, the Shapras will show the Swiss their careful and undeniable knowledge of how to care for the Amazon rainforests, and the Swiss will proudly display their watchmaking art, the Dutch their tulips and the Spanish their flamenco. And all will be happy to contribute to the improvement of the quality of life of our global village.

Please excuse this excess of images. But I believe that we all prefer a happy ending, whatever the story may be.

### Cooperation for Development and Indigenous Involvement

The indigenous movement, which has come more and more to define itself as a political movement, has developed modern indigenous organisations as a way to become involved with the surrounding society. It is not needed here to make a profound study of the characteristics which define the evolution of these organisations, but it seems convenient to clarify, once again, the effect of images on their effectiveness.

I would like to advance that, in general, indigenous organisations make their debut with heroic actions. A common example is crucial struggles for land, dignity and self-defence. They are moments in which the people are a single unit, moments in which nobody thinks of money or material goods, moments in which they make real the true and ideological understanding of 'indigenous'. These heroic moments give them strength and lead to a great respect for their surroundings.

For the North, it is these moments which move them and motivate support for these peoples capable of laying down their life for dignity. It is not uncommon to think of them immersed in tension, constantly committed to heroic attitudes. Daily nature and the petty needs of each day tend to be forgotten. And this happens not in the singular environment of idealism, but in the real setting of the violent aggression of market economies.

Indigenous organisations must attend to their members' needs if they want to maintain unity and strength for times of struggle. Because what these organisations will come to signify in the context of exclusion must be understood. They are not only trade organisations. If they have overcome the aggression of a merchant, the debilitating cultural invasion of a church and slave exploitation by a timber merchant or *patrón*, they should obtain the essential supplies which those social actors gave to their members (rope, seeds, schools, ham, a local market, remedies, communications, salt, mobility, etc.). And they are asked for even more because if the state excludes the communities, they turn to the organisations to fill the gap. On the other hand, it is not unusual that, in the face of a heroic process – especially if it is considered dangerous – existing state interests will enter the zone and offer development programmes which were never before offered and which allude to the ineffectiveness and lack of initiative on behalf of the organisation to solve basic domestic problems. They incite division and confusion. The *patrones*, merchants and churches do the same.

Then the moment of truth arrives. It is necessary to offer alternatives. It is clear that it is necessary that alternatives allow autonomy to be maintained. But, precisely what is lacking in the communities are alternatives capable of competing with a flow of investments like those that are within reach of the rest of the social actors intent on recovering control lost due to the intervention of the organised movement. The bottom line is that there is no money. But most of the alternative sources of income that are within reach or are not autonomous are in opposition to positive aims of the new organising era. And it is here that a new story begins, that of relations with foreign cooperation agencies. Before continuing, it is perhaps necessary to clarify certain ambiguities. The only monetary economies in many towns of the Peruvian Amazon have their origins in work with merchants and, later, the entry of economists from financial schools. This was a contribution which redistributed and created new power structures around those who entered a relationship with the foreign agent.

As the market's only offer, these privileged labourers had to adapt to the behaviour demanded of them and, at least in appearance, they did. The qualities of many of the teachers shaped by the Summer Institute of Linguistics for example, are the necessary qualities in order to gain access to an economic resource conditioned by a certain way of behaving.

A crucial moment in the break with the church was the suspicion that resources came from people whose intention was to help indigenous populations. The mediation was thus a widely known anathema, with all the justice on one side. And so it was that the indigenous organisations began a period characterised by direct relations with cooperation agencies.

It is now time to pose a question: how much of a change was there in this period of direct relations between cooperation agencies and indigenous organisations?

When an organisation requests help in order to heal the sick or for the purchase of medicine, a problem already overcome in the North thanks to their sophisticated social security system, the response is usually doubt about whether or not the issue is one of welfare or a denouncement of the reappraisement of indigenous health systems, previously satanised. When organisations request resources in order to acquire fuel and to be able to travel along the rivers in regions as big as some European countries – whose asphalt-covered road systems shorten all distances – they respond with doubts concerning the need for so much fuel if it concerns production programmes, the exploitation of timber or the raising of livestock, or else they quickly doubt its sustainabilıt̩, reject the true indigenous character of the initiative, or it ıs argued that it is going to create some sort of social hierarchy. A programme such as eco-tourism will have effects on cultural control. Assistance to a prisoner is not sustainable since the need for support will constantly be repeated. Patents are an aberration for the indigenous way of thinking. Property is contrary to a traditional vision. The sale of handicrafts should be agreed upon by the entire people because they are cultural heritage. It is inappropriate to introduce trade systems for manufactured products such as soap and others because it is nothing less than the introduction of capitalism, etc.

But nobody investigates other alternatives or climates as concerns how indigenous initiatives could enter into the capitalist world. And while we continue helping them to be perfect, *patrones* extract their wood, eco-tourism companies invade the communities, small-time dealers and merchants make a killing with surcharges, colonists obtain title-deeds to their lands, patents for indigenous products multiply, several hundred indigenes die from epidemics, the limited savings of labourers goes to paying for travel fares, regular contact between organisations and their members becomes unthinkable, other people's cattle invade all corners of the rainforest, and indigenous prisoners rot in gaol. And in this way the inevitable comes about. Indigenous organisations are forced to understand what the cooperation agencies want of them. And they begin to cover up their real needs in order to adapt themselves to the set of ideas acceptable to the agencies. This is no different from what occurred with the church or the politics of the moment.

It is the stage of cooperative surrealism. Solidarity sectors in capitalist countries deflected the view of the defects of their own economic systems, and they toss the ball to the indigenous peoples so that, without a foundation of at least minimally secured rights, without previous experience in the mercantile world, they resolve, within an unrestricted capitalist framework, the ethical problems of development.

Let us sum up. On the one hand, we have cooperation agencies which do not attack, at least where it can do any good, systems that make the expression of an indigenous economy impossible. On the other hand, we have an indigenous discourse which adapts to foreign demands, but in the process progressively distances itself from the reality it is supposed to represent.

On and off, specific lines of projects guaranteed to succeed appear. Words like ecology, genus and biodiversity appear for a time and then they go out of style again without having touched the political essence which beats in each one of these topics.

Let us remember that the pre-selection of topics and accepted ways to deal with them, the locations and dates in which fora are held to discuss them – with indigenous participation, of course – the discourse which develops them, the adequate amount of funding for the projects, etc., is nothing less than control.

And of course the speakers to represent the indigenous people are also selected because elders from remote communities (that is to say those who would best resemble the favoured image of the indigene) would not be able to understand the majority of the discussion as such and how it is dealt with in the world of cooperation aid.

The specialised interlocutors, who have made a great effort in order to understand what is demanded, often end up assuming a post which requires experience and certain expertise. Power becomes concentrated and is perpetuated, with few possibilities for a change-over. Additionally, they distort internal relations, creating real organisational problems which end up weakening the movement.

The result is a new type of mediation which masquerades as indigenous discourse. Let us clarify the terms. An intermediary is not a mediator. And the intermediary is just as much an intermediary regardless of whether or not it is an indigenous or a white person. Mediation, as a beneficial process, has no race.

Let me add an explanatory note: we must ask ourselves if this model does not also select the type of consultants. Along with indigenous people there are many more philosophers and academics/writers, including myself, than there are specialists and economists. It is a pity that these professionals are not being provided the opportunity to benefit from indigenous virtues and simultaneously help them develop.

In sum, it is possible that the failures of some organisations can be attributed, to a great extent, to the cooperation model.

**Getting Closer to Needs: A Return Trip from Wonderland**

It has become necessary to readapt cooperation systems. I think that a first step is to return to the needs and real problems and analyse their solution in the real-life setting in which they occur.

If indigenous peoples were to make an effort to understand what it is they were being asked they wanted, I do not think it would be so difficult for agencies to make an effort to understand what the indigenous people really want.

There have been distinct phases in the modern indigenous movement. At the beginning, when the organisation arose as a result of despair in the face of being excluded and marginalised almost to the point of extinction, very modest leaders appeared, with a very poor discourse, politically speaking, apparently acculturated as well. The alliances with missionaries, merchants or teachers were both local and based on a relationship of dependency. The type of support that was solicited was very limited and with pretensions to assistance. They appealed to sentiments of poverty and the like. They asked for a small school – to learn Spanish in order to protect themselves – or that a few hectares of land be respected. These requests were ignored, but they did explicitly state the needs of the time and the leaders were in close touch with those they represented.

With this space opened up by the leaders' first advances, a strong and proud indigenous movement emerged which has achieved major successes and has introduced a problem to the world which has come to be recognised as one of humanity's pending issues. They changed the relationships and alliances, acquiring political space previously thought unattainable, and they continued consolidating the platforms of grievances. The role of many leaders has been fundamental in this phase. They reached far, but their discourse also became condensed at such great heights and, in the real political arena, those indigenous people with their feet still on the ground were scarcely involved.

Many organisations now feel the urgent need to enter a third stage, a dialectical one, in which the leadership and the right to speech returns to the rank and file so that everyone can benefit from the movement's new possibilities.

With respect to cooperation efforts, if in the first stage they were charitable, integrating and set out to acculturate and create a patronage system, in the second stage being more ideological and not very realistic, they created conditions favourable for highly individualistic leadership.

It is important, then, to redistribute the message in order to come to know, without additional rhetoric, the problems of indigenous peoples. Instead of emphasising the act of discourse, we must stress the existence of horizontal, participatory approaches, liberating the organisations and the same leaders from the solitary or individualistic leadership that is the consequence of the model and which unfortunately characterises many of the indigenous organisations of the Amazon.

With respect to the topic of indigenous economy, or self-development, as the title of this talk indicates, I would like to raise some topics for discussion.

If the solidarity sectors of developed countries wish to support the self-development of indigenous peoples, it is understood that they must have their reasons. But if those reasons are founded on the opinion that indigenous peoples show a different, more humane path for the economy, then they should lay down coherent goals in order to create processes directed towards opening up that alternative through joint strategies, before sitting down like critical spectators to review the actions of actors who are unsure as to what to think of the workings of this new economic order in which they are compelled to act.

If self-development presupposes a minimum of control over economic conditions, it is necessary to support the indigenous peoples' struggle to gain the degree of self-determination that they demand in their countries. Self-determination has been defined, let us remember, as a cardinal right without which it is not possible to exercise other human rights.

If our economic system contains defects which dehumanise, let us work together to humanise them. Indigenous peoples will have much to gain, even if the events take place far away from their lands.

If we think that the models and approaches of indigenous economies are an example, let us work with technical experts, economists as well as, why not, images and ideas so that this alternative vision becomes a reality within the economic model which we are more familiar with than indigenous labourers.

Demanding that indigenous peoples continue in their traditional manner within a framework of economic injustice in which developed countries benefit is, I believe, a contradiction.

At the risk of seeming excessively hard, I want to provide an example that could shed light on the type of cooperation that I am referring to.

At this encounter I have found out that Switzerland has a national stock of trees which has remained unaltered for almost a hundred years. That demonstrates a great ability to control and extraordinary ecological care, something which, in the last hundred years, few indigenous peoples could have achieved. Then, why not explain to the indigenous peoples how they have achieved it? What type of legislation was passed and what are the civic rights and obligations which govern its usage? What prohibitions and responsibilities exist? In this way, indigenous peoples could learn that in Switzerland there are norms and laws which Swiss companies do not respect when operating in indigenous territories (and if it is not understood to what I refer, ask the Chilean Mapuche whose forests were converted into woodchips by Swiss lumber companies and others, taking advantage of laws passed during the inhumane Pinochet dictatorship). In this way, so that the Mapuches could show them their own ecological conceptions, a significant help would be to compel the companies of those countries to apply the same policies and the same respect demanded here in their oversees operations.

In the meantime, it seems inappropriate to deny support to those who are forced to plunder their forests in order to earn a pittance working in these companies.

In reference to this and in order to conclude, a very cruel story which circulates in Lima comes to mind. They tell that Father Christmas arrives at one of the very poor shanty towns in Lima loaded with gifts. He asks the children 'did you drink your milk today'? The children who only know the taste of milk from their earliest childhood memories answer in unison: 'Nooooo'. And Father Christmas, very angry, replies to them: 'then, there are no gifts'.

ANDREW GRAY

# DEVELOPMENT PRACTICE AND
# INDIGENOUS PEOPLES

The recent increased interest in the rights of indigenous peoples at the United Nations and its specialised agencies has led to several national initiatives in the field of development. During the UN Year of Indigenous Peoples in 1993, and now during the International Decade, countries such as Denmark, Norway, and the Netherlands have established or are in the process of drafting development policies targeted at improving the lives of indigenous peoples. These welcome initiatives are the result of two decades of lobbying by indigenous peoples and support organisations, and take the form of specific provisions for indigenous peoples within development policy and, in some cases, the allocation of funded programmes to promote their well-being.

Indigenous peoples appeared as specific subjects of development within the context of a discussion in the late 1970s about 'alternative' development or 'another development' (Hettne, 1982: pp.75ff). The small-scale, need-oriented, self-reliant and ecologically sensitive elements of indigenous development fitted well into the criteria established in publications about alternative approaches development (Nerfin, 1977). However, as resources become more available for indigenous peoples, agencies working with indigenous peoples have had to reflect on the extent to which indigenous self-development consists of a continuation of current rural and urban development principles or whether it demands specific techniques and methods of its own. This paper aims at contributing to these necessary reflections by tracing the contours of indigenous self-development and how it relates to contemporary development practice.

## Characteristics of Indigenous Development
Agencies and individuals working with indigenous peoples' development need to be sensitive to characteristic features of indigenous identity which are increasingly becoming central in the conceptualisation of the indigenous movement. This is not necessarily because

all indigenous peoples have the same intrinsic similarities, but because, as the indigenous movement spreads through the world, its participants increasingly recognise and gain a growing political self-consciousness. The characteristics reviewed here are neither universal nor comprehensive, yet they provide an insight into some of the recurring features in indigenous self-development.

Indigenous peoples' worlds are frequently described as holistic. This does not mean that each culture is totally integrated and isolated from the rest of the universe; on the contrary, every indigenous community has, to some extent, connections to other peoples and the national society, even those who are not recognised as 'in contact'. Holistic refers rather to the inter-connections between different aspects of indigenous world views. Whereas this is the case for many, if not all peoples, it is clearly articulated by indigenous peoples because of the strong and pervasive influence of the invisible spirit world, their close relationship with the environment and their distinct socio-cultural formations.

Resources and territories are intimately bound up with human and spiritual relations through the classification and behaviour of human and plant or animal species. Human inter-relationships also reflect relationships between the human and natural worlds through forms of reciprocity which ensure the continuation of life. It is difficult to carry out any action in one area of indigenous life without there being repercussions in others. For this reason, rural development programmes which concentrate exclusively on economic production and commercialisation, could well, in an indigenous context, encounter unintended consequences in other aspects of life.

Indigenous peoples have special relationships to features of their world which form parts of their collective identity and provide them with the means of life. For example, indigenous peoples' territories are frequently held collectively in trust from ancestors to descendants with the spirit world acting as guarantors. Households have access to resources in agreement with the rest of the community or people, and have the right to use the resources as long as they need, in accordance with the appropriate indigenous authorities.

Indigenous peoples vary considerably in how they solve the relationship between collective and personal ownership – some political organisations are more fixed and authoritarian than others – but all share a concern about alienating their territories to outsiders. In statements to the International Labour Organisation in its 1986 meeting of experts on indigenous peoples this relationship to resources was presented as a defining characteristic (Burgess 1987:136-7). The effect of this is that, for indigenous peoples, territories are inalienable which means that no person has the authority to hand them over to outsiders on a permanent basis.

When discussing other forms of collective property with indigenous peoples, the same principle applies. Indigenous knowledge and cultural heritage are usually conceptualised as pertaining to the people as a whole and not specifically to individuals. The effect of this is that inspiration, creativity and discoveries are added to the collective corpus of knowledge pertaining to the heritage of each indigenous people. Clearly, as with certain resources, aspects of knowledge will be shared, but in the same way as 'territory', heritage as a collective whole is inalienable. For this reason the commoditisation of culture can become problematic as it breaks up a collective heritage in the vain attempt to make it quantifiable. However, the extent to which the notion of inalienability is applied has to rest exclusively with the indigenous peoples concerned and not with outsiders.

The variety of indigenous culture is breath-taking. Indigenous peoples frequently live in parts of the world with high biodiversity and there is an interesting correlation between these areas and those with high rates of indigenous cultural diversity. Of the 5,000 or more peoples in the world over 90 per cent are indigenous. In parts of the Amazon, for example, each river or tributary contains a people with different customs, language and religions from their neighbours. Diversity is a crucially important principle for understanding indigenous peoples.

The importance of diversity becomes even more marked when looking at the relationship between the collective and personal aspects of indigenous life. Even though collective aspects of life are crucial for their survival, this should not create the mistaken idea that there is no room for personality and individualism. On the contrary, in many parts of the world, indigenous peoples are fiercely individualistic and internal alliances and conflicts are quite unpredictable from the perspective of outsiders.

The characteristics reviewed here are common throughout the indigenous world and can be tabulated in the following form:

**Indigenous Peoples**: Characteristics for Reflection in Development Work

**Holistic**: Social, natural and spiritual interconnections;

**Inalienability:** Territory, resources and knowledge part of a heritage;

**Diversity**: Between peoples, communities and individuals.

**Current Methodologies of Development and Indigenous Peoples**
The distinguishing features of indigenous peoples reviewed hitherto complicate the existing methodologies of rural and urban development. Since the Declaration of Cocayoc in 1974, development studies have experienced a gradual decline in the influence of large-scale theories such as those based on principles of modernisation or dependency (Schuurman 1993). The result has been a two-fold movement in development work. On the one hand there is an increased concentration on small-scale and participatory programmes putting local peoples first and emphasising self-reliance (Chambers 1983, Burkey 1993). On the other hand, there is a tendency for organisations to stream-line their development work, making it more efficient and cost-effective. Frequently, these two approaches come into conflict.

The participatory approach strives to listen to local people, respect their knowledge and construct a development partnership based on trust. The aim is to constitute 'reversals' whereby all disadvantaged sectors of society can overcome the poverty, discrimination and oppression which face them. The effect of the participatory approach is to slow down the speed of development to reflect the needs and desires of the recipients. A key method in this approach is Participatory Rural Appraisal (PRA) which has become prevalent in the 1990s (Chambers 1994). This involves working with local communities, often through visual mapping of communities and their problems, to produce analyses and proposals for seeking solutions. Based on ethnographic techniques, the method seeks to establish a rapport in less time than traditional anthropological fieldwork. Even so, the procedures need time and effort to be completed successfully (Mascarenhas et al. 1991).

At the same time as the participatory approach has increased in influence throughout development circles, the need for efficiency, streamlining and cost-cutting has given rise to several methods which strive to speed up even more the development process. Projects are now usually written in the logical framework style which combines a systems approach based on problem-solving, the classification of causality and establishing checks. By standardising development jargon and the use of tables, projects can be fitted into schema which make administration much easier.

As international agencies strive to decentralise their administration, an increasing amount of development work is being put out to tender for consultancy companies to implement. Many of these are subsidiaries of multinational corporations which have their own agendas and interests. At the same time, the need for efficient evaluation and monitoring has necessitated a search for quick methods of appraisal. The Rapid Rural Appraisal (RRA) method was developed in the 1980s, prior to Participatory Rural Appraisal, and is still very influential, using a mixture of systems analysis, observation and semi-structured interviews.

In spite of the fact that these two methodological approaches have to work together, they make uneasy bed-fellows. The 'participatory' approach advocates drawing the recipients of development into a closer partnership where development emerges through a relationship of trust, while the 'systems' or 'investigation' approach treats development as a process which is carried out by the donor on local peoples. The contradiction within current development practices rests on these contrasting methods, both of which have relevance in the context of indigenous peoples but which, if not adapted, can lead to unintended and unpredictable outcomes for projects. The only way in which these potential problems can be addressed is through careful preparation, sensitivity and flexibility on the part of the donor and consent, control and complete understanding and agreement on the part of the indigenous recipients.

Working with indigenous peoples would be impossible without extensive experience of a participatory approach. This is not to say that logical, cost-effective and efficient work can not be done with indigenous peoples; however, the key concept is to work with local indigenous peoples, not working on them. For this reason, the indigenous experience challenges both PRA and RRA in several areas. Indigenous peoples argue consistently and vociferously that they do not want to be consulted and participate in a development which is outside of their control and is without their consent.

This means that all development activities which take place with indigenous peoples have to be formulated within a collaborative framework. Each project or programme needs to have their full and informed consent which includes the right to veto its presence on their territories. Furthermore, development programmes should ultimately be under their control. This does not mean that donor policies and regulations need be ignored, but rather that they are accepted through a constructive agreement negotiated on a fair and equitable basis.

In certain circumstances the question of consent and control may lead to difficulties in projects, particularly where outside ethnocentricism, power relations and authoritarian attitudes become mixed in with rules and regulations. In this case the technocratic aspects of development practices can superimpose a new level of oppression on top of the problems already facing indigenous peoples. Nevertheless, providing that projects are well-prepared, transparent and conditions are agreed in advance, potential problems can be anticipated. If unintended problems arise during implementation, administrative flexibility becomes paramount in seeking solutions and adapting the project to changing conditions.

Indigenous development is usually carried out in a small-scale and culturally distinct environment. Donors therefore need to be sensitive and to appreciate the cultural and political difficulties affecting indigenous peoples in addition to incorporating other focal points of development work such as gender, age and environmental concerns. Such a wide variety of options and priorities can sometimes present problems; donors may not agree with each other; they may have differences of opinion with the recipients; and conflicts may arise among the recipients themselves. Sensitivity here means that all sides need to be prepared to give time and patiently strive to seek appropriate solutions based on the mutually agreed goals of the project.

The participatory approach strongly advocates a 'bottom-up' view of development projects. However indigenous development work should also be seen from an 'inside-out' perspective. This means that programmes and projects should be initiated from inside communities or indigenous organisations and not imposed from outside. Furthermore the term refers to the need for non-indigenous field-workers in development projects to turn themselves 'inside-out' by becoming self-aware and self-critical of their activities.

Projects with indigenous peoples should be seen as constructive agreements which lead to a process of learning, understanding and training for both donors and recipients. An analogy here is that the agreements made between indigenous organisations and agencies should be seen more as 'treaty' relationships between equal parties rather than business contracts between a patron and client.

The methodological factors which should be grafted onto the participatory and systems approaches to development practice are therefore:

1. Indigenous consent and control;
2. Administrative flexibility;
3. Political and cultural sensitivity;
4. Working from the inside-out;
5. Project agreements as 'treaties' rather than business contracts.

**'Cumulative Dialectic' Strategies for Indigenous Development**
The concept of development for indigenous peoples is distinct because it is based on the implementation of indigenous rights which focus not just on individual but, even more forcefully, on collective rights. As indigenous peoples articulate the injustices which they suffer, they seek solutions to the problems which face them in the form of the assertion of their rights. This provides the foundation for subsequent development activities.

Indigenous self-development is the implementation of rights in order to restore their control over their lives and territories. This section looks at three areas which embrace the subject matter of the majority of indigenous development projects:

territorial recognition and resource use; cultural strengthening and its implications for health and education; and organisational development.

Each area has a limitless number of strategies for development purposes which have been condensed here into a three-fold dialectical process. This process is based on the encounter between indigenous peoples and the influences of non-indigenous peoples. During the history of contact, indigenous peoples frequently want certain benefits from the national society but wish to protect themselves from other influences which they see as harmful.

These strategies of development are aimed at providing a framework for indigenous peoples to determine which elements of non-indigenous knowledge and practice they wish to incorporate through development projects and which ones they wish to reject. The decisions will vary according to the people, organisation, community or even household. However, a dynamic dialectical process is necessary to ensure that indigenous peoples themselves have the initiative and that the development is inside-out.

*The process of cumulative dialectical strategies has a common pattern:*
a) Start with what the local people know and need; strengthen this as the foundation for the programme.

b) On this basis facilitate indigenous recipients to determine what, if any, aspects of non-indigenous development they wish to incorporate into the programme – such as forms of production, health and education services or organisational training. This means that a project will necessarily need some collaborative indigenous research, training and experimentation within its framework.

c) The culmination of the process consists of each people, organisation or community (as appropriate) deciding how the internal and external aspects of their world should inter-relate and implementing the result.

These three aspects of indigenous development strategies are not stages, each of which has to be completed before moving onto the next. They are part of a dialectical and cumulative process which reflects the encounter between indigenous and non-indigenous worlds. The first part of the process establishes the basis onto which all outside influences will be related and then places the initiative on indigenous peoples to determine what elements they wish to incorporate into their lives. In this way it is possible to focus precisely on the open concept of self-determination within development practice.

## 1. Territories and resources – indigenous sustainable development

Throughout the world indigenous peoples suffer from the invasion of their territories and the plundering of their resources. Indeed, for many, development is a negative concept because it is frequently used as an excuse to deprive indigenous peoples of their livelihood (Sambo 1992:172). Poverty and hunger are encountered among indigenous peoples, not through over-population or over-exploitation of their resources, but from a social injustice which deprives them of control over their territories. Remedies for this problem can be found through a process of several strategies which should guarantee indigenous peoples' capacity to survive physically and secure their development in the future.

The first part of the process consists of strategies for indigenous peoples' sustainable development and consists of securing their territorial rights. All indigenous peoples have their own territories which they recognise; however, the problem arises when governments and members of the national society do not recognise these rights. The most appropriate method of securing indigenous rights consists of governmental recognition, preferably constitutionally. Projects working in this area need to understand state legislation and develop participatory methods whereby indigenous peoples themselves can demarcate their own territories and map them. This adds a new dimension to the notion of mapping in PRA, which concentrates on mapping for practical project planning. For indigenous peoples, mapping constitutes the basis of the legal recognition of their territories and resources. Included in any programme should be a legal territorial defence plan to ensure that future invasions are prevented so that the achievements of the territorial consolidation are not lost.

The second set of strategies for indigenous sustainable development is to secure a subsistence base for each community. The model used by a project will have to rely heavily on the particular social organisation of each community and discuss at length an approach which is favoured by all members. The model could be centralised at the level of the indigenous peoples, the community or the household, and this diversity of possibilities has to be considered from the very beginning of the project.

One approach which interests many indigenous peoples is the revival of old species and production methods which have been discontinued or forgotten, but which communities want to acquire again. There is always a marked diversity of crops which indigenous communities have used in the past and which can provide a basis for future use. Superimposed on this are crops which communities could grow but are inclined to buy from local markets. Alternative methods of production can all help to increase the self-reliance of each community. In this way indigenous peoples can work out the relationship they want between inside and outside production methods.

The third part of the process covers the need for indigenous peoples to control the way in which they relate to the market economy. Most indigenous peoples need access to financial resources. Commercialisation can, unfortunately, quickly gain the notion of a panacea for all ills. Studies completed by the Indigenous Coordinating Body of the Amazon Basin (COICA pers. comm.) demonstrate that commercialisation projects among indigenous peoples are of limited success unless territorial rights and a sustainable subsistence base are guaranteed. However, with these secured and the potential for sustainable access to the market economy ascertained, indigenous peoples can establish themselves locally from a position of strength, not weakness.

In this way indigenous access to resources, coupled with a sustainable and ecologically sensitive subsistence production, complemented by a well-researched and carefully controlled relationship with a cash economy, can establish conditions which will go some way to ameliorate the poverty facing indigenous peoples.

## 2. Local 'knowledges'

This heading recognises the diversity within and between indigenous peoples as to what constitutes their knowledge. It is important not to think of indigenous knowledge as a single criterion based on intellectual capacity. For indigenous peoples, the variety of ideas, hypotheses, theories and practical knowledge creates what could be seen as 'knowledges' or situational social practices where knowledge is embedded not only in intellectual speculation but in the actual activities of daily life and experience (Hobart, 1993).

The problem which indigenous peoples face from outsiders is the disrespect shown to and ignorance of their knowledge and experience. This affects their right to freedom of expression. The result is that many programmes are one-sided and only take non-indigenous factors into consideration – this can be particularly problematic in health and education programmes. As with territories and resources, there are several strategies in the cumulative dialectic of indigenous development which can guide people working on indigenous knowledge thereby implementing the rights which are so frequently violated.

The first set of strategies consist of collaborative work with indigenous peoples to secure and revitalise their cultural identity, religion and spirituality. Threats to the integrity of indigenous peoples should be taken into account in programmes and projects by providing support for strengthening their cultural practices. For example, elders and their youngers are responsible for keeping traditions alive by passing knowledge across the generations. Frequently, with the invasion of indigenous peoples' territories and the imposition of values from the national society, indigenous peoples have difficulty in keeping the relationship alive. Cultural revival, recuperation or revitalisation are preconditions for any projects which work with new ideas – no matter how progressive.

When indigenous peoples are confident that outsiders respect their views of life, it becomes much easier to incorporate the second range of strategies which concern a free and informed dialogue about their needs and desires. This will involve discussion and collaborative research as to what aspects of outside life, if any, they wish to bring into their communities while protecting and developing their cultural heritage. The result consists of establishing a plan which reflects community desires. The third aspect of the strategic process for projects consists of implementing the culturally appropriate plan. Particularly significant here are health and education because indigenous peoples usually want support in these areas; but without their control over programmes, projects will march over their own tried and tested methods.

Indigenous peoples have an enormous variety of responses to health and education needs. At one extreme there is a blending of the Western and indigenous education and health under indigenous control (such as occurs in the Mohawk schools in the United States and Canada) and at the other, there are peoples who advocate their separation (such as occurs among some of the Aboriginal peoples of Australia). Each of these approaches operates in a manner appropriate to and determined by the communities concerned (Aikman 1994). A broad and flexible approach in educational and health programmes is an important way for indigenous peoples to control their lives. It provides the means for them to benefit from outside support on their own terms without experiencing a detrimental effect on their cultural values.

## 3. Indigenous organisation

Throughout the world, indigenous peoples' own social and political institutions are not recognised. In some cases governmental institutions impose political frameworks within which communities have to operate. Often these do not work in harmony with traditional methods of organisation and communities can be in conflict over which to follow.

The first set of strategies aims to increase organisational strength and capacity. A constant problem for indigenous organisations is that they are formed in order to promote community resistance and expand the breadth of political mobilisation, yet they have no means to accomplish the numerous tasks they have to carry out. An organisation can only be successful with a secure infrastructural base, where leaders can be chosen according to the wishes of the constituent members, where travel and training is available and where internal and external communication is facilitated.

Frequently, projects with indigenous peoples expect newly fledged indigenous organisations to carry out project management with the same efficiency as professional non-governmental institutions. Often, a conflict arises between an indigenous organisation which was formed for political purposes and the development tasks which it is assumed to be capable of carrying out. Difficulties can occur in these circumstances, and the balance between a development which respects indigenous peoples' political right to decide their development priorities and the technical control over administration and project implementation can give rise to conflicts between donors and recipients.

The way to ensure that these problems are controlled is by incorporating the second aspect of the strategic process, administrative training, to ensure that technical staff are given the space to carry out their activities in an indigenous programme and that all decisions connecting the donor and recipient are negotiated fairly, sensitively and transparently. Indigenous organisations need to be supported both on the political level and on the economic-administrative levels. How these two levels inter-link should be defined at the outset of any project or programme and not fought over at a later stage. Flexibility is extremely important in dealing with organisational and administrative aspects of indigenous peoples' development programmes.

The third aspect of the dialectical process under the heading of indigenous organisation consists of strategies for working with, rather than on, indigenous organisations. This involves establishing constructive agreements with agencies over mutually acceptable projects. These may not necessarily conform precisely to the strict definitions of contracts and project documents because they should be drawn up with mutual agreement. Working together can only take place if the indigenous organisation has the means to fulfil the objectives which it initiated.

Self-representation and the recognition of indigenous peoples' own institutions are extremely important for implementing the organisational right of free association which indigenous development work addresses. By focusing on the problem, namely the violation of the right, development programmes can work to ameliorate the problems facing indigenous peoples. However, this has to be done with flexibility and sensitivity.

To summarise, three sets of problems facing indigenous peoples have been covered, here each of which is the response or solution to the violation of indigenous rights. Of the many different strategies for implementing these rights, a three-fold dialectical process consisting of several strategies has been highlighted which cumulatively become incorporated into each other so that at the end of the project or programme all aspects are operating simultaneously.

| Subject area | Problem (violation of right) | Strategic Process (implementation of right) |
|---|---|---|
| Territory | Invasion causes Poverty | i) demarcation ii) subsistence iii) commercialisation |
| Culture | Disrespect causes Discrimination | i) cultural revival ii) dialogue on needs iii) plan into action |
| Organisation | No recognition causes Oppression | i) strengthen organisations ii) train for development iii) work together |

### The All-Embracing Right to Self-Determination

The right which sums up the three problem areas mentioned above – rights to territories and resources, cultural freedom and to organise – is encompassed in the concept of self-determination. Like development, self-determination is an open concept and refers to the right of indigenous peoples to determine their own destinies. In this sense self-development by indigenous peoples is self-determination in practice carried out over time (Henriksen 1989).

The dialectical process of implementing strategies mentioned above is a clear example of how self-development and self-determination are interrelated. At each point in the process, indigenous peoples decide how they want to relate to the world outside on the

| Problem | Right | Implementation | Characteristics | Method |
|---|---|---|---|---|
| **Indigenous features** | | | | |
| Donor imposition | Indigenous control | Dialectical strategies | Holistic Inalienable Diversity | Consent 'Treaty' Flexibility Sensitivity Inside-out |
| **General – 'open-ended'** | | | | |
| Colonisation | Self-determination | Self-development | | |
| **Specific** | | | | |
| Invasion | Territorial | Titling Subsistence Market | | |
| Discrimination | Cultural | Revival Planning Action | | |
| Oppression | Organisation | Strengthen Train Collaborate | | |

basis of a strong territory, culture and organisation. The decision-making process is self-determination in action and as the process accumulates, a temporal self-development emerges.

The implementation of the right to self-determination is the basis for looking at a development method which includes aspects of the discussion reviewed hitherto. Self-determination embraces territory, culture and organisation in a way which is inter-connected. Development in many cases will involve all three areas. The administration of a project involves indigenous organisation while indigenous cultural identity is bound up in land, territory and resources. Furthermore, the contents of a territory constitute the components of culture and the relationships between the human, natural and invisible worlds.

Self-determination in development is also related to the notion of control of a programme and consent for its implementation. Indigenous peoples are responsible for their territories and their culture in ensuring that they pass from one generation to the next. To ensure that they are preserved, outsiders should not be able to take over the development process.

Self-determination is sufficiently open so that it encourages respect for the diversity among peoples, communities and persons which is such an important attribute of indigenous life. Diversity is built into indigenous peoples' views of the environment and they actively promote the principle in agricultural and other production methods. Personal and community freedom is a fertile ground for spreading a variety of cultural and religious practices embedded in the experience of daily life and the invisible world.

In this way self-determination covers the different topics we have discussed in this paper. In the following diagram the section 'indigenous features' is seen as including the all-encompassing criteria of indigenous development which embraces both the open-ended concepts of self-determination and the specific territorial, cultural and organisational projects:

## Conclusion

Self-determination covers rights to territory, culture and organisation. In order for these rights to be implemented through self-development, agencies need to become aware of the attributes of holistic inter-connectedness; inalienability of territory and heritage; and the diversity of peoples, communities and persons.

Indigenous self-development is distinct from other forms of development because it consists of the implementation of rights of indigenous peoples which have been discussed and drawn up over the last twenty years. The strategies for implementing indigenous rights involve building on the strengths of indigenous peoples such as their territories, cultures and organisational capacity, in particular. Projects should provide facilitation for indigenous peoples to determine how they want to incorporate outside influences into their daily lives in order to contribute to their well-being.

The boundaries between indigenous peoples and others lie on a spectrum where a difference in degree becomes a difference in kind. This occurs as distinctions become markedly more prominent when claims to territory, culture and freedom of organisation become intricately connected with the concept of self-determination. This blending of indigenous and other forms of rural or urban development can be seen also in the development methodology which is used with indigenous projects.

The current development dichotomy which is becoming more prominent shows that indigenous peoples are firmly on the side of participatory methods; but that these have to be adapted to embrace the diversity, flexibility and sensitivity needed in specific projects. Indigenous development has to begin on the inside and from below, but in many cases, the term participatory might seem strange as the initiative sounds as if it comes from the outside. In fact participation in an indigenous context means that donors participate in and facilitate indigenous-controlled development.

The other element of development methods – such as logical frame, cost-efficiency and tendering, all have to be adapted to suit the conditions of indigenous self-development. For example, although logical frame analysis covers multi-causal factors resulting in problems which development has to address, it does not deal with dual causality, and functional inter-relationships. Indeed, indigenous peoples in many parts of the world have their own causal models which would be far more appropriate for demonstrating their needs and proposals. Another danger is that cost-effective tendering increasingly attracts inexperienced organisations trying to graft an 'indigenous aspect' onto their other activities. Without due care this could lead to a continuation of the process undergone in the past twenty years where development has been imposed on indigenous peoples without their consent, thereby leaving it as a misnomer and negative term in community life.

Indigenous development is special and different but not so exclusively that it is separate from initiatives to support other impoverished or discriminated sectors of society. The distinctive characteristics of indigenous peoples arise from the conditions in which they live and their own colonial context, and these have to be addressed by reference to indigenous rights. This should not be seen, however, as a separation of development into exclusive indigenous and non-indigenous categories, but as a way of reflecting the needs, desires and aspirations of particular peoples in the development which affects them.

Rather than solely promote indigenous peoples as being different from other social categories, such as gender, age or class, it would perhaps be more useful to see what is distinct or similar about each sector, while promoting the consent and control of the people concerned over the development process. This will enable donors to enter into collaborative and coordinated development programmes with a variety of social sectors, clearly and coherently addressing the problems which they face. If such a sensitivity were possible there might be a chance of placing the 'human' within sustainable development. This would enable development work to address the problems facing the poor, ignored and oppressed of the world on their own terms.

## References

Aikman, S. 1994. Intercultural Education and Harakmbut Identity: A Case Study of the Community of San Jose in Southeastern Peru. Ph.D. Thesis, Institute of Education, University of London.

Burgess, H. 1987. 'Traditional Territories of the Earth', in *IWGIA Yearbook, 1986* pp. 133-140. Copenhagen: IWGIA.

Burkey, S. 1993. *People First: A Guide to Self-reliant, Participatory Rural Development.* London: Zed Books.

Chambers, R. 1983. *Rural Development: Putting the Last First.* Longman Scientific and Technical.

Chambers 1994. 'The Origins and Practice of Participatory Rural Appraisal' World Development, Vol. 22, No. 7. pp. 953-969.

Henriksen, G. 1989. *Introduction to Indigenous Self-Development in the Americas.* IWGIA Document 68, pp. 13-18. Copenhagen.

Hettne, B. 1982. Development Theory and the Third World Stockholm: SAREC Report R:2.

Hobart, M. (ed) 1993. *An Anthropological Critique of Development: The Growth of Ignorance,* Routledge.

Mascarenhas, J. et. al. (eds.) 1991. Participatory Rural Appraisal Proceedings of the February 1991 Bangalore Trainees Workshop. IIED & Myrada.

Nerfin, M. ed. 1977. *Another Development: Approaches and Strategies.* Uppsala: The Dag Hammarskjold Foundation.

Sambo, D. 1992. 'The Emerging Indigenous Human Right to Development' *IWGIA Yearbook 1992* pp.167-189. Copenhagen: IWGIA.

Schuurman, F. (ed.) 1993. *Beyond the Impasse: New Directions in Development Theory.* London: Zed Books.

# V
# NGOs, the State and the 'New Partnership': Lobbying for Indigenous Rights

GEORG HENRIKSEN

# INDIGENOUS PEOPLES, INTERNATIONAL CONVENTIONS AND DECLARATIONS AND THE STATE

In this article I am going to address a few questions relating to indigenous peoples, international conventions and declarations and the state. Since such conventions and declarations may be seen as both containing models of the reality in which we live, as well as models *for* the reality which we wish to create, I will present some reflections on the types of models we have of the relationship between indigenous peoples and the state. This is certainly a tall order, and all I can do is touch upon some of the issues which to me seem pertinent.

Let me begin with what I see as basic premises for the work that we all are engaged in:

1) The ultimate aim of our efforts must be to create strong and healthy individuals – people with a strong sense of self-worth and with resources and opportunities to realise their human potentials. Given the intimate relationship between the individual and the social body, individuals must be members of and active participants in strong and healthy communities in order to realise this. Article 27 in the Human Rights Convention on Civil and Political Rights points to the crucial relationship between the collective and the individual level; between collective and individual rights.

We have ample evidence from around the world which proves how catastrophic the effects may be both for individuals and communities when the larger social body of the state does not heed these interrelationships. I have observed this first hand in Labrador, Canada, where a group of Native Americans, the Innu, both as individuals and as a community, descended into a state of alcoholism and personal violence in a period of a few years.

2) The nation-state is not the permanent and once-and-for-all construction which we have thought it to be. Through all the

inter-ethnic conflicts and wars taking place in nearly all corners of the world, and also the break-up of the Soviet Union and Yugoslavia, we have ample evidence that the state, as a structure and dynamic system, is an ongoing project. Even my own country, Norway, small and homogenous as it is (4 million people), is facing the challenges inherent in a situation where a powerful majority relates to the indigenous Sámi people and migrants from other ethnic groups. Indigenous peoples play a crucial role in this huge project of redesigning the state so that it can accomodate both indigenous peoples and minorities. This is so, of course, because most indigenous peoples are seeking new solutions to the relationship which they have with the state without, except in rare cases, aspiring to create their own seperate states.

Therefore, in searching for and identifying integrative and disintegrative mechanisms in the complex social system which the state is, we can draw the conclusion that the integration of the state must build on recognition of indigenous rights and self-determination. In other words, it is truly in the interest of the state itself to recognise indigenous rights and to work with indigenous peoples in order to accomplish their self-determination.

What indigenous peoples are seeking is self-determination, and, in most cases, what some have called 'internal self-determination'. What this implies varies with the different circumstances in which indigenous peoples find themselves. In other words, self-determination can only be realised in a process of negotiation with the respective states of which the indigenous peoples are part. For these negotiations to be successful, they must result in settlements which are regarded as just and fair. If not, indigenous peoples will continue to experience powerlessness and to regard the excercise of state power as illegitimate. It is important, therefore, that all parties involved, including national and international agencies concerned with development, are conscious of the fact that both members of the powerful majority and the indigenous peoples each engage amongst themselves in moral narratives through which inter-ethnic relations are assessed and voiced. It is important to scrutinise these narratives because they give us clues as to what wrongs should be addressed. The moral narratives which people engage in fuel the grievances which representatives of indigenous people bring to the United Nations Working Group on Indigenous Populations, as well as the reactions of the states. We should also be aware, however, that such narratives often constitute the basis of negative and destructive sterotypes of *the other*.

In order to establish the state as a stable social order, indigenous peoples must experience that they are part of civil society in a meaningful way. One precondition for this is that *their voice* is both heard and respected in public discourse.

3) A people's sense of identity as a *people* is seldom or never eradicated. From all the evidence we have, we can conclude that, except for outright genocide, states cannot eradicate indigenous peoples' sense of identity and belonging to a national or social unit of their own. The history of the relationship between the Sámi and the Norwegian state would provide a very good example of this. First, there was a severe policy of assimilation. This was followed by the benevolent policy of the Norwegian welfare state in which all citizens had equal rights. In spite of this, the Sámi never relinquished their sense of a shared identity and belonging, and have, especially during the last two decades, forced the Norwegian Parliament to recognise an increasing degree of self-determination.

Shortly, the Norwegian Parliament will make a decision to fully incorporate into Norwegian law the European Human Rights Convention, the International Covenant on Civil and Political Rights and the International Covenant on Economic, Social and Cultural Rights. This means that these legal instruments will become Norwegian law in the full sense of the word, which implies that Norwegian judges cannot go against these international laws. Technically, this is called the monistic principle in contrast to the dualistic principle. In the latter, national law and international law, if it is ratified by the state, remains seperate. In practice, this means that national law ususally is given preference.

I should add here that Article 27 in the International Covenant on Civil and Political Rights (which states that members of a minority can not be refused the right to practise their culture, their religion and their language) can be interpreted as saying that minority/indigenous peoples must be given the necessary means and material resources in order to realise this (see for example the Sámi Rights Commission, NOU 1984: 18).

In spite of all the international conventions and declarations which we now have, (and we should add to the three above the ILO convention, the Draft Declaration on Indigenous Peoples' Rights, the declarations which came out of the 1992 Earth Summit in Rio, and the World Conference of Indigenous Peoples on Territory, Environment and Development which was held at Kari-Oca, north of Rio, and the Declaration from the World Summit for Social Development) we find that most states neglect them as soon as they run counter to the states' own strong interests.

Personally, I can report from Labrador that the air space of the Innu and Inuit people continues to be invaded by NATO fighter planes which are training in low-level flying, with detrimental effects on the wildlife and hunting activities of indigenous peoples. A huge deposit of valuable minerals (copper, cobalt and nickel) has recently been discovered within their territories, resulting in drilling and other preparations for major mining operations. Numerous prospectors and mining companies are flooding indigenous peoples' territory and staking claims to it, while indigenous peoples' interests are completely neglected. In other words, there seems to be a vast distance between the visions and goals in the declarations mentioned above and indigenous peoples' reality. Similar examples, and even worse, may be found in all parts of the world.

In Canada's case it is worth noting the discrepancies in the authorities' behaviour – comparing what is happening in Labrador and for example the establishment of Nunavut in Canada's North-West Territories, where the Inuit are given a significant degree of self-determination. The differential involvement of the federal and provincial levels is only part of the explanation. For example, the Newfoundland government refuses to deal with the Innu of Labrador as long as they insist on refusing the Provincial Court entrance to their communities, as the Innu want to apply their own standards of retributive justice.

If we want to stop the exploitation of indigenous resources and territories and the atrocities carried out against indigenous peoples, as well as the socio-cultural breakdown which often follows from this, we must work from several angles at the same time. Of course, there are the economic and political interests of states, dominant ethnic groups, national and multinational companies and other interest groups who devise and carry out their strategies with detrimental effects for indigenous peoples. These attacks must be met with counter-strategies by indigenous peoples and their organisations, as well as NGOs and other national and international bodies. The exchange of information and ideas which will take place at this forum will surely contribute to the production of future counter-strategies.

Another challenge consists of models people have developed and make use of to interpret the world and act in it. We all carry numerous models in our minds which makes it possible for us to understand the world. These models are, to a great extent, shared among members of the same culture, which entails that people in the same society tend to understand many things more or less in the same way. Many of these models are unconscious, but nevertheless they guide us as well as blind us.

The aforementioned declarations are all full of good intentions and aspirations, but as indicated above, it is doubtful that they are followed to any great extent by action. Yet, I do not think they are futile. Although many of them do not deal directly with indigenous peoples, it must be possible to assemble and mold them into new and alternative models of how to interpret indigenous peoples' situation and their relations with states, governments and other powerful institutions, as well as how to determine directions for development.

It is an important task to produce such models which can function as alternatives to those which normally inform the thoughts and actions of members of the powerful majority. What I am saying is that these conventions and declarations, which are the legal products of social experience and reasoning, so to speak, need to be forged into such alternative models which can function on a cognitive level amongst all members of the state, as well as being put to the real test through their implementation.

Growing up in a particular culture entails that we learn numerous concepts, some of which are linked so that they constitute systems of meaning, which we may also call cultural models. Often there will be barriers between such models so that when we are interpreting one particular phenomenon or event, we do not mobilise alternative or additional models with which we could have produced novel interpretations and instructions for action.

Thus, when journalists write about the mining activities in Voisey Bay in Labrador, they do this on the basis of some models they have in their minds, and which are associated with mining. These are predominantly concepts and models pertaining to economic activities. Thus, the journalists write about the magnitude of the mineral resources, the potential market value of the minerals, the capital costs involved in mining it, the strategies of different mining companies in what is perceived as a competitive game, the impact which the Labrador mining activities are having on the stock market and international business, etc. And these are models which they to a large extent share with the general public. Indigenous peoples hardly enter at all in these accounts of what is taking place in Labrador.

The same was the case with a group of environmental scientists who wrote a proposal to establish a Wilderness Resource Centre in Labrador. In this document they describe Labrador as a pristine wilderness, with an ecosystem without human beings. They want to establish knowledge of this wilderness but without mentioning the vast knowledge which the Innu and the Inuit already possess. And when they finally refer to the indigenous peoples in their report, they refer to them merely as another interest group and not as peoples who are stewards of social and cultural orders which are different from the Euro-Canadian. Now, I do not believe that these omissions of the indigenous peoples were done out of bad will, but rather were the result of a lack of understanding: a lack of the proper cultural models necessary to grasp the significance of the fact that indigenous peoples are living within these territories and have been living there since time immemorial. They also lack the proper models necessary to grasp the point of view of the indigenous peoples: the cultural models held by the Innu and the Inuit pertaining to the same issues as those the scientists were dealing with in their paper. At the same time the scientists were guided by the models held by members of the dominant population: models of what may be called 'science' and what is not 'scientific', implying that knowledge held and observations made by the indigenous peoples are not 'scientific', and, therefore, severely restricted both in their value and to what extent they can be used to argue a case, for example, that certain kinds of industrial developments will harm the environment.

Although the Labrador peninsula is huge, and the indigenous population is small, they do utilise the whole space as hunters. I do believe that these scientists have some awareness of this, but that they lack essential knowledge of how the hunters utilise their territory and its resources. To the extent they have an understanding of the indigenous peoples and their adaptation to the environment, the scientists do not easily connect these different models. Not surprisingly, there is a correspondence between the cultural models we activate and the 'sector' within which we operate. Hence, in the scientific interpretation of the environment as a wilderness ecosystem which the biologists and the ecologists were making, the Innu and Inuit had no place.

Also serving as a barrier to let the indigenous peoples enter into the scientific and economic models utilised by the Euro-Canadians when dealing with Labrador is the commonly held view of development and socio-cultural evolution as unilineal, and mainly measured in terms of economic and material progress. In these models of the future, which so many of us carry vaguely in the back of our heads, there is no room for indigenous peoples with self-determination, a factor enabling them to create their own histories. The fact that most indigenous peoples adopt the use of industrial products is taken as evidence of such a unilineal model of socio-cultural evolution. Indeed, many governments will give certain rights to indigenous peoples only on the condition that they remain 'traditional'.

Of course, in order to enhance self-determination indigenous people need an economic base. Once they have the necessary territorial rights, it is up to indigenous peoples themselves to what extent, and in what manner they will utilise resources within their territories in order to create income to finance their own development. However, we know that this raises a number of different issues that may even cause political cleavages within indigenous communities themselves. In order to deal with these questions, indigenous peoples also need to develop new cultural models in order to adequately deal with a rapidly changing world.

There is, of course, an essential interrelationship between self-determination and development. We cannot view development merely as 'progress' measured in terms of material wealth, health, education, etc. (although not excluding this). Development must be fully based on the indigenous peoples' own aspirations. In the words of the UN World Summit for Social Development Declaration: the Heads of state and governments are committed to create a framework for action to 'recognise and support indigenous people in their pursuit of economic and social development with full respect for their identity, traditions, forms of social organisation and cultural values' (23. m) (Draft Declaration).

As we very well know, the policies implemented by governments too often run counter to these commitments. This is first and foremost because of states' strong economic and political interests, but also because of the deeply ingrained views or models, on development, history and socio-cultural evolution held by the dominant peoples and their governments.

But let us not therefore dismiss the above government pledges. Rather, there lies an important challenge for us to combine into one model the above pledges made by governments on behalf of indigenous peoples, *as well as* the pledges they made concerning *all* members of their state societies. I believe many governments and their constituencies are worried about disruptive social processes linked with poverty, drugs, crime, interethnic hostilities and even war, xenophobia and political and religious fundamentalism. In order to avoid the marginalisation of individuals, groups and categories of people, processes which clearly constitute a threat to the social order, the state must ensure meaningful participation in the civil society for all.

In the same Social Summit declaration the governments pledge to:

> Support progress and security for people and communities whereby every member of society is enabled to satisfy basic human needs and to realise their personal dignity, safety and creativity ... Promote democracy, human dignity, social justice and solidarity at the

national, regional and international levels; ensure tolerance, non-violence and pluralism and non-discrimination in full respect of diversity within and among societies.

There is an obvious link between these goals and the needs and goals formulated by indigenous peoples both on the level of the individual and the collective. They are all important objectives which may contribute to the construction of cultural models; models which may also serve to secure the recognition of collective rights for indigenous peoples. On the basis of the evidence we have, we cannot but infer that collective rights and self-determination for indigenous peoples are crucial in order to meet the objectives stated in the Social Summit Declaration and, also, in order to maintain the social order of the state. Indeed, I sincerely believe that indigenous peoples through their political struggles and in developing novel cultural models are spearheading what will become an effort by many governments all over the world to cope with the needs of all their citizens, as well as the problem of social order.

We should recognise the importance of collective rights for peoples, not only in relation to territories and resources, but to educational systems, legal systems, health and social services, etc. Collective rights for all of these institutions are crucial in promoting social integration and cohesion, which again is crucial if the individual shall be able to realise 'personal dignity, safety and creativity'. As I have already stated, social systems and whole societies may disintegrate – with catastrophic results, also for the individual. In the Innu community in Labrador, mentioned above, out of a population of only 500 people, there were 90 suicide attempts in the period of only one year. These were suicide attempts which required intervention. So when we talk about development, we must of course also talk about social and cultural development, and about social integration and cohesion.

Clearly, if all the good intentions contained in the declarations which I have mentioned are to be realised, governments, as well as NGOs, must ensure that indigenous peoples are properly included in all discourses and negotiations which in any way relate to them, and with full respect for indigenous cosmologies, knowledge and aspirations.

National and international agencies involved in development have an important role in producing adequate models and, even more importantly, taking on the challenging task of promoting them vis-à-vis national governments and implementing them in different social, cultural and political circumstances.

JACQUES DE KORT

# TEACHING THE STATE: LOBBYING FOR INDIGENOUS RIGHTS IN THE EU

I wish to express my thanks to the organisers for inviting me here to share with you some of my experiences concerning lobbying for indigenous rights in the European Union over the past 25 years.

Whether the results of these lobby-activities have been succesful or not is to be judged by the indigenous peoples of the world. Only if, as far as their relations with Europe are concerned, the indigenous peoples experience in 1995 any positive and sustainable changes, compared to 25 years ago, then Europeans like myself, who have been involved in lobbying the European states, have a reason to be satisfied.

When they first met from people to people (in 1492) it took about 50 years for the present most dominant culture, the European Christian culture, to recognise the indigenous peoples of Abya Yala (the Americas) as human beings.

Only since 1993, the UN International Year of the Indigenous Peoples, has the existence of indigenous peoples on this planet been recognised by the dominant non-indigenous peoples who run this world.

But the rights of indigenous peoples do not yet exist on a universal basis. This means that there is not yet an international law protecting indigenous peoples everywhere on this earth. This endangers not only the lives of indigenous people but also cultural diversity (and to a certain extent biological diversity) on our planet.

The indigenous peoples have made several attempts to explain to the rest of the world who they are and what they think. Since the 1920s, when the Hopi people (Arizona, USA) made an unsuccessful effort to address the League of Nations (now United Nations), these attempts have been made in an organised way. Since 1953 some indigenous peoples from South America, connected to labour unions, managed to become involved in the drafing of ILO Convention 107, which was ratified in 1957. The first independent indigenous peoples organisations were founded in the 1960s in North and South America. Since 1976 more and more indigenous peoples' organisations from South, North and Central America and, since the 1980s, from the Pacific and Europe, and since the 1990s, from Asia and Africa worked their way up in the intergovernmental institutions. In May, 1992, indigenous peoples' organisations from all over the world held their first conference (on territory, environment and development) in Kari Oca, near Rio de Janeiro, Brazil. In June, 1992, for the first time in history, indigenous peoples could forward their messages directly to world leaders (UNCED II, Brazil). As a result, Agenda 21 mentions indigenous peoples as a neglected part of the world population that has the right to be involved in decision-making processes about the earth's environment and development.

The rights of indigenous peoples have been drafted by the UN Working Group on Indigenous Populations since 1982. A final draft was presented to the UN Commission on Human Rights in February, 1995. At present, it is quite uncertain when the General Assembly of the UN will adopt the Universal Declaration of the Rights of Indigenous Peoples. It is even less certain which version of the draft will be voted upon. Nevertheless, this drafting process has caused a growth in moral support for indigenous peoples among policymakers. In 1982 the World Bank adopted a code of conduct for dealing with indigenous peoples, which was revised in 1991. Since 1989 the European Parliament has adopted several resolutions supporting the rights of indigenous peoples. In 1989 the ILO revised its Convention 107 (ratified in 1957) into Convention 169 (ratified in 1990), which is more specific and updated on the rights of indigenous peoples. In the 1990s several transnational companies became aware of indigenous peoples' rights and some started to make efforts for a company code of conduct for dealing with indigenous peoples. Also, environmental organisations, peace groups and development agencies demonstrated a growing awareness for indigenous peoples' rights. In 1992, for the first time, Amnesty International ran a campaign for indigenous peoples (in Brazil).

This growing awareness was then also expressed by the United Nations, declaring 1993 as the International Year of the

Indigenous Peoples. As this year proved to be a period too short to even explain to all indigenous peoples about the existence of the Year, the General Assembly of the UN (in December 1993) adopted a resolution declaring 10 December 1994 as the first day of the International Decade of the Indigenous Peoples.

Behind this promotion of indigenous peoples' rights over the past three decades, there are two driving forces: one being the fast growing number of indigenous peoples' organisations (the Voices of the Earth), the other being the support-groups for indigenous peoples (the mouthpieces of the Voices of the Earth). Now, taking the Dutch lobby for indigenous rights as an example, we will look more into the background and strategies behind this lobby, applied over the past 25 years. Some results of this lobby will also be mentioned.

For the past 15 years I have been participating in this process of lobbying international policymakers, European politicians in particular, to pay serious attention to the many forms of discrimination, racism and slavery that indigenous peoples experience every day. In the Netherlands I followed the footsteps of others who had set this promotion campaign for the rights of indigenous peoples in motion in the late sixties. In this respect I would like to give credit to Mr. Ben Vermeer, Mr. Fons Eickholt and Mr. Viktor Kaisiepo. At present, I work for the Indigenous Council in The Netherlands, which at a national level makes an effort to coordinate the activities of indigenous peoples and their support-groups during the Decade of the Indigenous Peoples. The Indigenous Council in The Netherlands wishes to carry on the work, including lobby activities, that have been carried out in the Netherlands in the past under different names like WIZA, WIP and NCIV.

The history of the Dutch movement for indigenous peoples' rights coincides to a large extent with that in other parts of the world, where similar processes were set in motion about the same time and under similar circumstances. The International Work Group for Indigenous Affairs (IWGIA) (based in Denmark), Survival International (based in England), Society for Endangered Peoples (based in Germany) and Cultural Survival (based in the USA) played a coordinating role there. These and other support-groups for indigenous peoples, working together in an international network with indigenous peoples' organisations, succeeded in having the UN declare 1993 the International Year of the Indigenous Peoples and 1994-2003 the International Decade of the Indigenous Peoples.

The Dutch movement for indigenous peoples' rights has been supporting indigenous peoples over the past 25 years in many different ways. In the Netherlands this movement was set in motion in 1969 by anthropology students at the University of Leiden who were shocked by the information coming from anthropologists and missionaries about military attacks on indigenous peoples in the Brazilian Amazon. These students, influenced by the renowned social anthropologist Lars Persson, founded the South American Indians Working Group (WIZA) and merged in 1984 with the Indian Project Working Group (WIP) and four other Netherlands based support-groups into the Working Group for Indigenous Peoples (WIP). In 1993 this Working Group for Indigenous Peoples (WIP) changed its name into the Netherlands Centre for Indigenous Peoples (NCIV). Since February 1995 indigenous persons, there are about 200,000 of them living or staying in the Netherlands, have been taking control of this movement to certify that the profits of the Decade of the Indigenous Peoples in the Netherlands and the profits of everything that the movement for indigenous peoples' rights in the Netherlands has been doing in the past is shared with the indigenous peoples of the world.

In the late '70s the Dutch movement for indigenous peoples' rights was no longer dominated by anthropologists but changed gradualy into a multisectoral network of lobbyists, activists and researchers.

The Dutch movement for indigenous peoples' rights has always tried to link up its activities with initiatives taken by indigenous peoples themselves. Starting in 1969, relationships were established with indigenous peoples and their growing number of organisations in South, Central and North America. Since 1978 the scope was extended to the indigenous peoples in Europe, Asia and the Pacific. Since 1987 the Dutch lobbyists and activists established similar kinds of relations in Africa.

From its beginning in 1969, the Dutch movement for indigenous peoples' rights has launched several information campaigns, published many publications, set up a documentation centre, created networks, organised fact finding missions, was involved in funding indigenous peoples' projects, carried out lobbying activites, gave many trainings and courses to both indigenous and non-indigenous people and has been involved in elaborating policies of NGOs and governmental and intergovernmental bodies. All of these activities aimed at creating a better understanding of indigenous peoples and at strenghtening their chances for survival.

The lobbyists and activists in the Netherlands have been working on three geographical levels: national (Dutch speaking part of the world), Europe (since 1990 via the Brussels office of the European Alliance with Indigenous Peoples) and worldwide (since 1984 via the Human Rights Fund for Indigenous Peoples). In the field of education and information distribution the Dutch movement for indigenous peoples' rights has initiated and organised, among many other activities:

* the Fourth Russell Tribunal on the Rights of the Indians (Rotterdam, 1980);
* the campaign for the indigenous peoples of Peru (the Netherlands, 1982 – 1984);
* the creation of the Human Rights Fund for Indigenous Peoples (London, 1984);
* the Series of the Yearly Bertrand Russell Lectures on the Future of the Indigenous Peoples of the Americas (Amsterdam, 1984 – 1992);
* the campaign for the indigenous peoples of Amazonia 'Man and Environment in Amazonia' (the Netherlands, 1984 – 1989), including many publications, lobbied the World Bank, Inter-American Development Bank, European Union, the Dutch government and environmental NGOs;
* the First International Conference on Man and Environment in Amazonia (Vienna, 1987);
* the First International Conference on the European Community, Timber Trade and Indigenous Peoples (Brussels, 1987);
* the Aboriginal Solidarity Campaign (the Netherlands, 1988);
* the creation of the European Alliance with Indigenous Peoples (Brussels, 1989);

* the campaign 'Indigenous Peoples, Environment and Development' (the Netherlands, 1990 – 1992), focusing on the indigenous peoples of Aotearoa, New Zealand (1990), Africa (1991) and the Americas (1992), including the Symbolic Discovery of Europe 1992-project;
* the campaign 'Indigenous Peoples: a New Partnership!' (the Netherlands, 1993 – 2003), including the Voices of the Earth 1993-project (connected to the UN International Year of Indigenous Peoples) and activities connected to the UN International Decade of Indigenous Peoples.

In the field of providing direct services to indigenous peoples, on their request, the Dutch movement for indigenous peoples' rights has helped hundreds of indigenous peoples to organise themselves, to formulate their problems and to create conditions for a dialogue with the persons and institutions causing the indigenous peoples' problems. To do this in a responsible way, an internal code of conduct was formulated about how to deal with indigenous peoples' requests.

When the still very small movement for indigenous peoples' rights presented its first reports about the human rights violations of indigenous peoples (in Brazil) to the politicians and government in the Netherlands in 1969 there was hardly any response. The policy-makers and decision-makers in the Netherlands did not know much about indigenous peoples. The prevailing opinion among them was that these were only incidents, that only small cultures in a process of inevitable extinction were affected, and besides that, what did all this have to do with Dutch politics.

It was decided to choose the following strategy:

- first, making the issue of indigenous peoples' rights into an international issue;
- to develop educational materials for as many sectors in the Netherlands as a society as possible;
- to train volunteers, students and interns and introduce them to indigenous peoples;
- influence the education of students in anthropology, geography, archeology, history, journalism, tropical agriculture and other future professionals as to how to deal with indigenous peoples;

- illustrate the connection between Dutch society and indigenous peoples.

In the seventies this strategy was followed in short-term programmes. The focus was mainly on cases of violations of indigenous peoples' rights on the American continent.

This policy changed after the Fourth Bertrand Russell Tribunal, organised by the Dutch movement for indigenous peoples' rights in 1980, in Rotterdam, in cooperation with fellow organisations from other parts of the world. During this tribunal on the rights of the indigenous peoples of the American continent, the indigenous participants urged the organisers to present the conclusions and documentation materials of this meeting on their behalf to the Dutch government, the European institutions and the United Nations offices in Europe in order to persuade them to change their policies.

There was a clear need felt by the movement for indigenous peoples' rights in the Netherlands to work out a long-term programme to achieve these goals. The Dutch government had pointed out several times that it would not consider changing its foreign policy and development policy in favour of indigenous peoples unless it could be done in a European or UN context. Therefore, the movement for indigenous peoples' rights chose to elaborate a long term programme that was to be executed on 3 levels: United Nations, Europe and the Netherlands.

At all these levels we started to lobby with the results and documentation of the Fourth Russell Tribunal.

At the UN Centre for Human Rights in Geneva these results were welcomed. They helped to launch the UN Working Group on Indigenous Populations in 1982 and to open doors for indigenous peoples in the UN system.

At the European Parliament in Brussels the results of the Fourth Russell Tribunal were welcomed by its Human Rights Commission. But it was only after the presentation of an updated version of the final report of the tribunal, followed by meetings of indigenous peoples with members of the European Parliament (in 1987), that indigenous peoples became a topic on the agenda of the European Parliament. In 1989, for the first time in history, three resolutions were passed by the European Parliament. These resolutions were concerned with the human rights of indigenous peoples in the American continent, the indigenous peoples and environment in Amazonia, and indigenous peoples in the Philippines. These resolutions became important instruments, both for indigenous peoples and for their European supporters in the European Community. The next step, set by the movement for indigenous peoples' rights in the Netherlands, was to start lobbying the European Commission for political and financial support for indigenous peoples. For this reason, the European Alliance with Indigenous Peoples was set up, which opened its office in Amsterdam in 1990, and then moved to Brussels in 1991.

Immediately after the European Parliament had passed its resolutions on indigenous peoples, and when the ILO presented the revised Convention 169, and again when the UN had declared 1993 as the Year of the Indigenous Peoples the Dutch government was confronted with these changing attitudes. We were invited to inform one of the government parties in the buildings of Parliament about indigenous peoples' rights and explain why the Dutch government should support indigenous peoples.

But more was still needed in order to convince them. In 1992 a delegation of 75 indigenous peoples was invited by the Netherlands movement for indigenous' peoples rights to tour Europe and meet with European authorities, sponsored by the Dutch government and the European Commission. At the same time, the movement pushed for support by the Dutch government of the Kari Oca Conference. It all fit together, just in time. The Dutch Minister of Development Cooperation went to visit the Kari Oca Conference while attending UNCED II. In the meantime, the movement for indigenous peoples'rights had grown. Within the movement there was also a growing awareness that indigenous peoples should be given the opportunity to solve their problems themselves by negotiations. In this way the Dutch movement for indigenous peoples' rights has been supporting COICA (umbrella organisation of the indigenous peoples of Amazonia) its member organisations (in Brazil, Bolivia, Peru, Ecuador, Colombia, Venezuela, Guyana, Surinam and French-Guyana) and AIPP (umbrella organisation of the indigenous peoples of Asia) and its member organisations. The Dutch movement for indigenous peoples' rights administrated the First International Conference of Indigenous Peoples on Territory, Environment and Development (Kari Oca/Rio de Janeiro, 1992). Soon after the Kari Oca Conference the Dutch government received a copy of the Kari Oca Declaration from the hands of an indigenous delegation. As the Year of the Indigenous Peoples came closer, the movement was pushing the government and political parties in Parliament harder and lobbying on all levels. In December, 1992, the Minister of Foreign Affairs and the Minister of Development Cooperation requested two governmental commissions for advice on a possible indigenous policy paper. These commissions (one on human rights and the other on development cooperation) invited members of the Dutch movement for indigenous peoples' rights to brief them and make suggestions. These commissions presented their reports to the ministers in January, 1993.

In 1993 the Dutch movement for indigenous peoples' rights was finally recognised by the Dutch government. On 31 March, 1993, for the first time ever the Dutch government presented a policy concerning indigenous peoples, entitled 'Indigenous Peoples in Dutch Foreign Policy and Development Cooperation'.

As a result, the Dutch movement for indigenous peoples' rights, at that time cooperating under the umbrella of NCIV, was asked to administrate the so-called 'Dutch Conference Fund for Indigenous Peoples 1993'. This fund, containing about US$ 125,000 was made available to hundreds of indigenous peoples in Asia, Pacific, Africa, Siberia, Amazonia, Ecuador and Argentina in order to meet about the International Year of the Indigenous Peoples and work out common strategies. Altogether, the Dutch government, according to its own figures, spent about US$ 21 million in 1993 on projects that were related to indigenous peoples. According to the figures of the Dutch Council in the Netherlands, at least half of this amount was spent and used in a way that satisfied indigenous peoples. The other part of the money was spend on programmes where indigenous peoples had not been consulted but which were carried out in their name, as was particularly the case in India. Some projects were in fact education projects to raise public support for indigenous peoples, and executed in the Netherlands. We could not get further information about some of the projects. Internationally speaking, this is a reasonable score. But this should of course be turned into a 100% score duringe the Decade of the Indigenous Peoples.

In February, 1994, the policy paper of the government was debated and evaluated in Parliament, attended by several indigenous delegates. It received the official support of the majority in Parliament.

It has been important in this lobby process to convince the Dutch government and the European institutions of the following matters:

- face to face contact and high level meetings between representatives of indigenous peoples and the responsable policymakers and decision-makers;
- facts and figures that illustrated the relationship between indigenous peoples and the Netherlands or European institutions, but no overkill;
- references to adopted declarations concerning indigenous peoples, including the declarations of indigenous peoples themselves;
- concrete suggestions as to how the Dutch government could support indigenous peoples. In this respect I would like to mention the following examples that have been turned into practice and that might be helpful for the Swiss participants.

1. We asked for a symbolic amount to be spent on indigenous peoples' projects and suggested US$ 21 million, which equals a contribution of 0.10 Dutch guilder per indigenous person. To our suprise, there was no discussion on this amount.

2. We requested that the infrastructure of the Dutch government be made accessible to indigenous peoples in states where indigenous peoples are living. As a consequence indigenous peoples are welcome in the Embassies of the Netherlands around the world to deliver messages, to obtain information concerning the Dutch government's policies as well as international policies, and to deliver applications for urgent projects. Also, field offices of government related organisations such as the Netherlands Volunteers Organisation are providing facilities to indigenous peoples.

3. We requested that training courses concerning indigenous peoples be provided to embassy staff and staff in Dutch field offices. These training courses are now integrated in the preparations of this staff before leaving on a mission.

4. We requested an active attitude on the part of embassy staff and field officers. They now go on field trips and participate in indigenous peoples' meetings upon request.

A final piece of advice that I want to give to Swiss NGOs is: try to keep track of your members, volunteers, subscribers and interns. In the Netherlands we were able to do this and it turned out that some people who were once volunteers or interns, 20 years later happened to be in strategic positions in the Ministries, on Boards of Directors, or working for national media. These people proved to be of great help in turning the Dutch policy for indigenous peoples into reality.

I wish my Swiss colleagues the best of luck with their important mission.

# WORKSHOP RESULTS: TOWARDS A SWISS POLICY ON INDIGENOUS PEOPLES

The conference 'Indigenous Peoples, Environment and Development' (IPED) sought to identify criteria and principles for co-operation with indigenous peoples in development and environmental protection work. This was to be accomplished by the exchange of experiences in development and conservation programmes on indigenous territories by means of initiating a dialogue between all major parties. The indigenous participants and representatives of development and environmental NGOs, as well as Swiss governmental agencies were initially asked to present their positions in respect to such criteria during their preparations for IPED.

In the four workshops organised at the conference, the participants were engaged in the discussion of their demands and proposals and drew up a position paper summing up the results of each workshop. These workshop results were presented to the plenum in the closing session and constitute the basis for a resolution, called 'Working Paper on Indigenous Peoples, Environment and Development', which was presented to the UN50 NGO summit in Bern, on 30 June, 1995.[1]

This chapter summarises these workshop results. Not claiming to be exhaustive, it expresses the consensus on fundamental statements and points out differences where action and further negotiation is needed at the same time. Across the workshop topics these principles and demands to NGOs, governmental agencies and international organisations are grouped in four core areas: self-determination and land rights, information and communication, conservation of the environment, and development co-operation and legal instruments.

The resolution, which is based on these results and which was presented at the said NGO summit, is attached below.

## Self-determination and Land Rights
Indigenous peoples were placed upon our mother, the earth, by the creator. We belong to the land. We cannot be separated from

331

our lands and territories. Our territories are living totalities reflecting permanent vital relations between human beings and nature. Their possession produces the development of our culture. Our territorial property should be inalienable, unceasable and not denied title. Legal, economic and technical backup are needed to guarantee this (Kari Oca Declaration, IWGIA 1992: 57-61).

These statements formulated in the Kari Oca Declaration by indigenous representatives describe the close relationship between land, territories and indigenous cultures and emphasise the crucial significance of the concept of land that varies from culture to culture. The concept of land in general is intimately related to cosmology, economy and other social and cultural institutions. It is furthermore related to the concept of person and defines people's relation to each other and to the land itself.

Effective rights to land and territories[2] imply indigenous peoples' self-determination, as they are closely interrelated in the sense that one is conditioned by the other. This interrelation becomes evident when recognising that self-determination implies that all peoples can build their social order and legal institutions on the basis of their own concepts and systems of knowledge.

According to the importance of the link between territorial rights and the right to self-determination, there was a general agreement that self-determination *must have priority*, having consequences on all further rights, demands, principles and criteria. For instance, indigenous lifestyles are endangered without self-determination, while an indigenous lifestyle must be preserved in order to maintain cultural and biodiversity and sustainable resource use.

The participants in the conference basically recognised this specific situation and circumstances, and the non-indigenous representatives declared their solidarity with indigenous peoples. Based on the specific possibilities and means, all involved parties can support indigenous peoples in one way or another. Only when it comes to details and making such general statements concrete, do differing positions and approaches become evident.

Representatives of Swiss government agencies, for instance, asked for a clear and universal definition of the term 'indigenous'. As a matter of fact, such obstacles in the concretion of general statements force NGOs to further discuss the definitions of the crucial concepts and to seek for a consistent rhetoric in accordance with the indigenous peoples' demands.

At present, development of indigenous peoples according to their own conception is blocked, either by neo-colonial policies of national governments towards indigenous peoples or the lack of any policy, and by intergovernmental policies interfering with indigenous peoples' interests. As a consequence, the exploitation of natural resources without even consultation with indigenous peoples on their territories is encouraged, and free trade, including trade of intellectual property of indigenous peoples, and investment without consent is further advanced.

*Concrete Demands*
- If asked by indigenous peoples, NGOs could directly or through governments serve to function as foreign legal guarantors in order to induce national governments to respect indigenous management of land and territories.
- The NGOs which function as foreign legal guarantors can be linked with debt negotiation, including indigenous decision-making in the negotiation process.
- NGOs have to put pressure on state governments that oppress indigenous peoples with violence.
- NGOs have to put pressure on Swiss private companies violating indigenous peoples' rights.
- Governments should put pressure on and, if necessary, take measures against state governments that oppress indigenous peoples with violence.

**Information and Communication**
It is important to be aware that language, in general, and related specific concepts can be used as instruments of power because they convey the values and views of the particular society, group or institution of which they are part. As language can function unconsciously in hegemonic ways through indoctrination and international agreements, instruments must respect and include indigenous concepts of knowledge. This has consequences for how international legal instruments can and can not be used.

There is a strong need for a principled pragmatic approach when dealing with any strategy of change or with international instruments: the practical implementation of strategies and instruments consistent with indigenous peoples' concepts and knowledge will be determined by the effectiveness and its pragmatic use for the indigenous peoples in a particular circumstance.

Both the awareness of the importance of language and obvious disagreement on the meaning and implications of certain concepts force NGOs to discuss among themselves the definitions of concepts such as land rights, resource use, territories and self-determination. NGOs should seek to get their rhetoric right in accordance with indigenous peoples and seek to speak a *common language.*

Indigenous peoples claim to communicate in an open, listening, learning and receptive attitude giving the required time for a real dialogue. In order to provide the basis for a real dialogue with indigenous peoples, Western value systems and behavioural patterns have to be left behind.

The need for information has been located on different levels that are expressed with specific demands. Indigenous peoples should keep their Swiss partners informed of their situation and activities. Those NGOs with a wide international network of contacts should put more emphasis on their responsibility in terms of information and lobbying in the country, and at the same time be aware that indigenous peoples require all kinds of strategically helpful information that their partners can provide. NGOs should not only inform non-indigenous peoples about indigenous peoples by lobbying in their countries, and stress information about indigenous peoples to indigenous peoples in network programmes, but also provide indigenous peoples with information on multinationals and other companies operating in indigenous territories.

In order to intensify the flow of information, new mechanisms and structures should be worked out, whereby existing structures such as national embassies and field offices of international organisations could be integrated.

*Concrete Demands:*
-NGOs should organise a dialogue between Swiss policy-makers, Swiss decision-makers and indigenous peoples to solve the problem of different views on development.
- NGOs should organise a meeting between the Swiss government, government related organisations and indigenous peoples to find solutions for definition problems
- Swiss NGOs should use Channel 4 to broadcast indigenous documentaries and other information.
- NGOs should look into relations between Swiss society and indigenous peoples and look for ways to open a dialogue between indigenous peoples and Swiss companies
- The government should provide access for communication to indigenous peoples and soften the consular visa conditions for indigenous peoples.
- Private companies should be open for a dialogue with indigenous peoples.

## Conservation of the Environment
Indigenous peoples and conservationists agreed at the conference on the need to conserve and restore the environment in order to guarantee that land and other natural resources can be passed on to the next generations in good condition.

However, the situation worldwide is rather difficult for indigenous peoples. Nature conservation as an institutionalised global process is a recent phenomenon and is dominated by 'western' concepts. Human beings are mostly seen as a danger to nature and conservation strategies aim at excluding them and putting large areas under state control ('protected areas').

Such a model poses serious problems to indigenous peoples because it leads them to direct conflict with the state. Human rights abuses and forced relocation of indigenous peoples from their ancestral lands are known. In addition, external rules and regulations are imposed on indigenous peoples, and their own ways of managing natural resources are ignored.

Indigenous peoples demand that their own ways of nature conservation be supported, so that their own perceptions and ways of managing resources may have a chance.

Conservation in indigenous areas should observe the following principles: first of all, there should be respect for basic human rights and recognition of spiritual and philosophical distinctiveness of indigenous ways of life. Respect for indigenous lifestyles is important for the maintenance of biodiversity in the world. Collective rights of indigenous peoples in terms of collective territorial rights, sub-surface resource rights and the right to self-determination have to be respected. Indigenous peoples want their representative institutions to be recognised and they demand the right to development.

*Concrete Demands:*
- Government and environmental and conservation NGOs should develop clear policies in accordance with the above principles.
- No existing IUCN protected area category adequately recognises the principles listed above. Therefore, a new category should be promoted to recognise indigenous territories based on the principle of self-determination.
- In existing protected areas there should be a restitution of rights to the indigenous peoples (access, ownership, other rights).
- The Swiss government and NGOs should work for a redefinition of sub-surface rights (oil, minerals, water) and put pressure on the private sector involved in sub-surface exploitation in indigenous land.
- NGOs should help indigenous peoples to find solutions regarding the protection of traditional knowledge of agricultural and medicinal plants (intellectual property rights).
- The participation of indigenous peoples in the process of elaboration of environmental conventions is necessary (e.g. Biodiversity and Desertification conventions).

**Legal Instruments and Development Co-operation**
The participants at the conference recommended that due respect be paid to indigenous peoples by respecting and recognising their basic universal human rights and their cultural identity, their rights to self-determination, their knowledge and wisdom, as well as other rights as stated in internationally existing basic declarations.[3]

Indigenous peoples want to play an active role in the process of elaboration and improvement of such legal instruments. Because international conventions and other legal instruments are often dominated by 'western' concepts, indigenous peoples urge caution. With respect to ILO Convention 169 (Convention concerning indigenous and tribal people in independent countries, 1989), for instance, opinions are differing. Although it was agreed that there is no better legal instrument at the time, some representatives reject the convention because indigenous peoples were subordinate in its language, others seek adoption and ratification of the convention. The Swiss government and NGOs could work towards reopening Convention 169 for revisions to clarify those concepts and terms that cause disagreement.

Development co-operation has to respect existing legal instruments. Decisions that are taken here in industrialised countries may have an impact on indigenous peoples living elsewhere. Indigenous peoples demand that this impact always be taken into consideration and that their basic human rights be respected worldwide.

Indigenous peoples want to be invited and participate wherever and whenever they will be affected by the results of certain decisions. Swiss NGOs should work to ensure that indigenous peoples are fully involved in projects concerning them and support community decision-making. They are urged to make more time, energy and funds available for co-operation with indigenous peoples (co-operation both in the South and in the North).

In order to play this active part, indigenous peoples are therefore encouraged to organise themselves and exchange their experiences in development co-operation.

**Concrete Demands: a Swiss Policy for Indigenous Peoples**
- The government should work towards a Swiss policy for indigenous peoples in close contact with indigenous peoples.
- NGOs should enable the Swiss government to come up with such a policy statement. NGOs should work out a mechanism to make dialogue and partnership with indigenous peoples in this process come about.
- Swiss NGOs should coordinate among themselves on indigenous peoples rights.

## Concrete Demands: to International Institutions

- The Swiss government should sign and ratify ILO Convention 169
- NGOs should look at ILO Convention 169 and other such documents and conduct research to see to what extent they are useful in specific situations.
- The government should take an active lobbying role in favour of indigenous peoples in the United Nations system as well as in other international organisation, namely the WTO, WIPO (indigenous copyrights) and so on.
- The Swiss government and Swiss NGOs should lobby for free access for indigenous representatives to the higher levels of the United Nations so that they may directly participate in the process of elaboration of the UN Declaration on the Rights of Indigenous Peoples.
-The Swiss government and Swiss NGOs should help indigenous peoples to influence the recruitment policy of the World Bank and MDBs, and help indigenous peoples to gain better control over implementation of MDB guidelines.

## Notes

1. On the occasion of the United Nations 50th anniversary, Swiss NGOs working in the fields of human rights, environment and development among others, organised an event where specific concerns with respect to co-operation were discussed under the title 'NGOs shape the future'. IWGIA was engaged with the presentation of a resolution regarding the cooperation with indigenous peoples which was drawn out of the results of IPED (see Annex 1), in order to mediate and support indigenous peoples' demands among Swiss NGOs.

2. The term 'territory', as used in the sense above, does not necessarily mean that self-determination either vests only in land or implies a wish to secede. Out of fear and insecurity, the common use of the term 'land rights' and its practical application is still defined by colonial law and power, and used as a substitute for self-determination.

3. ILO Convention 169 concerning indigenous and tribal people in independent countries, Agenda 21, Chapter 26 ('Rec-

ognising and strengthening the role of indigenous people and their communities') of the United Nations Conference on Environment and Development, 14 June 1992, and the UN Draft Declaration on the Rights of the Indigenous Peoples, 1993.

**References**
IWGIA 1992. Newsletter No. 4. Copenhagen: IWGIA

## WORKING PAPER ON INDIGENOUS PEOPLES, ENVIRONMENT AND DEVELOPMENT

Presented to the UN50 NGO Summit in Berne, 30 June 1995

Elaborated by IWGIA Switzerland in conjunction with the results of the international conference from 15-18 May 1995 at Boldern, Switzerland (organised by IWGIA, GfbV, Incomindios, Bruno-Manser-Fonds and WWF Switzerland).

CONSIDERING THE FACT THAT indigenous peoples around the world contribute significantly to the variety of cultures on our planet; THAT their livelihoods rely more than any others on sustainability in an era of destructive exploitation of our environment as well as steadily diminishing natural resources; THAT the community of nations represented at the Conference of Rio (1992) have marked their position by proclaiming the Decade of Indigenous Peoples, clearly indicating that they are prepared to pay due attention to the rights of these people and to reinforce their efforts regarding all issues pertaining to development and environment; but THAT the current situations of most indigenous communities still form a stark contrast to such statements; AND, FINALLY, CONSIDERING Switzerland's role in trade relations and banking, as an importer of raw material from indigenous territories, as a country involved in development aid, as the origin of numerous far-travelled tourists, and hence the major responsibility it bears for the destiny of indigenous peoples, a responsibility which to this day has not been truly realised,

we express the hope and concrete wish

TO THE SWISS NON-GOVERNMENTAL ORGANISATIONS:

THAT they intensify their concerns about key concepts of indigenous peoples such as self-determination and land rights;

THAT they become especially aware of unique features of indigenous peoples regarding both their particular social structures and very own problem areas, which should be reflected in corresponding policies concerning development and environment;

THAT they outline the position of indigenous peoples in their current policies, clearly point out their projects in indigenous territories and coordinate their efforts in this area more efficiently;

THAT, specifically, larger development and environmental agencies establish clear principles in their work regarding indigenous peoples and their rights;

THAT they attempt to invest more time, energy and financial means in cooperation, projects and consultations with indigenous organisations;

THAT they facilitate access for indigenous organisations to Swiss NGOs through the establishment of an information centre or an index of organisations dealing with indigenous issues;

THAT they become more aware of their position close to the seat of the UN by assuming certain responsibilities for the promotion of indigenous concerns and the support of indigenous delegations at the UN;

THAT they strengthen their efforts to inform on indigenous concerns both in Switzerland and in countries where projects are carried out, i.e. by raising attention to existing conventions and declarations on indigenous rights, claims and requests;

THAT in all cases which affect indigenous peoples and in accordance with the significant international environmental agency IUCN, they attempt to foster the creation of a special category of parks, setting a major priority on the rights of affected communities;

finally, THAT they urge the Swiss government to assume responsibility towards indigenous peoples by underlining the protection of their rights in its foreign and development policies;


TO THE SWISS GOVERNMENT:

THAT Switzerland develop a carefully elaborated policy focusing on indigenous communities, thus following the examples of countries like Denmark, Norway, the Netherlands and Great Britain, and that it underline the protection of the rights of indigenous peoples in its foreign and development policies;

THAT Switzerland exercise diplomatic and economic pressure on countries known for violating the rights of indigenous peoples;

THAT the Swiss government recognise that the most efficient involvement to the benefit of indigenous peoples lies in the support of democratically influenced forces in respective countries, thus enabling the independent establishment of necessary bases of political freedom;

THAT the Swiss government ensure that its decisions do not have a negative impact on indigenous peoples;

THAT in future the Swiss Parliament, examine possible negative effects of constitutional revisions and changes on indigenous peoples;

THAT Switzerland call on its embassies and consulates all over the world to give special consideration and remain open to indigenous organisations and their concerns; especially visa matters should be treated in a more forthcoming manner, i.e. in view of participation in important conferences and human rights meetings;

THAT the Swiss government examine ongoing programmes and projects of both bilateral and multilateral (through development banks) national development aid with regard to their advantages or disadvantages for indigenous peoples;

THAT Switzerland assume an active role to the benefit of indigenous peoples in matters of justice in the UN as well as the World Trade Organisation and the World Organisation for Spiritual Property; especially THAT it actively support the indigenous request for the creation of a permanent forum for indigenous peoples within the UN;

finally, THAT Switzerland join and ratify ILO Convention 169 as soon as possible despite certain reservations among various indigenous organisations;

## TO THE UN:

THAT it pay particular attention in its human rights activities to indigenous peoples as an especially threatened group of people;

THAT it launch the Decade of Indigenous Peoples not only in word but also by participating actively (including financial support); this request is also directed to all specialised bodies and international organisations which form a part of the UN system;

THAT it does its best to support the process of acknowledgement of the general declaration on the rights of indigenous peoples by state governments and that it make sure that decisive points of the document and thus its entire significance are not weakened; to guarantee this it will be inevitable to also grant private organisations, especially indigenous ones, access and electoral rights on all organisational levels;

THAT it help put the decision of the 51st session of the Human Rights Commission (Resolution 1995/30) into practice, thus supporting the creation of a permanent forum for indigenous peoples within the UN.

# VI
# Concluding Remarks

MOANA JACKSON

# THE NATURE OF KNOWING: SELF-DETERMINATION, LAND AND THE DOUBLE HELIX

There is a certain symmetry in the sound of indigenous voices. A symmetry born of an ancestral birthright in the land, a common core of collective interests, and a painful shared history of dispossession in the process of colonisation. There is a symmetry too in the united wish to be free from the consequences of that dispossession and exercise once again the right to self-determination.

But symmetry of course does not mean sameness. While there is a shared pride in the ancient traditions and a fierce determination to be free from oppression, both the traditions and the nature of the oppression took different forms at different places and therefore caused different consequences. There is therefore a range of views among indigenous peoples about the best strategies to ensure decolonisation, to regain freedom and discourse even over the best language and terminology with which to express the strategies. But that is as it should be, for we are not some homogenised entities able to be easily classified and therefore controlled by colonisers or neo-colonisers. Rather we are peoples who are diverse yet similar, oppressed yet proud and independent yet united on the fundamental issues of what our rights are, what the earth really is and how self-determination will help us to protect all that is important to us.

At a conference such as this, it is inevitable that although the similarities and differences are both expressed, the symmetry of our indigenous lives, traditions and histories ensures that there is unity and oneness on the issue which must encapsulate who we are, and that is the right to self-determination. For it is this right which not only provides the political recognition of our authority, it also recognises that no one else has the right or the ability to define who we are and what it is we can do. In all of the contributions from the indigenous speakers at this conference there was a clear acknowledgement that from self-determination comes all other rights and obligations. If peoples are allowed to be free and determine their own destiny, the problems of how to live with our Mother Earth are easily contextualised. The environment and an ideal of development are inseparable from our relationship with our Mother Earth, and the protection of the resources which she has within or upon her are an unavoidable obligation which both our past and future impose upon us as her children.

Equally, inevitably the sense of obligation has been, and still is, obstructed by the states of Europe and their successors who since 1492 have assumed a right to colonise and rule the indigenous peoples of the world. The totalising act of genocide and dispossession which constitutes colonisation has attempted to control everything about us: the land with which we live, the faith in which we found comfort, the flora and fauna with which we shared our history, the resources from which we took sustenance and in which we found pleasure in the creation of art and music, the names and concepts by which we identified ourselves and our world, and the intellectual property and knowledge with which we tried to make sense of it all. Today, the old colonial powers or their successors continue to deny our rights and refine our worth in a new wave of colonial rhetoric and action.

In Bougainville the relationship between the people of the land and the land itself was firstly redefined and demeaned by a wave of political colonisers ranging from the Germans to the English, then almost totally destroyed by the advent of mining in an act of exploitative neo-colonialism. In Kenya the Maasai people struggle to protect unique forest areas that provide both physical and spiritual sustenance in the face of unregulated tourism ventures; and in Australia attempts to reintroduce and adapt Aboriginal resource management mechanisms meet with bureaucratic scorn and opposition. In India the western patriarchy which drove much of colonisation's aggression remains embedded and interacts with internal forces in an oppressive post-colonial behaviour that makes Adivasi women the most deprived and neglected group in that country. In Nigeria the 18th century colonial desire for profit from slavery finds new capitalist expression in a quest for oil that is as dismissive of the people's rights as any other dispossession, while in Peru, Colombia and many other South American countries the original dream for gold and El Dorado is expressed now in the desire for other land and forest resources. In my homeland of Aotearoa (New Zealand), the government has been embarked for five years now on a fast-tracked programme to sell land and other assets such as fishing rights to overseas interests. Acting like some new age colonial harlot, it sells off resources to the highest bidder. However, unlike most harlots, the body being used is that of our Mother Earth.

Three years after the hopes of the Earth Summit, colonial and neo-colonial control of what is called sustainable development continues apace. The Uruguay round of the GATT and the establishment of the World Trade Organisation has already opened the way for further exploitation of genetic cell lines, the patenting of all life forms, and perhaps eventually the creation of some new Robocop of multinationals, bringing obstructive indigenous peoples into line with one shot of his helix-disentangling gun.

Each of these scenarios, with their threats to the safety of Mother Earth and the lives of the people who live there, are variations on the old colonial theme. Although each is different in geographic place and method of operation, the similarities show the same frightening symmetry of all dispossession. The people most affected are indigenous and the pain is borne by our Mother the Earth, but the people seeking to profit and dispossess are the heirs and beneficiaries of the earlier colonisers. There is indeed truth in the old saying that the more colonisation changes, the more it stays the same.

Each of these challenges also poses various questions for NGOs, conservationists and developmentalists to constantly reassess their approach and strategy within the context of colonisation. For this, colonisation, which remains the base of all exploitation of indigenous lands and resources, and its ethos of control must be the starting point from which strategies for development with indigenous peoples must proceed. At a very basic philosophical level, this means accepting that indigenous peoples need and seek out allies; but we do not need ecological saviours nor patronising experts of any kind. In the United States there is a cliché that the typical Hopi Indian family consists of mother, father, two children and an anthropologist. In Aotearoa our people say that we have been cursed not just with the new diseases and militarism which colonisation always brings: we are also cursed by ethnographic trappers classifying who and what we are, and experts of all kinds who, in the same breath as they tell us of their support for our self-determination, seek to tell us what is best for us and what self-determination actually means. European discourses and strategies operated by NGOs or other groups which enter and alter indigenous efforts to be self-determining are simply new acts of colonisation cloaked in a rhetoric of 20th century feel good control.

Yet in spite of all the difficulties, there is clearly hope that the pain of the past and the destruction of the present cannot go on forever. And it is a hope born not out of some unrealistic optimism, but out of the fact that the struggle of indigenous peoples is based on a search for justice, and justice in the end can not be denied. As one speaker at this conference said, we have the moral high ground because in issues to do with the land and the environment we are fighting for ourselves and for the rest of humanity because we are the people of the land. The key to that struggle is to reclaim self-determination, already fought for for years in forums such as the United Nations Working Group on Indigenous Populations and expressed in documents such as that group's draft Declaration and the Kari Oca Declaration prepared at the Earth Summit.

Self-determination must be the starting point from which each indigenous struggle should proceed, whether it is a fight to protect the biodiversity of our land, the pharmaceutical and other information therein or an effort to preserve traditional practices. If indigenous peoples can once again make their own decisions, determine their own destiny, there is hope that we, and our world, can be saved. For NGOs and other non-indigenous organisations who wish to be effective allies, the challenge is not to be narrowly focused on specific and discrete issues only to do with one piece of land or one particular resource. Rather, the challenge is to contextualise the particular issue within the broad reaching context of the colonising paradigm.

Only by seeing the origins of the particular environmental or resource threat within the inevitability of colonisation's will to dispossess can we find solutions that will move indigenous peoples from the lonely post of last sentry at the entrance to the world's forests, deserts and waters. The contemporary relationship between indigenous peoples, environment and development is one unavoidably shaped by colonisation and the lust for greed. The strengthening and development of the relationship which indigenous peoples hold so dear will depend in the end on how free the particular indigenous peoples are from the chains of colonisation, how able they are to once again exercise their self-determination.

This conference has given us a chance to share and develop insights on how this might be achieved. The immediate challenge will be how effectively we can transform the ideas discussed here into effective strategies for change. As indigenous peoples we know that our ancestors will be watching us; as Jeremy Narby said, even the double helix, in calm reason or hallucinatory ecstasy, will cry out in joy or sadness depending upon how we fare.

# CONTRIBUTORS

**Marcus Colchester** received his D. Phil in Social Anthropology from the University of Oxford after first qualifying in Zoology. Between 1975 and 1983 he spent nearly four years studying the social ecology of Amazonian Indians. He played a key role in initiating the process of securing the Yanomami lands of the Upper Orinoco; an area that has now been defined as a Biosphere Reserve. As Projects Director with Survival International he worked on indigenous rights issues globally. Among the issues which he has researched and published on in detail are: the transmigration programme in Indonesia; the resettlement programme in Ethiopia; the Narmada dams in India; and logging in Sarawak. He now acts as Director of the Forest Peoples Programme of the World Rainforest Movement. In this role he has undertaken a twofold role of promoting indigenous networks and supporting indigenous control of their forests at the same time as pressing for changes in top-down development policy and projects that threaten these objectives.

**Christian Erni** studied social anthropology at the University of Zurich. He has done extensive research on the economy and environmental adaptation of the Buhid of Mindoro Island in the Philippines, for which he received his Ph.D. from Zurich University. From 1990 to 1996 he was scientific assistant and lecturer on Ecological and Economic Anthropology at the Department of Social Anthropology, University of Zurich. He currently works as Project Coordinator at the IWGIA International Secretariate in Copenhagen.

**Margeret Friel** is a member of the Jawoyn Association, an Aboriginal Association that successfully stopped mining at Coronation Hill, but which later went on to surrender native title to another area of land for mining interests. In the 1980s Ms Friel was an active anti-apartheid campaigner, and more recently she has been actively involved in the Australian debate surrounding native title.

Her educational and employment background is in law and education, including teaching and Aboriginal student support services. She is currently the Director of the National Aboriginal Youth Law Centre in Darwin, Northern Territory. The current focus of her work includes children and youth legal and educational issues.

**Pedro García Hierro** is a lawyer and has been consultant to indigenous organisations in Peru for 25 years. He has above all worked for the Peruvian national indigenous organisation AIDESP (Asociación Interetnica de Desarrollo de la Selva Peruana) and is currently a member of the NGO Racimos de Ungurahui. He has published several articles and a book on the indigenous territories and the agrarian legislation in Peru (Territorios Indígenas y la Nueva Legislación Agraria en el Peru. IWGIA Document No. 17, 1995).

**Andrew Gray**, anthropologist Ph.D., studied at Edinburgh and Oxford University. He has done extensive fieldwork among the Harakambut people of the southeastern Peruvian Amazon and worked as consultant with many indigenous peoples in Asia and Latin America. Between 1983 and 1989 he was the executive director of IWGIA (International Work Group for Indigenous Affairs). At present he works for the Rainforest Movement and is a member of the International Board of IWGIA and the board of the Anti Slavery Society International.

**Rikha Havini** graduated from high school in Sydney in 1992 and is currently undertaking college studies in Brisbane. He was born in Bougainville, is a young activist and well versed on all issues, including politics, environment and mining. Rikha Havini joined the conference on behalf of his father, Moses Havini, International Political Representative & Human Rights Advocate for the people of Bougainville.

**Georg Henriksen** is Professor at the Department of Social Anthropology, University of Bergen. He has done field and consultancy work with the Innu of Labrador and the Mic Mac of Nova Scotia in Canada, with the Turkana in Kenya and the Sámi of Helgeland in Norway. He is at present Chairman and has been a member of the International Board of IWGIA since 1981.

**Moana Jackson** is a member of the Ngati Kahungunu and Ngati Porou Maori tribal nations of Aotearoa (New Zealand). He graduated in law from University of Wellington (Victoria), Columbia and Arizona state Universities and is presently visiting

Professor at the University of Wellington Law School. His full-time work is with the Maori Legal Service, the first indigenous legal office in Aotearoa. The organisation is dedicated to ensuring the honouring of the Treaty of Waitangi signed with England in 1840, and reaffirming the Declaration of Maori Independence, promulgated in 1835. Moana Jackson's specific areas of work are in treaty issues and the pursuit of Maori sovereignty.

**Elizabeth Kemf** is a Swiss/American environmentalist. She has a Masters degree in creative writing and has worked as journalist, photographer and instructor of filmmaking and communications.

She has worked with WWF International since 1981. Her first post was as information officer and editor of the organisation's flagship publication, the WWF news. In 1991 she founded WWF's Conservation News Service, which she headed until she was assigned to undertake a global review of indigenous peoples and protected areas, which was commissioned by WWF/IUCN and the European Commission.

Elizabeth Kemf is the author of several books and over 150 popular and technical articles on a variety of topics ranging from literary and film criticism to alternative energy and agricultural systems and the links between cultural and biological diversity.

**Jacques de Kort** was born in 1953 in the Netherlands and studied Human Geography with a specialisation in developing countries at the University of Amsterdam.

Jacques de Kort has a long history of experience in lobbying for indigenous peoples in the Netherlands as author of many articles on indigenous issues, as coordinator of education campaigns in the Netherlands, as consultant to the European Parliament on the human rights of indigenous peoples (1984-89) and consultant and co-producer of the 'First World Conference of Indigenous Peoples on Territory, Environment and Development' in Kari Oca/Rio de Janeiro 1992.

From 1992 to 1995 he was director of the Netherlands Centre for Indigenous Peoples Foundation (Stichting Nederlands Centrum voor Inheemse Volken, NCIV) in Amsterdam. Presently he is consultant to the Indigenous Council in the Netherlands and consultant for the Decade of the Indigenous Peoples Foundation.

**Jonathan Kamomon Ole Lekuruon** was born in Loita Location, Kenya, in 1964 and educated at Narok High School and Embu Development Institute, where he obtained a Diploma in Social Work.

He is currently a Training Officer for the Ilkerin Loita Project, where he works as a youth coordinator and is in charge of audiovisuals and the Moran Basic Education programme. Apart from youth training and development, his many tasks include audiovisual coverage, adult training and education; pastoralist mobilisation, organisation and empowerment; community awareness and conscientisation; and environmental protection and management.

Mr. Kamomon was also involved with Oxfarm Samburu, Farm Africa in Samburu, ASAL Programme in Kajiado and the government Department of Social Services, prior to joining Ilkerin.

**Lorenz G. Löffler** was born in Thüringen, Germany, Mr. Löffler studied ethnology, sinology and anthropology at the universities of Jena, Leipzig and Mainz. He did field studies in East Pakistan, Bangladesh and West Bengal and has been professor of ethnology as well as head of department at Zurich University, Switzerland.

**Jeffrey A. McNeely** was educated as an anthropologist at the University of California at Los Angeles. Mr. McNeely lived in South-East Asia for 12 years, contributing to a wide range of conservation activities for governments, United Nations agencies and private conservation organisations.

In 1980 he started at IUCN as the Executive Officer of the Commission on National Parks and Protected Areas. He was the Programme Director for the Third World Congress on National Parks, held in Bali, Indonesia, in October 1982. Subsequently, he served IUCN as Director of the Programme Division (1983-1987) and Deputy Director General (1987-1988), taking responsibility for guiding all conservation activities of IUCN. He was Secretary General of the Fourth World Congress on National Parks and Protected Areas, held in February 1992 in Caracas, Venezuela.

Currently, he is Chief Conservation Officer at the International Union for Conservation of Nature and Natural Resources in Switzerland. He has published over 75 technical articles and 100 popular articles.

**Sonajharia Minz** was born in 1962 in Bihar, India. Sona Minz belongs to the Oraon people and her mother tongue is Kurukh. She is an educated mathematician and computer scientist and is currently employed at the School of Computer and Systems Science in New Delhi.

She is involved in the Indian Confederation of Indigenous and Tribal Peoples in India as a member taking part in the local activities of Delhi zone.

In an individual capacity she is working towards awareness-building amidst tribal students doing their higher education in urban areas, especially Delhi. Sona Minz is also active in working among tribal girls and women working as domestic helpers in Delhi who are exposed to various kinds of exploitation.

**Ben Naanen** received his Bachelor degree in History and Archaeology, his Masters in economic history and wrote his dissertation on the problems of development and social change in Nigeria.

He considers himself a historian and political economist. Ben Naanen is currently an Assistant Professor at the University of Port Harcourt, Nigeria. He also engages in journalism, serving as a columnist and editorial board member for a publishing house in Nigeria. He has been the General Secretary of the Movement for the survival of the Ogoni People (MOSOP) since December 1992.

**Jeremy Narby** is a Canadian anthropologist. In the early 1980s he worked with the Anthropology Resource Center in Boston, one of the first NGOs involved with indigenous peoples' rights. He did a doctorate in anthropology at Stanford University, after living 2 years in an Ashaninka village in the Pichis valley in the Peruvian Amazon, where he investigated the relationship between indigenous land use and land rights.

Mr Narby worked with OXFAM-England on their field-guide for NGOs working with indigenous peoples, and since 1989 he is the Amazonian project coordinator for Nouvelle Planète, a Swiss NGO involved in community development projects around the world. As such, he is funding and supervising indigenous land titling projects in the Amazon Basin.

**Euclides Peña Ismare** was born in 1959 and is a member of the Waunaan ethnic group in Colombia. He studied Public Administration at ESAP from 1986-1992. He is currently a student of Administración de Empresa de la Economía Solidaria at the University Santo Tomas Regional Pereira.

He was Vice-President of OREWA in 1980-81 and President during 1982-86. From 1986-1990 he was Project Coordinator of 'Producción-Salud' in the Zona Baja y Media San Juan. He was also Accountant for the 'Movimiento Campesino de los Negros' ACADEZAN in Rio San Juan.

Since 1991 Mr. Ismare has been Deputy of the Departemental Assembly of Choco and he is also the Coordinator of the 'Equipo Politico'.

**Darrell Addison Posey** was born in Henderson, Kentucky, USA, in 1947. His Ph.D. in anthropology was completed in 1979 at the University of Georgia.

Since 1977 Dr. Posey has worked in the Brazilian Amazon. He is Titled Researcher (Pesquisador Titular) for the Brazilian National Council for Science and Technology at the Goeldi Museum, Belem, Brazil.

Since 1989 he has coordinated the International Working Group on Traditional Resource Rights.

He was Founding President of the International Society for Ethnobiology and President of the Global Coalition for Bio-Cultural Diversity. He was the recipient of the first 'Chico Mendes Award for Outstanding Bravery in Defense of the Environment' and is one of the recipients of the United Nations 'Global 500' award. Currently Mr. Posey is a Senior Associate Member of St. Antony's College (Oxon) and Associate Fellow of the Oxford Centre for the Environment, Ethics, and Society of Mansfield College (University of Oxford).

**Victoria Tauli-Corpuz** is chairperson of the Cordillera Peoples' Alliance (CPA), a federation of around 120 indigenous peoples' organisations in the Cordillera region of the Philippines. This federation, which was organised in 1984, promotes the struggles of the Igorot peoples of the Cordillera for self-determination and regional autonomy. She is also Chairperson of the Centre for Development Programmes in the Cordillera, a consortium of 13 development NGOs, based and working in the Cordillera.

She is Founder and Executive Director of the Cordillera Women's Education and Resource Center, Inc. (CWERC), an NGO which is mainly engaged in raising social and feminist awareness of indigenous women in the Cordillera. Today she is also convenor of the Asian Indigenous Women's Network (AIWN).

From 1994 to 1996 Ms Tauli-Corpuz has been a Member of the Board of Trustees – United Nations Voluntary Fund for Indigenous Populations (a UN Body which administers the UN fund that helps to bring indigenous peoples to attend the UN Working Group on Indigenous Populations each year in Geneva).

**Prasert Trakansuphakon** was born 1954 in Chiang Mai, northern Thailand, and belongs to the Karen people. He studied political science and obtained an M.A. at the Candidate Faculty of Education at Chiang Mai University.

Presently, Prasert Trakansuphakon is Director of IMPECT Association (Inter-Mountain People's Education and Culture in Thailand) and president of the Center for the Coordination of Non-governmental Tribal Development Organization (CONTO).

**Luis Never Tuesta Cerrón** was born in 1946 in the Amazon region of Peru. His mother tongue is Aguaruna but he did his studies in Spanish. He has been a professor of technical education since 1970. As a member of the 'Grupo de desarrollo Alto Maraon' he worked as promoter for agriculture and cattle breeding with the Aguaruna communities along the Rio Cenepa in the Peruvian Amazon. His work with the Ministry of Education, among others as a Regional Director for Education in Imacita, led him to his present position as Executive Director of the Programme for Education of Bilingual Teachers within AIDESEP.

His task for AIDESEP and the programme is to legally represent the organisation in Iquitos. In addition to his administrative function, he is integrating ecological questions in the programme. Furthermore, he is coordinating the cooperation with various indigenous regional organisations.

The main objectives of the current programme and activities are to educate teachers with the capacity to focus indigenous education on solving present socio-economic and ecological problems indigenous peoples are facing.